QUALITATIVE METHODOLOGY

QUALITATIVE METHODOLOGY

editor
John Van Maanen

An updated reprint of the
December 1979 issue of
Administrative Science Quarterly

SAGE PUBLICATIONS
The International Professional Publishers
Newbury Park   London   New Delhi

For information address:

SAGE Publications, Inc.
2455 Teller Road
Newbury Park, California 91320

SAGE Publications Ltd.
6 Bonhill Street
London EC2A 4PU
United Kingdom

SAGE Publications India Pvt. Ltd.
M-32 Market
Greater Kailash I
New Delhi 110 048 India

Printed in the United States of America

Library of Congress Cataloging in Publication Data

Main entry under title:

Qualitative methodology.

    Bibliography: p.
    Includes index.
    1. Social sciences—Research—Addresses, essays, lectures. 2. Social sciences—Methodology—Addresses, essays, lectures. I. Van Maanen, John.
H62.Q35   1983   300'.72   83-14332
ISBN 0-8039-2117-9 (pbk.)

    94   10   9   8

Contents

The Seminar

Qualitative Researcher:

"Many people these days are bored with their work and are. . . ."

Quantitative Researcher
(interrupting):

"What people, how many, when do they feel this way, where do they work, what do they do, why are they bored, how long have they felt this way, what are their needs, when do they feel excited, where did they come from, what parts of their work bother them most, which. . . ."

Qualitative Researcher:

"Never mind."

Reclaiming Qualitative Methods for Organizational Research: A Preface

John Van Maanen, Editor

THE TERRITORY IS NOT THE MAP

The label qualitative methods has no precise meaning in any of the social sciences. It is at best an umbrella term covering an array of interpretive techniques which seek to describe, decode, translate, and otherwise come to terms with the meaning, not the frequency, of certain more or less naturally occurring phenomena in the social world. To operate in a qualitative mode is to trade in linguistic symbols and, by so doing, attempt to reduce the distance between indicated and indicator, between theory and data, between context and action. The raw materials of qualitative study are therefore generated *in vivo,* close to the point of origin. Although the use of qualitative methods does not prohibit a researcher's use of the logic of scientific empiricism, the logic of phenomenological analysis is more likely to be assumed since qualitative researchers tend to regard social phenomena as more particular and ambiguous than replicable and clearly defined.

The data developed by qualitative methods originate when a researcher figuratively puts brackets around a temporal and spatial domain of the social world. These brackets define the territory about which descriptions are fashioned. These descriptions are essentially idiographic maps of the territory, which must then be read and interpreted by the investigator if any nomothetic statements are to result from a given study. Doing description is then the fundamental act of data

collection in a qualitative study. But, the map cannot be considered the territory simply because the map is a reflexive
product of the map maker's invention. The map maker sees
himself quite as much as he sees the territory. There are
however better and worse maps and qualitative researchers
seek to construct good ones by moving closer to the territory they study in the physical sense as well as in the intellectual sense by minimizing the use of such artificial distanc-
ing mechanisms as analytic labels, abstract hypotheses, and
preformulated research strategies.

Qualitative methodology and quantitative methodology are
not mutually exclusive. Differences between the two approaches are located in the overall form, focus, and emphasis of study. As demonstrated by several of the research
accounts in this issue, qualitative methods represent a mix-
ture of the rational, serendipitous, and intuitive in which the
personal experiences of the organizational researcher are
often key events to be understood and analyzed as data.
Qualitative investigators tend also to describe the unfolding
of social processes rather than the social structures that are
often the focus of quantitative researchers. Moreover, no
matter what the topic of study, qualitative researchers in
contrast to their quantitative colleagues claim forcefully to
know relatively little about what a given piece of observed
behavior means until they have developed a description of
the context in which the behavior takes place and attempted to see that behavior from the position of its
originator. That such contextual understandings and empathetic objectives are unlikely to be achieved without direct, firsthand, and more or less intimate knowledge of a
research setting is a most practical assumption that underlies and guides most qualitative study.

From this perspective, qualitative methods are rather similar
to the interpretive procedures we make use of as we go
about our everyday life. The data we collect and act upon in
everyday life are of the same sort a qualitative researcher
explicitly attempts to gather and record. Such data are symbolic, contextually embedded, cryptic, and reflexive, standing
for nothing so much as their readiness or stubbornness to
yield to a meaningful interpretation and response. When
crossing the street, for example, the sight of a ten-ton truck
bearing down on us leads to an immediate and presumably

prudent action. We do not stop to first ask how fast the truck is traveling, from where did it come, how often does this occur, or what is the driver's intention. We move. Our study of the truck involves little more than a quick scan, a glance up the road which reveals to most of us a menacing symbol of such power that a speedy, undeliberated response is mandatory. It is the aim of qualitative researchers to identify such symbols and, as a way of assessing their meaning, to record the pattern of responses these symbols elicit.

This example also suggests that the linking of sign and signified, representation and conduct, proximal and distal, awareness and phenomenon in social research is always dependent upon an interpretive framework. And, when a given interpretive framework becomes firmly accepted and more or less set by a researcher, analytic formulas can be established and focusing devices put into place such that the investigator is able to engage in quantitative study. It is in this sense that quantitative and qualitative work are connected. But, if one is to consider for example the almost 25-year history of *ASQ*, such linkages are rarely made explicit when a study is eventually published. Perhaps, Gresham's Law is at work in organizational studies wherein the programmed research is driving out the unprogrammed.

There are however a number of organization theorists beginning to question the wisdom of allowing Gresham's Law to take its course unquestioned. There is a growing concern about where quantitative techniques are carrying us. For example, questions have been raised about the extent to which our methods are guiding our theory and concern has been expressed about the degree to which our procedures have become so ritualized that the necessary connection between measure and concept has vanished. Since quantitative methods have held an almost monopolistic grip on the production of knowledge in the field, any serious reflection regarding current organization theory must at some point consider the value of alternative methods.

Several unresolved but interrelated and crucial problems of organizational inquiry currently exist which are both epistemological and methodological in nature. First, there is a rather curious and troubling distance between the generalized principles which have been postulated for the behavior of individuals, groups, and organizations and the specific, always contextual understandings and explanations given by social actors that provide purpose and meaning to their behavior. Second, the gap between the theoretical constructions we use to construct our study and the availability of data to render such theories testable appears also to be growing. Third, our data manipulation techniques have become increasingly complex, mathematically sophisticated, and governed by strict assumptions, but, paradoxically, our interpretive frameworks which make such data meaningful have grown looser, more open-ended, fluid, and contingent. Fourth, there is an increasing distrust among organizational observers of the claims made for such analytic conveniences as the formal interview, the paper-and-pencil survey, the lab study, the use of official statistics, records, documents and the like. Indeed, there seems to be rather widespread skepticism surrounding the ability of conventional data collection techniques to produce data that do not distort, do violence to, or otherwise falsely portray the phenomena such methods seek to reveal. In particular, the overwhelming role played by the survey instrument in organizational research has led some observers to suggest that the field is becoming simply the study of verbally expressed sentiments and beliefs rather than the study of conduct. To further refine our data analysis techniques, however, is not to improve the quality of the data which is, in the final analysis, at issue.

Given this abbreviated list of commonly voiced concerns, it is worth pointing out as a final prefacing matter that there is something of a quiet reconstruction going on in the social sciences and some of the applied disciplines. It is hardly revolutionary, but a renewed interest in and felt need for qualitative research has slowly been emerging among sociologists, educators, urban planners, psychologists, public interest lawyers, welfare administrators, health care personnel, political scientists, labor economists, and others. There has come of age the significant realization that the people we study (and often seek to assist) have a form of life, a culture that is their own and if we wish to understand the behavior of these people and the groups and organizations of which they are a part, we must first be able to both appreciate and describe their culture. As a society, we have become increasingly aware of the fact that we live, work, and play in multicultural surroundings. Moreover, within this society at least, it is becoming clear that the origins of many of these cultures are not coupled conceptually to matters such as geography, ethnicity, or social class but are grounded in organizational experiences. Whether we are examining the organizational worlds of middle managers, tramps, stockbrokers, high school principals, police officers, production workers, or professional crooks, we are certain to uncover special languages, unique and peculiar problems, and, more generally, distinct patterns of thought and action. What this rather profound realization means for our own scholarly work in the organizational areas is an essential theme that runs through each of the articles presented in this special issue.

A STUDY OF STUDIES

A call for papers on qualitative methods was printed in the March 1979 issue of ASQ. From the pool of potential authors with firsthand qualitative research experience, we requested short contributions to the journal dealing with the meaning, use, and function of the various types of data with which they had worked. But, since the number of papers submitted far exceeded the journal space available (even when expanded to a full issue), we were faced with the difficult task of further specifying and making explicit our standards for what would constitute a worthy contribution in this area. Unlike quantitative approaches, there are few guidelines to follow when assessing the soundness of a given qualitative technique. Moreover, there is, as this issue attests, a large and increasing number of rather specific qualitative methods available for use in organizational research. Yet, what was most difficult to deal with was the fact that the papers we received each represented something of a unique meshing of problem, theory, method, and the person(s) standing behind it all. To say one paper was somehow more valuable than another required the further elaboration of the somewhat loose and inarticulate standards we began with last March.

Four criteria eventually emerged as the reviewers attempted to decide what papers would be most appropriate for this special issue. First, we tried to eliminate those papers where prescription dominated description. Second, we looked for the practical importance of a given paper to organizational researchers. That is, we tried to eliminate those papers that appeared to be primarily epistemological or methodological in favor of those papers which illustrated the actual use of qualitative methods. Third, we wanted to achieve a disciplinary mix among the papers published. The intent was to demonstrate the utility of qualitative methods to a variety of distinct, discipline-based problems. And, fourth, we tried to select papers that presented novel themes in organizational studies. This fourth criterion presented something of a dilemma since many qualitative methods (e.g., content analysis, participant observation, constitutive ethnography, the construction of life histories, semiotics, conversational analysis, etc.) are by definition quite novel to organizational research since they have been so infrequently employed in the area. Our resolution here (and it is not without ambiguity) was to examine the findings uncovered by the method discussed in a paper and judge whether or not such findings would be relatively predictable given what is currently known about organizations and the life that goes on within them. Essentially, what we were after was at least a partial answer to the question: What can we learn about organizations that we do not already know by the use of a particular qualitative method?

Looking at the thirteen papers of this volume collectively, three somewhat distinct thematic groupings can be discerned. The first and most heavily represented set of articles addresses the use of what Peggy Sanday calls in the lead article, "ethnographic paradigms." That there are multiple ethnographic paradigms is perhaps the crucial point of Professor Sanday's informed review of the variety of anthropological methods currently in use. John Van Maanen, commenting upon the mix of participant observation and ethnographic interviews used in his studies of the police, makes the point in the second article that the key analytic decisions of qualitative study are most often accomplished by the investigator in the research setting itself and that the selection of substantive topics to pursue in a given study cannot be disembodied from the actual research process itself. Donald Light then suggests in the next paper that the structure of organizational life invariably lies well beneath the surface in a given research setting. To begin to describe what such structure looks like requires that the investigator develop careful descriptions of the daily routines and concerns of the members of the studied organization over a lengthy period of time. Structure, from Professor Light's perspective, is a label for various social processes which, in his research on professional training, are virtually impossible to comprehend over the short run or by simply relying on the publicly articulated and rationalized understandings presented by the members of the organization. Michael Piore, in the following paper, makes a similar point. Essentially, the author calls for what amounts to a "new economics," one that views the economy (both at the macro and micro levels) as a social process. Since the qualitative tradition in economics has largely disappeared from view, Professor Piore's comments on the role played by direct, firsthand involvement in his own highly respected research has particular interest. Andrew Pettigrew, in the next to last paper of the set, also displays an interest in unscrambling social processes. In his case, however, the social process of concern is that of leadership. By examples taken from his current research project, Professor Pettigrew demonstrates the crucial importance of taking a qualitative stance toward the key events, figures, and transition points in an educational institution as a way of understanding how organizational cultures are shaped and reshaped over time. Henry Mintzberg closes out this first set of papers with a crisp summary of the assumptions that underlie his own extensive research on the management of organizations. "Direct research" is the tag that he uses to capture the critical aspects of his method and, in large measure, the points he articulates provide a rather comprehensive synopsis of the methodological positions taken by the authors of the preceding papers.

The second set of papers represents methods less dominated by ethnographic, observational, and on-site, in-depth interview techniques alone. Instead, these papers succinctly suggest that the quantitative versus qualitative distinction drawn among social science methods is often an arbitrary and oversimplified distinction. Authors of papers in this set demonstrate that quantitative indicators ranging from the crude to the sophisticated can and do emerge from the use of field methods and the direct observation of organizations. Matthew Miles argues that it is a mistake to think that qualitative researchers are somehow against measurement. Moreover, as Professor Miles demonstrates in his discussion of fieldwork crises, researchers should develop quantitative indicators where possible. By so doing, they can guard against the entropic tendencies that are involved in team research wherein team members seek to go their own ways leading to an empirical defocusing and quite possibly the analytic deterioration of the study. Todd Jick takes up this same theme in the following paper bluntly titled "Mixing Qualitative and Quantitative Data." After a review of the surprisingly rich literature on triangulation in social research, Professor Jick displays the practical utility of having intimate familiarity with a research setting as a means of building several quantitative indicators of what to outsiders might seem to be rather impressionistic and ill-defined concepts. Closely related to the multiple methods explored by Professor Jick as a way of handling messy research topics, Charles McClintock, Diane Brannon, and Steven Maynard-Moody in the next selection argue for a more systematic approach for constructing case studies. In this paper, a method based on the logic of survey analysis is described that seems to have considerable potential for producing, in the authors' view, "thick and generalizable analyses." The final paper of this set is by Kirk Downey and Duane Ireland and deals with the relative advantages and disadvantages of both quantitative and qualitative methods. The authors here show that the supposed analytic match that is ideally sought between problem and method invariably leaves considerable latitude for the use of both quantitative and qualitative techniques. Taking the assessment of an organization's environment as an illustrative substantive domain, Professors Downey and Ireland show how it is possible and, in many cases, clearly desirable to assess an organization's environment in qualitative terms. Moreover, they suggest that many researchers in this area may well have been pushed inappropriately (and perhaps prematurely) toward the quantification of environmental concepts without giving due consideration to the meaning of the concepts they measure.

The third and concluding set of papers presented in this issue is distinguished solely by the novel themes explored by the authors. Unlike the previous two groupings of papers, the authors of the papers in this third set share neither a similar approach to data collection nor a similar stance toward data as they are produced. What these three papers do share however is a fresh outlook upon the legitimate topics of organizational inquiry. The writings that appear in this set are not only rich with tightly drawn and worked out examples, but are full of the subtle ironies that challenge us to think more clearly about organizational research. The first paper is Gerald R. Salancik's seductive plea to tickle, provoke, and otherwise stimulate organizations to see what, if anything, will occur. Professor Salancik essentially calls for the application of a natural experimentation model in organizational study. This can be accomplished, for example, retrospectively through close inspection of the artifacts of organizational research such as the non-response of organizational members to survey questionnaires. Some of the previously overlooked assumptions and implications associated with the use of unobtrusive measures in organizational research are spelled out in the following paper by Eugene Webb and Karl Weick. Arguing that while research designs and analytic techniques have become far more complex in recent years, the task of data collection still plods along the relatively parochial self-report path with researchers devoting little effort to considering the range of alternatives available to them. In brief, Professors Webb and Weick issue a lively call for the creative and playful use of unobtrusive measures in organizational studies and suggest in passing the intriguing proposition that as the popularity of the governing theories of the field declines, the interest in qualitative methods may well increase. It is these "governing theories" that interest Peter Manning in the concluding article of this issue. Taking deadly aim at the correspondence theory of truth whereby the independence of the observer and the observed is assumed, Professor Manning displays how the language chosen to represent a given social world serves also to constrain and perhaps prefigure the analysis of that world. Since language or "styles of discourse" can be seen to shape organizational analysis, the author suggests that the researcher's own use of language become subject to methodological concern. Although the analysis of discourse has long been a key method of literary criticism, its use in social analysis is particularly pertinent and overdue since such analysis involves not only the interpretation of a "natural text" (social behavior) but the creation of another text as well through the descriptive accounts of social behavior generated by the researcher.

In closing, it must be said that the intent of this issue is to encourage the further develpment of qualitative study as a way of increasing the diversity of the field, thus increasing the sources of insight and discovery. We wish to encourage additionally a more penetrating and reflective approach to the study of organizations than has been the case to date. If this special issue sharpens the dialogue among observers of organizations and helps to create an increased awareness of the methodological options available to them, our purposes will have been achieved.

The Ethographic Paradigm(s)[1]

Peggy Reeves Sanday

Among the qualitative methodologies currently in use, the ethnographic method has a long and distinguished history. As practiced by anthropologists, ethnography involves a particular set of methodological and interpretive procedures that evolved primarily in the twentieth century. Ethnography, however, is at least as old as the work of Herodotus. With great and sometimes disdainful zest, that ancient Greek ethnographer recorded the infinite variety and strangeness he saw in other cultures.

Current anthropological ethnography is governed by a continuously developing paradigm which, according to Wallace (1972: 469), had its origins in the image of "Franz Boas stepping off the boat in an Eskimo village with his suitcase in hand, preparing for a long stay in residence." Using the term paradigm in the Kuhnian sense, Wallace says (p. 469), "this image is the paradigm." This image, which emerged early in the twentieth century, constituted a new paradigm because it was "opposed in a revolutionary way to a nineteenth century tradition of library scholarship and of uncritical use of the comparative method to derive models of cultural evolution" (p. 469). As Wallace (p. 469) points out, although Boas was not the first to do fieldwork and his fieldwork did not meet all the standards of his own paradigm, "he did effectively establish the fieldwork paradigm for American academic anthropology."

Since the days of Boas, the importance of a long residence and participant observation has not changed for ethnographers. However, a number of more specialized data collection procedures and differing interpretive emphases have been added to broaden the ethnographic paradigm. The purpose of this paper is to review some of the procedures and interpretive patterns guiding current ethnographic practice that have relevance for studying institutional settings within the United States.

THE RESEARCHER AS INSTRUMENT

Before discussing some of the divergent trends in the practice of ethnography, the consistency with which extended participant observation has remained central can be underscored. Most ethnographers, regardless of their theoretical persuasion, would agree on this point. Extended participant observation means that at least a year is devoted to the task. A long residence applies both to the comparative study of other cultures and to the study of institutional settings within a culture. In doing ethnographic studies of schools, for example, it has been recommended that the time of study should, at the very least, span the school year (Wolcott, 1975).

Participant observation demands complete commitment to the task of understanding. The ethnographer becomes part of the situation being studied in order to feel what it is like for the people in that situation. In addition to the time required, participant observation saps one's emotional energy. The ethnographer who becomes immersed in other people's realities is never quite the same afterward. The total immersion creates a kind of disorientation — culture shock — arising from the need to identify with and at the same time to remain distant from the process being studied.

When anthropologists explain their craft they often claim that "the anthropologist is the main instrument of observation" (see Mead, 1959b: 38; Metraux, 1959; Pelto, 1970; Wolcott, 1975). Fieldworkers learn to use themselves as the principal and most reliable instrument of observation, selection, coordination, and interpretation. Ethnography, as Metraux (1959: iii) says, "depends on this highly trained ability to respond — and to respect that response — as a whole person."

Participant observation is supplemented by a variety of data collection tools. Other tools are employed depending on the problem, access to data, and theoretical orientation. They may range from key-informant interviewing, collection of life histories, structured interviews, questionnaire administration to the less well-known techniques of ethnoscience. The main reason for employing a variety of data collection procedures is that it enables the investigator to cross check results obtained from observation and recorded in field notes.[2]

Two questions are frequently posed by anthropologists regarding the methods of ethnography. The first concerns the criteria by which a person's qualifications for conducting an ethnographic study are to be judged. One of the most important criteria in the past has been prior experience in another culture. George Spindler, a key figure in educational anthropology, has said that "no anthropologist-of-education-to-be should start with his or her first significant piece of empirical research in a school in our own society" (quoted in Wolcott, 1975: 115).

Such a restriction may appear overly demanding. Its rationale is based on the assumption that one comes to understand something by seeing it as an outsider. An anthropologist who has had experience studying another culture is likely to be more sensitive to the nuances observed at home, which otherwise might be ignored. As Clyde Kluckhohn has said, "It would hardly be fish who discovered the existence of water" (quoted in Wolcott, 1975: 115).

In teaching students the practice of ethnography, it is now common to place them in unfamiliar settings in their own society. Students may become cocktail waitresses, teachers' aides, sit behind the desk at a police station, or while away hours at a fire station. My experience with these students has been that it is possible to train those who are highly motivated to see the world from another's point of view without sending them to exotic foreign lands.

This capacity for empathy is not enough. One must also be able to record, categorize, and code what is being observed, that is, to take field notes. An empathetic fieldworker who does not know how to take field notes or how to use other data collection techniques is likely to take in a lot and give little in return. It is not sufficient to read in a grant or thesis proposal that the fieldworker intends to "do an ethnography using the standard fieldwork techniques." The aspiring fieldworker should indicate what categories of behavior will be attended to, how observations will be recorded, and how results will be cross checked. Because the categories of behavior may change while the fieldworker is in the field as the unexpected occurs, it is necessary also to judge the flexibility of the prospective fieldworkers.

The second question in connection with doing ethnographic studies concerns the criteria for judging the descriptive adequacy of the completed ethnography. These criteria are at once very simple and enormously complex. If, after having completed the ethnography, the observer can communicate the rules for proper and predictable conduct as judged by the people studied, he or she has produced a successful product. The ethnographer is like the linguist who has studied and recorded a foreign language so that others can learn the rules for producing intelligible speech in that language. As Frake (quoted in Wolcott, 1975: 121) says, the adequacy of ethnography is to be evaluated "by the ability of a stranger to the culture (who may be the ethnographer) to use the ethnography's statements as instructions for appropriately anticipating the scenes of the society."

STYLES OF PARADIGMATIC ETHNOGRAPHY

Since the ethnographer filters the data, the question arises as to whether we treat the product as science, art, journalism, or even fiction. Does ethnographic problem solving constitute "normal science" so that we can speak of an ethnographic paradigm, or is "doing ethnography" largely an effort to hold, as it were, a mirror up to nature in whatever way the individual deems fit?

The answer to these queries is, in the end, a matter of individual taste. For an understanding of British life in other centuries we may turn to Chaucer, Shakespeare, Boswell, or to a host of other contemporary commentators. For a view of contemporary American life we may turn to journalists, novelists, poets, or to ethnographers. Clearly, the latter are not the only or even the keenest observers of human cultural behavior. As for observers of other cultures, some of the early ethnographic classics were written by men who carefully recorded life in other cultures and who were not anthropologists. These writers, many of whom were missionaries or colonial officials, can be called ethnographers although they did not operate within an ethnographic paradigm. This means that they did not formulate a conscious concept of culture nor did they organize their materials according to a theory of culture. In short, there is an intersection but not a union between the domain of good ethnography and the domain of paradigmatic ethnography.

Paradigmatic ethnography begins when an observer, trained in or familiar with the anthropological approach, gets off the boat, train, plane, subway, or bus prepared for a lengthy stay with a suitcase full of blank notebooks, a tape recorder, and a camera. Paradigmatic ethnography ends when the masses of data that have been recorded, filed, stored, checked, and rechecked are organized according to one of several interpretive styles and published for a scholarly or general audience. In general, the styles that can be distilled from the body of ethnographic literature are (1) holistic, (2) semiotic, and (3) behavioristic.

Holistic Style

The holistic style is the oldest and is represented by at least two opposing cultural theories. On the one hand there are the configurationalists represented by the work of Benedict and Mead (Boas' students) and on the other there are the functionalists of British social anthropology represented by the work of Malinowski and Radcliffe-Brown. These four scholars were alike in their commitment to the study of culture as an integrated whole. They were different in the integrative models they chose in the inevitable dialogue between ethnographic fact and theory.

Benedict began her training under Boas in 1921 when the prevailing cultural theory was expressed in the notion, published by Lowie, that cultures were built over time out of unrelated "shreds and patches" (Lowie, 1920: 421).

Benedict was committed to the "historical particularism" of the Boasian program and to Boas' Baconian dedication to the primacy of induction. Boas profoundly disliked premature generalization and continually warned his students against making generalizations before all the facts were recorded, sifted, compared, and carefully analyzed (Mead, 1959b: 29; and Harris, 1968: 286–287).

During the 1920s the interaction of Mead, Benedict, and Boas led to a shift in the particularist framework. In 1930 Boas wrote: "An error of modern anthropology, as I see it, lies in the overemphasis on historical reconstruction, the importance of which should not be minimized, as against the penetrating study of the individual under the stress of the culture in which he lives" (Boas, 1948: 269). Benedict's configurationist concept emerged in this climate along with the notion that culture can be seen as "personality writ large," that is, as Mead (1974: 43) describes it "that each historical culture represents a many-generational process of paring, sifting, adapting, and elaborating on an available areal form, and that each culture, in turn, shapes the choices of those born and living within it."

In *Patterns of Culture,* published in 1934, Benedict emphasized a culture's tendency toward consistency. The central theme of this book is that each culture "selects" or "chooses" from the infinite variety of behavioral possibilities a limited segment which sometimes conforms to a configuration. Benedict (1932: 4) said that configurations in culture "so pattern existence and condition the emotional and cognitive reactions of its carriers that they become incommensurables, each specializing in certain selected types of behavior and each ruling out behavior proper to its opposites." She applied this point of view to three cultures and found two dominant types, the now well-known Apollonian distrust of excess and orgy which she contrasted with Dionysian cultivation of emotional and psychic excesses.

Mead, who was a student of both Benedict and Boas, made extensive use of the configurationalist framework during her formative period. She attributes to herself the first published statement of the configurationalist idea (see Mead, 1959a: 207; see also Harris, 1968: 407). In the winter of 1927–1928, Mead (1959a: 247) wrote, "So human societies, left to themselves, will select parts of their heritage for elaboration, and the original choice will gain in impetus from generation to generation until a coherent individual culture has been developed."

Mead differed from Benedict in that she did not sum up a whole culture in terms of a few dominant categories. She was more particularistic than Benedict and throughout her ethnographic career described dominant attitudes in terms specific to the culture in question. For example, after stating the configurationalist position Mead (1959a: 247) goes on to describe dominant cultural attitudes in Samoa, thereby shunning the universalistic terms that attracted Benedict:

A strong religious interest, a premium upon aberrant individual gifts, a permission to love without social sanction and give without stint to that which is loved; all these would disturb the nice balance of Samoan society and so are outlawed. Samoa may be said to have a formal social personality, to be a devotee of a careful observance of all the decreed amenities.

Mead and Benedict were interested in describing and interpreting the whole, not in explaining its origin beyond the effect of individuals on it. Moreover, Benedict did not think that all cultures could be fit into either the Apollonian-Dionysian scheme or into any other comparable configuration. "All cultures," she wrote (1934: 196) in *Patterns of Culture,* "have not shaped their thousand items of behavior to a balanced and rhythmic pattern; lack of integration seems to be a characteristic of certain cultures as extreme integration is of others." This disinterest in generalizing antagonized Radcliffe-Brown and Malinowski who were devoted not to the characterization of the cultural whole but to how each trait functions in the total cultural complex of which it is a part.

Although Radcliffe-Brown and Malinowski disagreed rather sharply they were more alike then their differences might suggest. Both employed an organismic analogy as their major analytical model and denied the value of speculative historical reconstruction. Both conceived of cultures as wholes and employed the term function in considering the social effect of customs and institutions (see Harris, 1968: 545–546 for a discussion of the similarities between these two men). According to Radcliffe-Brown (1949: 320–321), Malinowski defined functionalism as "the theory or doctrine that every feature of culture of any people past or present is to be explained by reference to seven biological needs of individual human beings." Radcliffe-Brown rejected this notion "as useless and worse," and said "as a consistent opponent of Malinowski's functionalism I may be called an anti-functionalist" (Radcliffe-Brown, 1949: 320–321).

Radcliffe-Brown (1952: 178) hailed Durkheim's definition of "function" as "the first systematic formulation of the concept applying to the strictly scientific study of society." He rejected definitions of function (such as the definition proposed by Malinowski) that did not relate function to "social structure." This combination gave rise to the label "structural-functional." The only acceptable definition of function for Radcliffe-Brown was the "contribution" an institution makes to the maintenance of social structure. "This theory of society in terms of structure and process, interconnected by function," Radcliffe-Brown (1949: 322) wrote "has nothing in common with the theory of culture as derived from individual biological needs." (See Harris, 1968: 515).

Radcliffe-Brown (1952: 9) partitioned the total social system into three "adaptional" analysis units: (1) social structure, or "the arrangements by which an orderly social life is maintained" ; (2) the "ecological," or the way the system is adapted to the physical environment; and (3) the culture, or the mechanisms by which an individual acquires "habits and mental characteristics that fit him for participation in social life" (Radcliffe-Brown, 1952: 9; see also Harris, 1968: 517).

The current structural-functional approach is widely employed in the conduct of school ethnography. In presenting the assumptions upon which school ethnography is based the Spindlers (1971: ix) say:

Education is a cultural process. Each new member of a society or a group must learn to act appropriately as a member and contribute to its maintenance and, occasionally, to its improvement. Education, in every cultural setting, is an instrument for survival. It is also an instrument for adaptation and change. To understand education we must study it as it is — imbedded in the culture of which it is an integral part and which it serves.

The key concepts in this statement are process, maintenance, survival, adaptation, change, imbedded in, and integral part of. Such concepts convey the image of a dynamic system straining toward maintenance and equilibrium. Each part of the system has its function, no part can be studied without considering its relation to other parts, and each new part which is added to the system must find its accepted fit. This image of social behavior as a dynamic system is one which most social scientists share. Regardless of the method employed most social science research of today is devoted to uncovering causal relationships and explaining covarying patterns.

The desire to interpret behavior as it fits a particular configuration is almost lost. This may be because explanation as opposed to interpretation has been the anthropological fashion of the past few decades. Perhaps it is time to return to the holistic style as practiced by Benedict and Mead. It would be interesting to see whether one could take a variety of organizational settings and compare them for their configurational texture as Benedict compared the Zuni, Dobuans, and Kwakiutl, or as Mead compared three New Guinean societies for the relationship between sex and temperament. Along these lines, one might ask to what extent do organizational settings in the United States select different aspects of the American culture to emphasize and to demand of their members? How are newcomers initiated to the constraints of the organizational culture? Another question of interest concerns the historical process by which organizations come to emphasize certain behavior as acceptable and to regard certain behavior as deviant.

Semiotic Style

The explanatory and interpretive modes can be discerned in the semiotic approach to the study of culture. The core of the semiotic style lies in the search for the "native's point of view." "The whole point of a semiotic approach to culture is," Geertz (1973: 24) says, "to aid us in gaining access to the conceptual world in which our subjects live so that we can, in some extended sense of the term, converse with them." The basis for the semiotic approach can be traced to Boas' notion that the main task of the anthropologist was "the adoption of an informant's mode of thought while retaining full use of his own critical faculties" (Mead, 1959b: 38).

In recent years the semiotic approach has produced the highly specialized field of "ethnoscience" on the one hand and "thick description" on the other. These two prongs of the semiotic approach, guided by different epistemologies, have produced the usual exchange of prickly remarks between the major adherents, in this case Geertz and Goodenough.

Geertz (1973: 5–6) believes that "man is an animal suspended in webs of significance he himself has spun." Geertz (pp. 5-6) takes culture to be those webs and the analysis of culture to be "not an experimental science in search of law but an interpretive one in search of meaning." For Geertz anthropological analysis requires "thick description," that is, wading through the clusters upon clusters of symbols by which man confers significance upon his own experience. According to Geertz "doing ethnography" is not a matter of methods — of establishing rapport, selecting informants, transcribing texts, taking genealogies, mapping fields, keeping a diary, and so on. What defines the ethnographic enterprise, Geertz (pp. 5-6) says, "is the kind of intellectual effort it is: an elaborate venture in, to borrow a notion from Gilbert Ryle, 'thick description.'"

Geertz shares the Boasian disdain for generalization and scientism. Geertz (p. 5) declares, with complete seriousness, "operationalism as a methodological dogma never made much sense so far as the social sciences are concerned, and except for a few rather too well-swept corners — Skinnerian behaviorism, intelligence testing, and so on — it is largely dead now." For Geertz anthropological writings are second- and third-order interpretations. They are "fictions; fictions, in the sense that they are 'something made' " (p. 15). To describe the actions and involvements of people with one another, he says (pp. 15-16), "is clearly an imaginative act, not all that different from constructing similar descriptions of, say, the involvements with one another of a provincial French doctor, his silly, adulterous wife, and her feckless lover in nineteenth century France."

Despite what Geertz says about ethnography as art, he does in fact work within the ethnographic paradigm. His comments on building cultural theory can be compared with those of Mead, for example. He says (1973: 26) that "the essential task of theory building is not to codify abstract regularities but to make thick description possible," "not to generalize across cases but to generalize within them." He likens this process to clinical inference which begins with a set of symptoms and attempts to place them within an intelligible frame. In culture the symptoms are symbolic acts or clusters of symbolic acts. Theory is used to ferret out the unapparent import of things. Cultural theory is diagnostic, not predictive.

Such a view of how theory functions in an interpretive science suggests to Geertz the distinction between "inscription" (thick description) and "specification" (diagnosis) as contrasted with the distinction between description and explanation found in the experimental or observational sciences. The distinction Geertz favors (1973: 27) is "between setting down the meaning particular social actions have for the actors whose actions they are, and stating, as explicitly as we can manage, what the knowledge thus attained demonstrates about the society in which it is found and, beyond that, about social life as such."

Similarly, Mead (1962: 134) declared no sympathy for the attempt to build a science of man which "would conform to the ideal science, physics" and her sympathy for "those who have insisted on the complexity and uniqueness of significant events in the life of a bird or the life of a human being." Even more to the point, Mead argued against the relevance of statistics for problems that required complex situational and emotional statements of context and compared her role to that of an insightful medical diagnostician. The student of the more intangible and psychological aspects of human behavior, she said (1949: 169), "is forced to illuminate rather than demonstrate a thesis" just as the physician and the psychiatrist "have found it necessary to describe each case separately and to use their cases as illuminations of a thesis rather than as irrefutable proof such as it is possible to adduce in the physical sciences."

The second prong of the semiotic style is variously called "ethnoscience," "componential analysis," or "cognitive anthropology" — a terminological wavering, Geertz says (1973: 11), "which reflects a deeper uncertainty." This school of thought is committed to the notion that culture is located in the minds and hearts of men. Goodenough (1971: 41), the leading proponent of this view, defines culture as consisting of whatever it is one has to know or believe in order to operate in a manner acceptable to its members. Goodenough (1971: 41) defines culture in ideational terms as "a system of standards for perceiving, believing, evaluating, and acting." In order to be competent in a given cultural scene one must learn the prevailing standards in order to act appropriately and to anticipate the actions of others.

Cultural description in Goodenough's terms involves the writing out of systematic rules, of formulating ethnographic algorithms, which make it possible to produce acceptable actions much as the writing out of linguistic rules makes it possible to produce acceptable utterances. On close analysis the differences between Geertz and Goodenough are not in aim but in method, focus, and mode of reporting. Goodenough (1974: 435–436) discusses some of these differences in his review of Geertz' book *Interpretation of Cultures.*

By refusing to recognize that symbols are located in the minds and hearts of men, Goodenough says, Geertz' view of culture entails a paradox. Symbols and their meanings are at once social and public and "at the same time learned by processes that, however much stimulated socially, are intrasomatic and incapable of being observed directly" (p. 435). Goodenough believes (1974: 435) that the resolution of this paradox is "the crux of the problem of cultural theory." By stressing the public nature of symbols, Goodenough argues, Geertz rivets attention on only one of two relevant areas. When people manifest themselves to one another through symbolically governed behavior they make it possible for each to go to work cognitively on what has been symbolically communicated. The job of cultural analysis and cultural theory, thus, is to examine what gets publicly exchanged and cognitively recorded.

The cognitive anthropologist supplements participant observation with a battery of specialized techniques. Videotapes, tape recorders, and ethnoscience elicitation procedures are used to gauge the underlying rules for behavior and the implicit categorizations by which people order their world. These rules and categorizations are framed by the ethnographer in a kind of grammar of culture. The mode of reporting is also highly technical, more like the lexicon and grammar published by the linguist than like "thick description."

There are several differing methodologies which can be subsumed under the heading "ethnoscience." These methodologies vary in quantitative emphasis and in the degree to which the unit for analysis corresponds with the whole. At one extreme there are the multi-dimensional scalers whose goal is to derive orthogonal dimensions representing meaning from a self-contained universe of terms such as terms for firewood, plants, diseases, colors, and so on. In a sense scholars employing ethnoscience techniques for these ends are doing semantic analysis and not ethnography. The unit of analysis in these cases is the terminological universe under study and the main information gathering tool is a set of questions designed to elicit the terms in question.

At the other extreme are scholars like Goodenough whose interest is in building the whole from careful study of the parts. The parts are more broadly conceived in Goodenough's schema than in the more technical applications. Goodenough conceives of standards for perceiving, evaluating, believing, and doing at various levels. For example there is what he calls the "individual propriospect" which is the set of all standards an individual attributes to other persons as a result of his experience of their actions and admonitions. Then there is a person's "operating culture" which is the particular standards used on a given occasion to interpret the behavior of others or to guide one's own behavior. Above the level of operating culture there is a group's "public culture" consisting of the set of all individual versions of expected behavior in a given setting. A society's "culture" is the overall system of mutually ordered public cultures pertaining to all activities within a society. Finally, there is a society's "culture pool" which is the sum of the contents of all of the "propriospects" of all of the society's members, including every system of standards of which any member happens to have knowledge (Goodenough, 1971).

Though widely discussed and admired, "thick description" is less frequently applied than the different uses of "ethnoscience" (or "ethnomethodology" as it is called in sociology). The reason for this may be that, though difficult to learn, the methods of cognitive anthropology can be more precisely stated and followed. It takes more than method to do thick description. It requires an almost artistic insight which can be perfected in those who have it but which can not be taught.

Goodenough's approach is useful for making the leap from description to comparison. Anthropologists have long recognized that the same cultural element, such as the concept of property or the term for father, may mean different things in different cultures. Hence, when comparing cultures it becomes necessary to reduce categories of behavior to comparable forms. Goodenough makes the leap from description to comparison by employing the distinction, first proposed by the linguist Kenneth Pike, between the emics and etics of socially meaningful human behavior.

Emic analysis involves isolating and describing the ideational elements of cultural behavior and how these combine to form larger patterns. For example, when Goodenough began to prepare an account of the workings of Truk's social organization he found that he could not describe kin-group organization without first describing property transactions. Examining property relationships forced him to look at the forms of entitlement that Truk's rules of the social game allowed. Definition of Truk descent groups had to be made in terms of these forms of entitlement. Goodenough found that he had to build up an account of the culture of social organization in Truk from a set of what he calls the "elementary or primitive concepts in Trukese culture" (1970: 108–109).

The task of developing typologies of cultural behavior for cross-cultural comparison rests on etic and not emic concepts. When we compare cultural forms, such as property relationships, Goodenough says, we must look not at the content of these forms but at their function. The emic entities in different cultures are transformed to an appropriate set of etic concepts by virtue of some kind of function. Thus, we would label "property" in Truk the cultural forms that seem to be the functional analogues of what is labelled property in Anglo-American culture (1970, 120–121).

Behavioristic Style

With the emphasis on form and function in comparison we leave the domain of meaning and enter the domain of behaviorism. Behaviorism in anthropological ethnography involves the formulation of deductive propositions. The ethnographic portion of such studies is not meant to uncover meaning or to diagnose the whole. Rather, its purpose is to provide observational data on preselected functionally relevant categories. A good example of this approach is the well-known "Six Culture Study" associated primarily with the Whitings (see B. Whiting, 1963).

The Six Culture Study was aimed at exploring cross-culturally the relation between different patterns of child rearing and subsequent differences in personality. It was designed to study the degree to which the treatment a child receives in the first years of life determines his behavior and in adult life influences his perception of the world, his philosophy, religion, and code of ethics.
To ensure general comparability of data a field guide was developed that presented the overall research plan and hypotheses to be tested. Implicit in the research design was a general model of the relation of personality to culture which guided the types of observations made in the field. In addition to collecting data for testing this model cross-culturally the design included assessing intracultural differences. While the cross-cultural measures were based on the standard ethnographic techniques of participation, observation, and recording, the intracultural measures were more structured and included sampling, timed observation, and interviewing in a standard manner (Whiting, 1963).

This approach is labeled "behavioristic" here because its main goal is to uncover covarying patterns in observed be-

havior. The main adherents seek to form an integrated behavioral science approach by drawing their hypotheses from
"a combination of the psychoanalytic theory of personality
development, learning theory, and cultural anthropology."
The independent variables are labelled "behavior systems."
A "behavior system" is defined as "a set of habits or customs motivated by a common drive and leading to common
satisfactions" (Whiting et al., 1966: vi). In addition to the
Whitings' work, such an approach is associated with the
work of Robert LeVine and George Murdock. This approach
departs the most radically from the Boasian particularistic,
inductive framework.

CONCLUSION

Obviously the ethnographic paradigm in anthropology is in-
ternally differentiated. The main differences are whether the
primary focus is on the whole, the meaning, or the behavior
and the degree to which the analytic goal is diagnosis or
explanation. Which mode one adopts in one's own work is a
matter of taste and not of dogma. Most anthropologists
who go into the field have probably been trained by scholars
who employ some combination of these ethnographic
styles. Hence, upon return from the field anthropologists
may hear echoes of various intellectual ancestors as they
write their findings. Accordingly their ethnographic product
is likely to be embraced by some and rejected by others.

What counts in the long run is not how the facts are
dressed but whether they make sense. The men and
women whose work has been described above have all provided us with ethnographic pictures that have managed to
capture our imagination and to advance knowledge. Which
mode one adopts in studying an institutional setting within a
culture depends on one's goals as well as one's taste. For
example, if one wants to understand the inner workings of a
bureaucracy in all its complex detail the interpretive mode
seems the most relevant. If, on the other hand, one assumes that there are general rules by which bureaucracies
function, the explanatory-comparative mode may be more
appropriate.

Perhaps of greatest interest is whether any given scholar interprets or explains — makes a "fiction" or a "science" out of — the ethnographic product. It is worth repeating that the choice depends on a combination of individual temperament and the accidents of academic training. Within the field of anthropology there exists a strong undercurrent of interpretation that affects most practicing anthropologists in varying degrees. An equally strong urge to produce verifiable propositions can also be discerned. It is difficult to predict the future. How scholars in other disciplines make use of the ethnographic paradigm has been and will continue to be instructive. At this point there is ample evidence that the ethnographic paradigm is "alive and kicking." Certainly, no new symbol or image is current from which a new paradigm may evolve to become opposed in a revolutionary way to the twentieth century tradition of ethnography.

NOTES

1

Preparation of this paper has been assisted by a purchase order, P-79-0029, from the National Institute of Education. The views expressed are the author's, of course.

This paper owes its inception to Fritz Mulhauser of the National Institute of Education who asked me to prepare a paper on the comparative uses of school ethnography as part of my activities as a member of NIE's Organization Research Study Group. Karl Weick, then chairman of this study group, encouraged me in this effort. Weick's metaphoric use of "loose coupling" to describe the structure of school bureaucracies reminded me of those days in anthropology when a well-turned metaphor did not compete with quantitative modes for communicating. At a conference on ethnographic methodology, sponsored by the Organization Research Study Group, Murray Wax gave additional shape to this paper when he spoke of writing up one's field notes as a kind of "dialoguing with one's anthropological ancestors." John Van Maanen provided another important impetus when he suggested that I frame my views on the ethnographic craft in a historical perspective.

The term "paradigm" is used in this paper along the lines explicated by Thomas Kuhn in *The Structure of Scientific Revolutions* (1962). There is some question in anthropology as to whether there is more than one paradigm currently guiding ethnographic practice. If the term "paradigm" is used to imply a model for collecting data and a theory for interpreting results then there is more than one ethnographic paradigm as this paper will show. However, if the term paradigm is used to mean doing "normal science" within the continuously developing domain of interpretations which have evolved since Boas established the importance of a lengthy residence and of understanding reality from the native's point of view, then the ethnographic paradigm can be seen as changing with respect to method and theory but not with respect to basic intent.

2
See Pelto (1970) for an extended discussion of ethnographic methods and Wolcott (1975) for the application of these methods to the ethnographic study of schools.

REFERENCES

Benedict, Ruth
1932 "Configurations of culture in North America." American Anthropologist, 34: 1–27.
1934 Patterns of Culture. New York: Houghton Mifflin.

Boas, Franz
1948 Race, Language, and Culture. New York: MacMillan.

Geertz, Clifford
1973 The Interpretation of Cultures. New York: Basic Books.

Goodenough, Ward
1970 Description and Comparison in Cultural Anthropology. Chicago: Aldine.
1971 Culture, Language, and Society. Reading, MA: Addison-Wesley Modular Publications, No. 7.
1974 "On cultural theory." Science, 186: 435–436.

Harris, Marvin
1968 The Rise of Anthropological Theory. New York: Crowell.

Kuhn, Thomas
1962 The Structure of Scientific Revolution. Chicago: University Press.

Lowie, Robert
1920 Primitive Society. New York: Boni and Liveright.

Mead, Margaret
1949 Coming of Age in Samoa (orig. 1928). New York: New American Library, Mentor Books.
1959a An Anthropologist at Work: Writings of Ruth Benedict. Boston: Houghton Mifflin.
1959b "Apprenticeship under Boas." Walter Goldschmidt (ed.), The Anthropology of Franz Boas, Memoir 89: 29–45. Washington: American Anthropological Association.

1962 "Retrospects and prospects." In T. Gladwin and W. C. Sturtevant (eds.), Anthropology and Human Behavior. Washington: Anthropological Society of Washington.
1974 Ruth Benedict. New York: Columbia University Press.

Metraux, Rhoda
1959 "Foreword." in M. Mead, An Anthropologist at Work: Writings of Ruth Benedict. Boston: Houghton Mifflin.

Pelto, P. J.
1970 Anthropological Research, the Structure of Inquiry. New York: Harper & Row.

Radcliffe-Brown, A. R.
1949 "Functionalism: A protest." American Anthropologist, 51: 320–323.
1952 Structure and Function in Primitive Society. London: Oxford University Press.

Spindler, George, and Louise Spindler
1971 "Foreword." In G. Rosenfeld, Shut Those Thick Lips!: ix. New York: Holt, Rinehart and Winston.

Wallace, Anthony F. C.
1972 "Paradigmatic processes in culture change." American Anthropologist, 74: 467–478.

Whiting, Beatrice, ed.
1963 Six Cultures. New York: Wiley.

Whiting, John, Irvin L. Child, and William W. Lambert
1966 Field Guide for a Study of Socialization. New York: Wiley.

Wolcott, Harry
1975 "Criteria for an ethnographic approach to research in schools." Human Organization, 34: 111–128.

The Fact of Fiction in Organizational Ethnography

John Van Maanen

"The temptation to form premature theories upon insufficient data," remarked Sherlock Holmes to Inspector Mac-Donald in *The Valley of Fear* (Baring-Gould, 1967), "is the bane of our profession." The same could be said of those of us conducting social research in organizations since, following the customary and respected practices of the day, we tend also to theorize well in advance of our facts thus allowing for the possibility that the facts that emerge from our studies are twisted to fit a given theory. Yet, it is still the case that provisional hypotheses, tentative speculations, commonsensical hunches, and other tenderly held presuppositions about the world often represent the best we can do when attempting to see, grasp, and perhaps decode empirical phenomena. Faced with routine uncertainty and doubt, the most we can do with or without the scientific method is to wait for time and fuller knowledge to explode whatever theoretical constructions we have built.

From this perspective, the amount of time an investigator spends constructing a theory by actively seeking the facts is a variable and one that presumably should be related to the quality of the theory that emerges from the field of study. The Sherlockian prescription as applied to organizational research is therefore simple, sequential, and reflexive: less theory, better facts; more facts, better theory.

Methodologically, organizational researchers schooled in an ethnographic tradition take this prescription rather seriously. In essence, ethnographers believe that separating the facts from the fictions, the extraordinary from the common, and the general from the specific is best accomplished by lengthy, continuous, firsthand involvement in the organizational setting under study. Although capable of generating massive amounts of data, the strategy is risky nevertheless. Ethnographic research is guided as much from drift as design and is perhaps the source of far more failures than successes. Assuming an ethnographic stance is by no means a guarantee that one will collect accurate and theoretically useful data no matter how long one remains in the field. Much of this operational difficulty lies in the rather wide-spread confusion that surrounds the various kinds of empirical information generated by an ethnographic study as well as the confusion that surrounds the theoretical uses to which such information can be put. My objective in this paper is to reduce some of this confusion by tying empirical discovery and conceptual development in ethnographic work to the specific experiences of the researcher.

BACKGROUND

The ethnographic approach is that of anthropology, and, to a more limited extent, sociology, under the stiff but precise tag, participant observation.[1] As practiced, this approach allows a fieldworker to use the culture of the setting (the socially acquired and shared knowledge available to the participants or members of the setting) to account for the observed patterns of human activity. In organizational studies, the patterns of interest are typically the various forms in which people manage to do things together in observable and repeated ways. Procedurally, the ethnographic method is described by Conklin (1968: 172) as involving "a long period of intimate study and residence in a well-defined community employing a wide range of observational techniques including prolonged face-to-face contact with members of local groups, direct participation in some of the group's activities, and a greater emphasis on intensive work with informants than on the use of documentary or survey data."

My own work has attempted to be true to this procedural decree and over the past decade I have been involved in several projects of which ethnographic fieldwork was the principal data-gathering method.[2] Analytically, the aim of these studies has been to uncover and explicate the ways in which people in particular work settings come to understand, account for, take action, and otherwise manage their day-to-day situation. Specifically, much of my work has taken place in police agencies and has addressed such matters as recruit socialization (Van Maanen, 1973, 1975), police careers (Van Maanen and Schein, 1976; Van Maanen, 1978a), the street behavior of patrolmen (Van Maanen, 1974), and police labeling practices (Van Maanen, 1978b).

In the sections that follow, I discuss certain aspects of the information I have managed to collect, categorize, and publicly report as a result of my police studies. First, a fundamental distinction is made between an informant's first-order conception of what is going on in the setting and the researcher's second-order conceptions of what is going on. Second, working with first-order concepts, the differences between presentational and operational data are described. In this section, I argue that maintaining the separation between these two types of first-order data is the key analytic task faced by the ethnographer in the field. Third, the various ways in which an ethnographer can be misled in the research setting as to what constitutes operational data are denoted. If undetected, such deceptions allow for the distinct possibility that fictions will be reported as facts (and facts as fictions). Fourth, the analysis is brought to a close by observing that ethnographers merge the empirical and analytic aspects of research work and by so doing create an elusive and everexpanding procedural mandate.

First-Order and Second-Order Concepts

Put simply, first-order concepts are the "facts" of an ethnographic investigation and the second-order concepts are the "theories" an analyst uses to organize and explain these facts. The facts come in varying forms however. At one level, certain descriptive properties of the studied scene serve as facts, for example, the number of arrests made by the vice squad or the particular rules enforced by a certain patrol sergeant. Of course, such facts do not speak for themselves and the fieldworker must therefore deal with another level of first-order fact, namely: the situationally, historically, and biographically mediated interpretations used by members of the organization to account for a given descriptive property. Thus, the arrest pattern may be seen by some as the result of an administrative attempt to "crackdown" on prostitution. The sergeant's activities might be rendered sensible to certain members of the organization by assigning the sergeant to an indigenous character type known to the police as "brown-nosers" (those aggressively amibitious supervisors who struggle to make rank by zealously enforcing departmental rules and regulations). Both the descriptive properties of the studied scene and the member interpretations of what stands behind these properties are first-order concepts. At the empirical level, then, both behavior and member depictions of such behavior must be viewed within the framework of the observed.

Second-order concepts are those notions used by the fieldworker to explain the patterning of the first-order data. Descriptively, many second-order concepts are simply statements about relationships between certain properties observed to covary in the setting and may occasionally converge with first-order interpretations. Arrest patterns, for example, may be seen by the ethnographer and the police administrator alike as sensitive to the organizational policies regarding pay for overtime and court time. On the other hand, second-order concepts are perhaps most interesting when they do not converge for it is here that the fieldworker may have something novel to say. Typically, the more theoretically engaging second-order concepts represent what could be called "interpretations of interpretations."

Consider everyday police talk. Here the ethnographer is often handling first-order conceptions that reveal an informant's formulation of social structure (i.e., the informant's version of an ordered set of social relationships). If a patrolman claims, for example, "I don't want nothing to do with Horton, he's a fucking call jumper,"[3] that patrolman is displaying his sense of social structure. Implicit in the statement are at least three second-order conceptions bearing upon: (1) the role relations existing among patrolmen; (2)

the competitive structure of policing; and (3) the centrality of a patrolman's assigned territory or "turf" to the practice of policing. To the ethnographer, these matters are seen as deeply embedded in the commonsensical though unarticulated understandings carried by virtually all members of the police culture. They represent what Cicourel (1967) calls "background expectancies" and as such they must always be inferred by the fieldworker since such assumptions are regarded as fully unproblematic by members of the studied organization. To draw out such second-order concepts is perhaps the most difficult yet most interesting goal of the ethnographic enterprise.

It should be clear however that when first formulated such second-order conceptions are relevant primarily to the culture of the researcher, not the researched. Consciously selected strategies must then be employed by the ethnographer to build such concepts. The strategy most commonly employed by a fieldworker is to explicitly examine the linguistic categories used by informants in the setting to describe various aspects of their routine and problematic situations. To continue my illustration, initially the label call jumper first suggested to me a class of phenomena apparently important to the police but one with which I was unfamiliar. Thus, having generated the category, I attempted to distinguish between the category as *seen* and the category as *heard.* Only by observing the phenomena firsthand and questioning the police about the actions they had just taken (or not taken) was I able to corroborate and elaborate upon what my informants were telling me. This is simply to say that my second-order conceptions of the first-order class of events known to policemen as "call jumping" rested upon both my talking to the police and observing the contextual contingencies upon which the use of the label was based. On the other hand, the understanding of this class of events carried by my informants rested on their continuing socialization in the natural setting and the sense of normality that results from such a process (Van Maanen, 1977). Thus, the meaning of "call jumping" to an informant was self-evident and in no need of explanation while to me its meaning was almost totally obscured by my [initial] ignorance of police work.[4]

Given that one aim of ethnography in organizational settings is to derive second-order concepts, it is obvious that such concepts are dependent upon the faith the fieldworker can sustain in the first-order concepts uncovered in the setting. In brief, most first-order concepts can be typed as being primarily presentational or operational. A central task then is to correctly type first-order concepts for if they are mis-typed, many second-order concepts developed by the ethnographer are likely to be rather thin, hollow, and perhaps altogether faulty.

Presentational and Operational Data

Field data represent primarily the ethnographer's recording of first-order concepts as they arise from the observed talk and action of participants in the studied scene. This informa-tion is of two generic but distinct types. First, there is the "operational data" which documents the running stream of spontaneous conversations and activities engaged in and ob-served by the ethnographer while in the field. These data surface in known and describable contexts and pertain to the everyday problematics of informants going about their affairs. Second, there are the "presentational data" which concern those appearances that informants strive to main-tain (or enhance) in the eyes of the fieldworker, outsiders and strangers in general, work colleagues, close and intimate associates, and to varying degrees, themselves. Data in this category are often ideological, normative, and abstract, deal-ing far more with a manufactured image of idealized doing than with the routinized practical activities actually engaged in by members of the studied organization. In short, opera-tional data deal with observed activity (behavior per se) and presentational data deal with the appearances put forth by informants as these activities are talked about and otherwise symbolically projected within the research setting.

The line separating these two strains of data is not always distinct. Verbal depictions are invariably recorded along with the concrete activities observed to be taking place. What the researcher is told cannot always be observed or assessed with any confidence as to its accuracy. Even when dealing with directly observable behavior, it is sometimes quite dif-ficult for an observer to grasp its contextual meaning to those whose behavior is being described. Often one only sees (and, hence, understands) what is happening after having been first told what to look for. A wink, a blink, or nod is not merely a fleck of behavior to be described without ambiguity but is rather a potential sign that must be read as to what is signified.

These bothersome facts suggest rather pointedly that separating operational and presentational data is an *analytic* accomplishment that must be attended to continually by a fieldworker. If the researcher somehow loses sight of this distinction there is the possibility that the presentational data will literally swamp the operational data, thus masking the difference between fact and fiction in the findings generated from ethnographic study. Fieldwork, despite the best intentions of the researcher, almost always boils down to a series of endless conversations intersected by a few major events and a host of less formidable ones. The information as recorded by the fieldworker is then primarily talk based not only because this is what occupies the vast majority of the ethnographer's time but also because, as noted above, understanding the concrete activities taking place in the field is grounded largely upon what members have to say about what such activities mean to them. Moreover, because the ethnographer focuses on both behavior and the symbolic worlds within which such behavior is located, the meaning and significance of the events of interest to one's informants can not be known merely by analyzing the number of times such events are observed to take place.

To hear patrolmen talk of "street justice," for instance, might lead a listener to believe that its application occupies a fair amount of work time in police organizations.[5] Attempting to find out about "street justice" by talking to my informants, I collected information cast in ideal terms. At times, when asked to explain or describe what the phrase meant, a patrolman would respond by giving a recent example but on the basis of the example alone I was unable to assess whether the case cited was imaginary or real, exceptional or ordinary, unusual practice or standard. In order to separate the presentational from operational, I had to not only check the various features of the talk against other stories I had heard (and would later solicit), but, most important, I had to see the implementation of "street justice" firsthand and compare my direct observations with the accounts provided to me by others. In other words, if "street justice" was to be set in operational terms, it was imperative that I observe at least a few of its occasions. Yet no sample could be used. Indeed, in a year and a half of fieldwork, I have seen what my informants would unhesitatingly call "street justice" on only four or five occasions. The relative availability of operational data will of course vary by topic, by site, by informant, by time spent in the field, and so forth. But, it is nonetheless true of fieldwork that when it comes to the events one's informants regard as significant, one must often lean far more on what one hears than on what one sees.[6]

Given this unavoidable aspect of fieldwork, the ethnographer always runs the risk of mistaking presentational for operational data. Worthy of further note in this regard is the nasty fact that the fieldworker may find it difficult to generalize (to develop second-order concepts) from specific practices (operational data) without merely parroting back the normative abstractions (presentational data) used by members of the studied group to both describe and account for their behavior. Events bearing on an individual's behavior are often quite literally hidden from view. For both the fieldworker and the informant, particular events take on significance and meaning insofar as at least one cultural interpretation exists for what is taking place. From this standpoint, ethnography (and everyday life) is as much "believing is seeing" as it is "seeing is believing." Inference and trust are central matters here and therefore evaluating the believability of what one hears and sees is critical in the analytic task of separating the operational from the presentational data.

Lies, Ignorance, and [Taken-for-Granted] Assumptions

Do informants speak the truth as they know it to the fieldworker? Does a particular *in situ* activity have the characteristics ascribed to it by the fieldworker? These issues (and more) must be addressed by the researcher and, in some way, handled by typing the information obtained as true or false from the informant's perspective, as operational or presentational from the fieldworker's perspective, or as ambiguous and uncertain from one or both perspectives. This is not to say, however, that lies, deceptions, evasions, conjectures, and so on are categorically disregarded by the ethnographer. To the contrary, false and misleading information is exceedingly valuable to the fieldworker when it is recognized as false. Given this methodological premise, it is important to examine the ways ethnographic data, primarily talk-based data, can mislead the fieldworker.

First, the researcher can be misled because informants want it that way. People lie, evade, and otherwise deceive the fieldworker in numerous and inventive ways. I have often been purposely led astray by patrolmen in my police studies. Consider the recurring statements I heard from many officers attesting to the "fact" that they felt under no pressure whatsoever to make certain kinds of arrests when on patrol.

It was of some importance apparently to these patrolmen that they be seen as autonomous, independent actors in the police drama for they took great care to present themselves in such a manner. But, their actions often belied their words for, on many occasions, I sat with these same officers in their prowl cars outside dimly lit taverns simply waiting for the first unsteady (and unlucky) patron to drive away. In this fashion, any number of drunk driving arrests could be enacted with dispatch and assured "quality." More to the point, however, on such occasions, these not-so-cunning arrests were said by the men to be necessary for "getting the drunk-hunting sergeant off our backs for awhile."

A central postulate of the ethnographic method is that people lie about the things that matter most to them. Penetrating fronts, a phrase used with powerful effect by Douglas (1976), then becomes one of the more important goals of the competent fieldworker. If the ethnographer can uncover the lie, much is revealed about what is deemed crucial by the individual, group, or organization. Evasion too enters the calculus of deception for it is unfortunately true that most informants are only as good as the questions put to them. For example, after having become rather close to a particular informant over the course of a year, I learned from an ex-partner of his that he had twice been suspended from the department for alleged misconduct (brutality) on the street. When I later asked my friend why he had never bothered to mention this aspect of his police career to date, he remarked with a wry but embarrassed smile, "You never asked."[7]

Three kinds of discrediting information are most often shielded by the conscious deception. "Hidden failings" represent one category and deal with a particular informant's own private and personal flaws, disreputable interests, or shameful errors. Disclosures of this type are relatively rare in fieldwork for such information surfaces only when the researcher inadvertently stumbles over it or creates a very special relationship with a given informant. Another category is represented by certain "rotten apple" disclosures which refer to those perceived character defects, flagrant individual mistakes, or taboo-violating local activities thought to be associated with a specified other in the organization. Materials of this sort are again notoriously difficult for an ethnographer to come by since most informants are quite aware of the rather deep interpersonal rule that suggests the protection of one's own self is based in large measure on the protection of the selves of others. In police circles at least, peer protection at the street level is almost a point of honor though fleeting glimpses are sometimes provided of others by certain members of the organization (notably the most marginal and least occupationally committed members). The last category concerns those disclosures of "collective secrets." Information in this domain typically deals with certain widely known, but controversial practices engaged in by members within certain social segments of the organization. Once, after having been uncharacteristically but unmistakably waved from a dispatched "investigate open door" assignment by another patrol unit, my partner for the evening remarked: "those fucking mopes in Charlie Three, ripping the goddamn place off [a department store warehouse] and on my call yet." Information in this domain is relatively easy to come by — though not always easy to check — since such practices are often deeply resented (or strongly supported) by others and many people in the setting are only too eager to express their disdain (or approval).[8]

The second way a researcher can be misled in ethnography is when one's informants are themselves misled and wrong about matters of their concern. To wit, several informed observers of the police are woefully ignorant (yet still assertive) of the laws they are charged with enforcing (e.g., Banton, 1964; Black, 1971; Manning, 1977). Of methodological interest is the notion that randomness per se is of relatively little value to an ethnographer when assessing the believability of the data produced. A fundamental principle of fieldwork is that the researcher's account of the studied scene should be built on the information provided by the most knowledgeable (and candid) members of that scene. For example, several police recruits were convinced that the "policeman's discount" on retail goods in many downtown shops was a thing of the past. However, others in the department told me the opposite. To check these contradictory statements, I occasionally "buzzed a clerk" (displayed my police badge) when paying for certain goods in certain downtown stores and was rewarded with information as to who was more knowledgeable among my informants.

There is a general point underlying this cautionary tale. Not all informants are good informants since the information they possess — regardless of their willingness to part with it — is hardly equivalent. In the police world (as perhaps in all organizational worlds), those persons who strictly adhere to most departmental rules and regulations are unusual and are considered by many others on the scene to be culturally incompetent in the local setting. Patrolmen who always read an accused suspect their rights upon an arrest or patrolmen who answered every call dispatched to their unit were considered by most of their colleagues to be stupid. What is proper may not be either popular or rational to all members of an organization and informants will differ greatly along these lines. The distribution of knowledge about what is going on in any organization is an important part of the sociology of that organization and the fieldworker must take care to establish the limits of an informant's expertise.

The third way an ethnographer can be misled is because informants are sometimes totally unaware of certain aspects underlying many of their own activities. Like fish who are presumably unaware of the water in which they swim, there are things associated with police work that all policemen take more or less for granted and therefore have a difficult time articulating. All the patrolmen I studied, for example, talked of their "duck ponds" where it was felt they could write as many moving traffic citations as they so chose. Such duck ponds would be described, for example, as those busy but poorly marked intersections in the city where illegal turns were frequent or those unobtrusive side streets located just beyond certain hills where motorists would speed by. What was never mentioned when talking about these territories was, however, the crucial fact that pedestrian traffic was by and large virtually absent from the most popular duck ponds. Yet, this fact alone was what was common to duck ponds across the city since a working policeman had no desire to be pestered or otherwise bothered by the passing pedestrian who, if not seeking aid or direction, might accuse the officer of loafing on the job, being unnecessarily sneaky in the performance of the job, or acting as mere automaton in meeting what to the citizen might be seen as an obnoxious ticket quota. At any rate, by simply relying on the stated rationale supplied by patrol officers for choosing their duck ponds, I would have been easily misled and missed this rather taken-for-granted but critical aspect of police work.

Another class of "things everybody knows" (but are not typically aware of) are discovered in what Goffman (1971) refers to as "negatively eventful occasions." What is meant by this phrase is simply that the obviousness of certain features in a social scene comes about only when something else in that scene has been removed, goes awry, or is in some way altered. As Emerson (1970) so pointedly demonstrates, the notion of normality can only be described in reference to what is considered deviant. For instance, to answer a "barking dog" call when first dispatched was an occasion worthy of note to my informants since such calls were typically ignored by most patrol units (though routinely cleared as "unable to locate"). The example of "call jumping" is also good in this regard since the label itself arises from a breach in the taken-for-granted and usually unproblematic assumptions that surround police activity. In the interplay between theory and data as both are generated in the field, it is the empirical exception that often displays the analytic rule.

The potential the taken-for-granted features of an organization have for misdirection in fieldwork goes, however, far beyond what an informant may or may not say or do. The ethnographer's own taken-for-granted understandings of the social world under scrutiny are also tied closely to the nature and quality of the data produced. Take, for example, my surprise and initial puzzlement at the positive reactions a number of police officers expressed regarding the stiff, formal, thoroughly bureaucratic treatment they received from certain court officials, hospital personnel, and ranking officers — all of whom represented people with whom my informants had frequent dealings. As a middle-class academician, such treatment seemed improper and hence noteworthy to me since it violated my own sense of propriety about the "correct tone" for interpersonal conduct among people quite familiar with one another. Eventually, however, I came to realize that the police grow comfortable with this sort of orderly and highly predictable treatment from certain types of people and not only expect it but are sometimes confused, dismayed, and perhaps angered when this formal treatment is not forthcoming.

Another illustration is useful in this regard for it suggests an important constitutive base underlying the ethnographic enterprise. Consider here the fact that I was initially jolted by the visceral disdain most patrolmen expressed toward those citizens who, for some reason or other, required aid in settling a family dispute. At first, I attributed such vociferous distaste to occupational concerns: that such calls were considered open-ended and messy, that they were thought to be quite dangerous, that they interfered with what most police took to be their "realwork" of crime control and crook catching, that the typical "family beef" involved people whom the police regarded as beneath them both socially and economically, and so forth. But the matter went deeper because after exploring the various contextual contingencies upon which patrolmen expressed their most vehement reactions, it became apparent that they were reacting not to the call per se but were reacting to the specific kind of persons they encountered on such calls whom they saw in very personal terms as quite different from themselves since these people were obviously unable to control their own households. At an unstated level, it was a moral matter to them. Because the police believe that they would never require public assistance in attending to family matters, those that did request aid were viewed as craven, stupid, repugnant, or, in the idiom of the police, "the dumb fucks of the world." In this case, I was blinded by my own perceptual screen and did not see that persons who regarded themselves as very independent, self-reliant, and decisive would, naturally enough, find others who appeared to require outside help in what were thought to be private and usually trivial matters to be persons unworthy of human respect.

In sum, misdirection in fieldwork arises from several sources not the least of which is the ethnographer's own lack of sensitivity for the discrepant observation and lack of appreciation for the tacit bases of one's own understanding of the social world. The vast amount of what is unremarkable to me about police organizations is therefore underrepresented no doubt in my writings. The same bias informs all ethnographic work in that it is by and large the differences from one's own world (and unexpected similarities) that find their way into one's field notes. Without overlooking the lies and the areas of informant ignorance, it is clear that knowledge based on incongruity is as central to fieldwork as it is to any other area of scientific endeavor.

THE ETHNOGRAPHIC ILLUSION

I have tried in this paper to detail what I consider to be the crucial analytic distinctions to be drawn when assessing the kind of data one must deal with in ethnographic studies. First, I noted the necessity of separating first- and second-order concepts, a separation based primarily on whose point of view is being reported, the informant's or the researcher's. Second, I suggested that the various bits of recorded information generated by the ethnographer as to the features of the studied organization must be typed as presentational or operational, a distinction resting in large part upon the ethnographer's ability to both see and understand what is occurring within the informants' framework. Third, I noted that the ethnographer must continually assess the believability of the talk-based information harvested over the course of a study, an evaluation dependent upon the fieldworker's interest, skill, and good fortune in uncovering lies, areas of ignorance, and the various taken-for-granted features of the studied organization. These tasks represent the essence of sound fieldwork and lie at the heart of any faithful description of a studied organization.

Accomplishing such tasks involves continual and careful attention to the details of one's adventures in the field. From this perspective, then, analysis and verification in ethnography is something one brings forth with them from the field, not something which can be attended to later, after the data are collected. When making sense of field data, one cannot simply accumulate information without regard to what each bit of information represents in terms of its possible contextual meanings. Moreover, such an analytic assessment can be accomplished only in the field where one has the opportunity to check out certain bits of information across informants and across situations. It is true of course that much of what one learns at the time is not fully understood and may in fact be reinterpreted and seen later in new ways. The theories developed by ethnographers in the field have an alterable and fluid character to them. Since ethnographic theories are tested, retested, and tested again in the field, they tend to be rather resistent to high-level abstractions. Even at the end of a long study, the theories proclaimed by ethnographers are likely to be only tentatively asserted, full of reservation and qualifying detail. But, if this is the typical version of a given social world that arises from those who study it most closely, it is also an argument for paying stricter attention in all forms of social research to the distinctions of the sort made in this paper regarding the kinds of data one collects.

This normative discussion raises a final concern because it suggests that the expressed aim of ethnography, "to depict," in Goodenough's (1964: 14) terms, "the system for perceiving, believing, evaluating and acting" is a shockingly broad and preposterous one. Culture is itself an interpretation and therefore most of the facts one goes into the field to discover are themselves already known about and interpreted in a particular light by the people one talks to in the setting. The results of ethnographic study are thus mediated several times over — first, by the fieldworker's own standards of relevance as to what is and what is not worthy of observation; second, by the historically situated questions that are put to the people in the setting; third, by the self-reflection demanded of an informant; and fourth, by the intentional and unintentional ways the produced data are misleading. Though most ethnographers are well aware of this irreducible dilemma, they still maintain the stance that if they spend some more time in the field to dig a little deeper and probe a little further, certain crucial facts will be revealed which will tie up loose ends and provide closure to a study in danger of infinite expansion. Ultimately, this is an illusion although, I hasten to add, it is an altogether necessary one. "The world," according again to Sherlock Holmes, "is full of obvious things which nobody by any chance will ever see."

NOTES

1

Ethnographic research is of course more than a single method and can be distinguished from participant observation on several grounds one of which is that of its broader aim, the analytic description of a culture. This paper conveniently glosses over many of the fine points of methodological nuance and regards any social study at least partially ethnographic if it allows a researcher to become immersed in the everyday life of the observed. In essence, the use of such techniques in organizational studies literally forces the researcher to come to grips with the essential ethnographic question of what it is to be rather than to see a member of the organization.

2

Though the main thrust of this paper is upon the kind of social information generated by ethnographic study, I have elsewhere considered other methodological aspects of my field experiences: the process of securing access and building a research role (Van Maanen, 1978c); the use of informants in fieldwork (Van Maanen, 1980); the process of collecting, recording, and reporting ethnographic data (Van Maanen, 1978d); and the moral and ethical implications of doing ethnographic work (Van Maanen, 1982). While much of this work can be viewed as proselytizing on my part, some of it is not for I agree with Becker (1970: 3) that methodology in the social sciences is far too important to be left to the methodologists.

3

"Call jumping" refers to those occasions where a patrol unit other than the unit taking the dispatched call arrives on the scene first and "handles" the call. Such behavior is relatively rare in police agencies and is considered, both officially and unofficially, improper though, under some conditions, call jumping may be considered a favor and be welcomed by the unit whose call was jumped. But that is another story.

4

This is an important distinction to make because, in the final analysis, fieldworkers can never fully apprehend the world of their informants in its "natural" form. Even though ethnographers may sense the situated meanings various informants attach to the objects of their concern, such meanings will remain largely exhibits of how informants think rather than the "true" meanings such objects have to informants. While I tried to listen, to see, to talk, to feel, and to get into every odd cultural corner I could, it would still be absurd to suggest that I understand the police world as my informants do. A fieldworker is not interested solely in what things are for themselves as are the people studied, but rather the fieldworker is interested specifically in what things "stand for" to the people observed. Bittner's (1973) discussion on the ethnographer's "specimen knowledge" and the native's "innate knowledge" is revealing in this regard.

5

"Street justice" was a tactic employed by the patrolmen I observed (Van Maanen, 1974: 116–120) to rectify what they believed to be a situation badly in need of rearranging. Practically, "street justice" represented a "thumping" or "beating" administered, under certain conditions, on the street, though not quite in public. Typically, street justice was reserved for those who brazenly challenged an officer's definition of who was in charge of an interaction.

6

The importance of observing key episodes and how one decodes what is learned from their observation are covered nicely by Manning (1984). The notion of "event sampling" is somewhat related to these issues as it is discussed under various labels in Glaser and Strauss, 1967; Lofland, 1976; and Douglas, 1976.

7

It is worth noting that there is often a good deal of symbolic violence involved in fieldwork since people are, to a degree, coaxed, persuaded, pushed, pressured, and sometimes almost blackmailed into providing information to the researcher that they might otherwise prefer to shield. Simply because the ethnographer is there may create problems for people. And, despite the preachings of modern moralists, many people feel that it is the unexamined life that is worth leading, not the examined. Ultimately, it is the researcher's own sense of morality that will determine how such symbolic violence will be used in the field. There are then limits, individually drawn, that will restrict the degree to which the believability of field data will be checked out. Failure to push another on delicate matters or voluntarily withdrawing from a scene embarrassing to another are good examples in this regard.

8

This segmentation of interests raises a related point for it is the very existence of such social division in organizations that makes fieldwork so valuable within them. It seems almost universally true that the secrets of one group are revealed most readily by members of another group. Were this not true, ethnographers would always be left to construct their field reports out of appearances, cliches, pieties, and conventional wisdom. Aside from the obvious race and rank divisions among the police, other social cleavages were important to my work. For example, lines of discord could be seen between the young and old, men and women, patrol officers and detectives, professionally-oriented and traditionally-oriented officers, and even patrolmen working different sectors and shifts were occasionally openly contemptuous of one another. These major and minor feuds and factions provide vital sources of information for the watchful but prudent fieldworker.

REFERENCES

Banton, Michael
1964 The Policeman in the Community. New York: Anchor.

Baring-Gould, William S., ed.
1967 The Annotated Sherlock Holmes, 2 Vol. New York: Clarkson N. Potter.

Becker, Howard S.
1970 Sociological Work. New Brunswick, NJ: Transaction Books.

Bittner, Egon
1973 "Objectivity and realism in sociology." In George Psathas (ed.), Phenomenological Sociology: 108–125. New York: Wiley.

Black, Donald J.
1971 "The social organization of arrest." Stanford Law Review, 23: 1087–1111.

Cicourel, Aaron V.
1967 The Social Organization of Juvenile Justice. New York: Wiley.

Conklin, H.
1968 "Ethnography." In D. L. Sills (ed.), International Encyclopedia of the Social Sciences, 5: 115–208. New York: Free Press.

Douglas, Jack
1976 Investigative Social Research. Beverly Hills, CA: Sage.

Emerson, Joan
1970 "Nothing unusual is happening." In Thomas Shibutani (ed.), Human Nature and Collective Behavior: 208–222. New Brunswick, NJ: Transaction Books.

Glaser, Barney G., and Anslem Strauss
1967 The Discovery of Grounded Theory. Chicago: Aldine.

Goffman, Erving
1971 Relations in Public. New York: Harper & Row.

Goodenough, Ward H.
1964 "Introduction." In Ward H. Goodenough (ed.), Explorations in Cultural Anthropology: 3–21. New York: McGraw-Hill.

Lofland, John
1976 Doing Social Life. New York: Wiley

Manning, Peter K.
1977 Police Work. Cambridge, MA MIT Press.
1984 "Making sense of field data." In Thomas J. Cottle and Robert Weiss (eds.), The Narrative Voice. New York: Basic Books (forthcoming).

Van Maanen, John
1973 "Observations on the making of policemen." Human Organizations, 32: 407–418.
1974 "Working the street." In Herbert Jacob (ed.), The Potential for the Reform of Criminal Justice, 3: 83–130. Beverly Hills, CA: Sage Criminal Justice System Annuals.
1975 "Police socialization." Administrative Science Quarterly, 20: 207–228.
1977 "Experiencing organization." In John Van Maanen (ed.), Organizational Careers: Some New Perspectives: 15–45. New York: Wiley.
1978a "People processing." Organizational Dynamics, 7: 18–36.
1978b "The asshole." In Peter K. Manning and John Van Maanen (eds.), Policing: A View from the Streets: 221–238. Santa Monica, CA: Goodyear.

1978c "Watching the watchers." In Peter K. Manning and John Van Maanen (eds.), Policing: A View from the Streets: 309–349. Santa Monica, CA: Goodyear.

1978d "Notes on the production of ethnographic data." In Robin Luckham (ed.), Anthropological Methods in the Study of Legal Systems: 112–157. Stockholm: Scandinavian Institute for African Studies.

1980 "The informant game." Urban Life, 9: 469-494.

1982 "The moral fix." In Peter K. Manning and Robert N. Smith (eds.), Social Science Methods, 1—Qualitative Social Research: 115-139. New York: Ballinger.

Van Maanen, John, and Edgar H. Schein

1976 "Career development." In J. Richard Hackman and J. Lloyd Suttle (eds.), Improving Life at Work: 30–95. Santa Monica, CA: Goodyear.

Surface Data and Deep Structure: Observing the Organization of Professional Training

Donald Light, Jr.

Directors and managers of professional training programs want to know whether they are effective. To find out, evaluation instruments, questionnaires, and scales are used — often at considerable expense — which promise to measure what the trainees have mastered or how they have changed. These devices often produce surface data that describe certain attributes of the candidates but say nothing about the underlying structure of the training program and how well it is working. The usual evaluation produces data on *individuals* to answer questions about the *organization*. Often directors of programs want to know how their training affects *behavior* but get data on *attitudes*. The evaluation instruments usually contain preconceived *artificial* questions or probes that do not measure the *natural* development of trainees as they progress through the program.

These three disjunctures and how to overcome them are the subject of this article. The first principle is that the methods of analysis should fit the questions asked. It follows that the method can only be as clear as the questions. Thus the second principle is that what one wants to know must be understood and clearly stated. As obvious as this may be, many people do not clearly state their objectives, often because professional trainers and educators have hidden agenda. For example, they often want trainees to emulate them, although they could not perform professional work well themselves. Most business school faculty would not make good executives; most medical faculty are too socialized to practice medicine effectively in a typical community. Given such cross-cutting agenda, how does one know when a program is effective? This question becomes more complex when a program aims at more than mastering facts. If the goal of a program is to produce shrewd managers or humane clinicians, those in charge should sit down with a sympathetic but firm outsider and work through all their assumptions, contradictions, multiple agenda, or vague notions to clarify what they wish to accomplish and evaluate. This experience alone can greatly improve the quality of any training program.

INADEQUATE METHODS FOR COMPLEX PROGRAMS

Once objectives and values are clarified, a central concern is how the training program affects those in it. This by its nature is an organizational question (Van Maanen and Schein, 1979). Thus one needs organizational data to evaluate organizational activities. It is surprising how often we collect individual data and aggregate it to analyze organizations. Of course, information on individuals is important, but it can rarely give the insight program directors need to improve their program. Holistic rather than analytic methods can better provide that insight (Weiss, 1966). With analytic methods, the investigator attempts to isolate the various elements in a complex situation, such as professional training. To do this, the evaluator usually knows (or assumes he or she knows) what the elements are, and to separate them out he or she usually employs predeveloped instruments and analyzes the results quantitatively. He or she then identifies the dependent, independent, and intervening variables, and assesses the links between them.

A lot can be missed by such analytic methods partly because predeveloped instruments are used which may not suit the particular situation and partly because these methods cut reality up into discrete fragments of surface behavior which are then recombined into statistical clusters. By contrast, the holistic method considers a complete activity like training as an interrelated system with a deep structure (Weiss, 1966). Part or all of it may be hidden from view, implicit in the analytic elements. By focusing on the system as a whole, this method obtains a better sense of how the training program works. Outcome measures on defined objectives are important data, but until they are combined with a holistic analysis of the training program, they do not explore the "black box" that candidates enter at one end and leave at the other. One gains no insight into what the outcome measures *mean* in terms of the program itself. Of course, those running the program are sure *they* know how the program works; after all they designed it and run it. But this may be the biggest deception of all for the deep structure of the program may be quite different from what its designers assume it to be. This is particularly true in terms of values, habits, self-esteem, self-identification, and the more subtle aspects of professional training. The idea that prisons socialize first offenders into a life of crime is a disturbingly familiar one. Certainly they were not designed to be schools of crime or betrayal funnels to the underworld, yet that is their organizational impact. Can we comfortably assume that matters are any different in professional training programs? We accept that elementary school weans children from family life and teaches them how to cope with organizational life. Schools were not designed to do this, and although one could call it a "by-product" it may be as profound as anything else they learn. What are the latent functions or unanticipated consequences of various professional training programs?

THE MERITS OF OBSERVATION

To find out how a training program really works and to get beneath stated objectives and surface behavior, one must use observation. Although questionnaires and interviews have their value, systematic observation has a number of advantages for organizational analysis (Reiss, 1975). First, it offers much greater precision in measuring the time and duration of events. Second, it enables one to discover the interrelationships between elements of the whole, such as the interaction between instructors and trainees, the impact of training experiences on other related experiences, the influence of peer culture among those being trained, and the implicit messages which the organization gives about itself in the training process.

A third advantage of observation over interviews is that people are not good at recalling past events, especially if they are involved in a confusing or intense experience (Cannell and Fowler, 1963: 8; Yarrow, 1963; Yarrow, Campbell and Burton, 1964). Yet most studies of professional socialization are based on interviews. Direct, current observation can not only document attitudes more accurately, but it can also record what trainees actually *do*. This subsequently allows one to compare attitudes with actions and even recollection with actual behavior. Inaccurate recall is more insightfully seen as the reconstruction of past events to fit a new sense of self, an emerging professional identity. Thus, what is commonly considered a source of error can, with holistic data, become a source for insight.

Finally, observation allows one the vital flexibility to discover. Scales, instruments, and questionnaires require that one presumes prior knowledge of all the key forces that shape trainees and all the key dimensions on which they change. Worse, they do not allow one to measure or discover anything else. And worst of all, one often does not know that the variables measured were the wrong ones. If Gallup and Harris have taught us anything, it is that if you ask people a question they will give you an answer regardless how irrelevant or peripheral it is to their lives. Thus, questionnaires or paper-and-pencil tests will always produce answers, which then get quantified and characterized as "hard data" regardless how irrevelant they are to the training process.

Observation, which can be combined with instruments, is naturalistic. When done by a trained, astute observer, *its categories emerge from what is actually happening* rather than from artificial, preconceived notions. When these notions reflect the goals of the program they are important to measure, but more relevant is how trainees behave in relation to them. Observation also allows one to develop hypotheses, test them, alter them, and retest them while the study is going on (Glaser and Strauss, 1967). Fixed instruments tend to lock one in until external information suggests that new instruments need to be developed and another study conducted. Observations are as easy to quantify as any other data (Merklin and Little, 1967; Worby, 1970), so the issue is not whether to use quantitative or qualitative data. Rather, the central point is that organizational behavior requires holistic analysis and that direct observation is a vital part of that analysis.

OBSERVATION OVER TIME

Implicit in this discussion is the importance of longitudinal data. If one wishes to analyze a continuing process, such as a training program, then one needs continuous data that measure each stage in the process. This can be done using questionnaires, interviews, and observations but since observations focus on process, they are the most likely of the three to provide valuable information about how the program affects the trainees.

Manifest Stress and Latent Structure

A good illustration of these points is the training of psychiatrists. Many investigators have studied psychiatric training, and most have observed signs of stress among the residents (Halleck and Woods, 1962; Klagsbrun, 1967; Merklin and Little, 1967; Worby, 1970; Pasnau and Bayley, 1971). Given that the observers are often psychiatrists or psychiatrically-oriented behavioral scientists, it should be no surprise that many of them have concluded that the training program merely brings out neurotic tendencies already there. An official task force on emotionally disturbed psychiatric residents was formed and conducted a national survey that produced sobering results (Russell, Pasnau, and Taintor, 1975). Nearly 7 percent of all residents did not complete the year, a rate that becomes considerably higher for a given cohort over the three years of post-M.D. training. Another 6 percent finished the year "despite marginal performance and/or emotional illness" (Russell, Pasnau, and Taintor, 1975: 265). Nearly two-thirds of these continued to perform marginally or badly but were not dropped. The suicide rate was among the highest in medicine. Other studies of individual programs note depression, anxiety attacks, disruption of marriages, inappropriate behavior with patients, and the like (Hawkins, 1976). The question is why.

Personal pathology may be the answer, though those who suggest it have not investigated it. Rather, they assume it because it fits their preconceived notions about how people behave. Organizational variables are not part of their paradigm. But observers further note that these signs of stress particularly occur in the middle of the first year. While this may seem a clear indication that some organizational event is triggering it, most psychiatric educators find the psychological, individualistic explanation satisfactory: a certain proportion of residents have emotional problems, and exposure to a program where emotional problems are openly examined and discussed brings them out. Once brought out, they are "worked through" and in time the signs of pathology subside. In a rough way, this is itself an organizational explanation. It assumes that if the program did not examine emotional problems they would not surface, but the emphasis is on the preexisting problems that the program brings to the surface.

Holistic observation, however, has produced a much richer and more detailed account of the deep structure of psychiatric residency and the way in which programmatic features are the latent cause of unanticipated results (Light, 1980). It found that residents went through five stages of socialization behind which lay structural features of the program.

First, residents were actively, if subtly, discredited. They were told that medical training would be an obstacle to providing good therapy, that they would have to abandon many of their hard-won professional habits and values. The desire to patch up and cure the patient, a driving force in the clinical years of medical school and internship, was labeled a "rescue fantasy." Active, direct intervention would overwhelm mental patients and frighten them, supervisors said.

It is important to realize that on the whole the instructional staff did not appreciate the extent to which they were discrediting who the residents were and what they had accomplished in medical school. They saw themselves as very supportive, which they were at the same time that these messages kept coming through. A respected trainer of American psychiatrists asked me what I was finding, and I told him about the initial discrediting with specific examples.

He replied with kind concern, "Well, if you find *any* evidence of this going on please let me know." Since I had just given him clear evidence, I concluded that he was requesting me *not* to let him know.

Second, a period of confusion and turmoil followed. Trainees struggled to get their bearings; yet the tools they had to fall back on were the old tools that were being discredited. They found their values and identities challenged. The vagueness of psychiatric principles and procedures further increased their anxiety, because they lacked the precision of lab tests and specific therapies. They struggled to do the right thing, but were not sure what it was. As Merkin and Little (1967: 195) put it, "Threatened by his strange environment, his feelings of discontinuity with his past, and his lack of preparation for great responsibility, the new resident is in a hazardous position. His fears for his sanity are more intense, as are those of people who experience cultural shock when suddenly required to adapt to a foreign civilization."

By now it should be clear that stress and its emotional manifestations were not just the surfacing of neurotic predispositions. When we make the same arguments about Blacks and Hispanics, it is called "blaming the victim." We put the victim in a structure that creates obstacles and then attribute an unsatisfactory or troubled performance to the victim. We then react as a conservative (by telling the victim to sink or swim) or a liberal (by helping the victim) but in neither case do we examine how structural forces shape the victim in the first place. In understanding those forces, holistic observation was needed to get beneath the surface behavior and attitudes that had been measured in previous efforts to study how psychiatrists are trained.

The period of confusion ended in a third stage of numbness and exhaustion. Some called it a slump during which trainees did not seem to care. They became cynical or nihilistic in order to protect themselves against the pressures they felt. The degree to which this or the other stages were manifest varied by individual and by program, but I would argue that discrediting, which leads to a confused groping and ends in apathetic fatigue, is fairly common in professional training programs.

Yet life went on. The work continued. And as the trainees pushed on one noted that they began to discover that there *is* a way to make sense of their new tasks. In this fourth stage of renewal, trainees discovered there *are* techniques that work and values that make sense. Psychologically, the period of numb fatigue is a turning point, the end of resistance put up by the old values and ways against the new. As trainees continued, they began to realize that what they were doing all along was part of a coherent, effective approach. This does not necessarily mean that in some objective way the techniques necessarily worked or the approach was coherent — only that trainees came to perceive them in this way. There is a strong tendency for people to resolve anomalies, to reduce anxiety, to understand what they are doing.

The stage of renewal is the crucible of socialization, the period when students assimilate the program's techniques and values into a new professional identity. The great anthropologist, Clifford Geertz (1973: 5), has written that man is "an animal suspended in webs of significance he himself has spun." Pure symbolic interactionists go as far as to argue that each trainee can spin any web of significance that he or she wants. But organizational constraints and forces make only certain patterns available; so it is no surprise to see that most trainees in the fourth stage of renewal discovered as if for the first time the truths, techniques, and folk wisdom that their supervisors had espoused and made available to them.

Role playing is a crucial part of this fourth stage. The more residents acted as if they were psychiatrists, the less false it seemed, particularly when patients and supervisors took their performance seriously. This daily role playing helped both to push out what remained of the old perspectives and to make real the new way of doing things, which was embodied in the very roles they were performing.

The fourth stage of renewal led to the final stage of self-affirmation. As bonds of identification strengthened and individuals gained confidence, they began to wean themselves from those on whom they had depended. Increasingly they attributed to themselves a sense of mastery. One interesting mechanism that may be at work here is "effort justification" (Lawrence and Festinger, 1962). Most trainees found it difficult to admit that they learned little from all the effort and strain they went through in the program, so they were inclined to accentuate what they learned and how much more professional they were at the end of the program. This was particularly true if trainees had been given serious responsibilities.

A driving force in the last two stages is ideology, a set of rationalizations to explain why the new ways promoted by the program are worthwhile. To paraphrase Jerome Frank (1971), people succeed only if they are convinced that what they are doing makes sense and that they are good at it. The new paradigm or ideology embodied in the training program provides this rationale and allows trainees to collect success stories, which they regard as evidence that the beliefs are valid. Often, the beliefs and methods of a program emphasize techniques; one change trainees made is from an emphasis on externally measured results to an emphasis on technique. A good job is a job well executed according to the techniques emphasized in the program, rather than a job that produces some externally measurable results. To the extent that a program has this emphasis, many worrisome questions about effectiveness are evaded.

Deep Structure

In the case of psychiatric residency programs, a number of structural arrangements underlay the stages of socialization described (Light, 1980: Ch. 12). The first was that residents started with the sickest patients on the wards rather than with outpatients. On one hand, there is nothing "deep" about this at all. It was such an obvious part of the program that no one talked much about it. If asked why they had residents begin with inpatients, the senior staff said that disorders and defenses were most easily seen in very sick patients, thus new residents could learn more easily the basic dynamics of the psyche. Also, some senior staff felt that residents first had to learn how to sit with psychotic patients. If they could do that, they could sit with anyone. But these arguments are not very persuasive. The first assumes that the disorders and defenses of psychotics are just like those of you and me, only more so, and there are a lot of experts who would question that assumption. Moreover, psychosis has its own complexities so that it cannot be assumed that psychotic patients openly display their psyche. Psychotics come in all shapes, and bearing their pain does not necessarily prepare one for effective therapy with outpatients. But no matter. Careful observation of how starting with psychotic inpatients affected the residents indicated that other lessons were learned.

First, psychotic inpatients were a shock. If one wanted to disabuse bright young physicians of the idea that they were competent, one could not do better than to start them with inpatients. They did not look ill like medical patients; yet they were quite disturbed. Residents found that relating to them was very difficult, and their efforts to improve them had frustrating results. Some improved rapidly, others moved sideways to other disorders, while others did not respond at all. Early in training, before residents had assimilated the psychiatric ideology and were focusing on results, they openly admitted that they could not credit themselves even with those who improved, because they could discern no regular pattern in how patients responded. They worked hard at improving these patients and became discouraged at the results, not realizing that distinguished therapists had done no better.

Second, starting with inpatients led to a modified medical model that ultimately allowed residents to see continuity between their professional status and their new roles. While medical techniques and previous knowledge are not very relevant, inpatients on a ward being treated by people who are called "doctors" preserved the fundamental trappings of status. Moreover, the patients were called "sick" with "mental illness," though the analogy to medicine was open to question. While the brain and the nervous system can sustain disease, that spiritual-psychological presence called "the mind" cannot. But the effect of starting with inpatients was to make the analogy as plausible as possible. Within this medical framework, residents learned new definitions of the old terms "illness" and "therapy" without finding the shift implausible.

Another important contributor to the deep structure of the program was intensive supervision. If starting with inpatients was a major force underlying the first three stages that broke down old habits and resistance, then intensive supervision made a central contribution to renewal and self-affirmation. During the early stages of resocialization, supervisors within the program contained much of the emotional and psychic turmoil where it could be channelled toward the goals of the program. Supervisors also provided role models which then became vital as residents began to identify with the new way of doing things. These two functions increased the residents' emotional investment in the program.

CONCLUSION

A full understanding of how a training program works requires field observations that examine the deep structure as well as the surface behavior of those in it. The example above, though greatly simplified, illustrates the kind of comprehensive understanding that is not possible from questionnaires and interviews. The point is well made in another context by the Coleman Report, the most massive analytic study ever made of achievement in school (Coleman, et al., 1966). As is the case so often, the method determined what was measured and Coleman measured "teacher quality" by highest academic degree and number of years teaching, "student achievement" by grades, and "school quality" by the age of the building and how many labs it had. With these kinds of measures, most of the variance went unexplained, and the correlations were low; but he concluded from them that (among other things) schools have little impact on student achievement. This was big news to parents, who had been choosing homes near good schools, and Congress which was trying to improve Black education by improving the schools they attended. To those who know schools, this conclusion appeared to be an artifact of the data, regardless how well it was analyzed by the nation's leading social scientists.

In contrast, a recent study from England (Rutter et al., 1979) systematically observed students in schools and came to very different conclusions. With richer, more holistic data, it found that schools made an enormous difference in the proportion of students who passed national exams or got arrested for delinquency. A detailed analysis of how different educational programs work and why emerges from the study. While the investigators collected output data, they also went into the schools to find out what social processes lay behind the successes and failures of the students. In contrast to the wastefully expensive Coleman Report, which tried to analyze a training program by isolating a few variables from the whole, the British study examined the whole and discovered key dimensions of educational programs that only systematic observation over time could uncover. If we are to train people well and evaluate our efforts wisely, we need to follow this example of organizational analysis.

REFERENCES

Cannell, C. F., and F. J. Fowler
1963 "A Study of the reporting of visits to doctors in the National Health Survey." Ann Arbor, MI: Survey Research Center, University of Michigan.

Coleman, James S., E. Q. Campbell, C. J. Hobson, J. McPartland, A. M. Mood, F. D. Weinfeld, and R. L. York.
1966 Equality of Educational Opportunity. Washington: U.S. Government Printing Office, Catalog No. FS 5–238: 38001.

Frank, Jerome
1971 "Psychotherapists need theories." Psychotherapy and Social Science Review, 5: 17–18.

Geertz, Clifford
1973 The Interpretation of Cultures. New York: Basic.

Glaser, Barney G., and Anselm L. Strauss
1967 The Discovery of Grounded Theory. Chicago: Aldine.

Halleck, Seymour L., and Sherman M. Woods
1962 "Emotional problems of psychiatric residents." Psychiatry, 25: 339–346.

Hawkins, David R.
1976 Conference on the Education of Psychiatrists — Preparatory Commission III: The Resident. Washington: American Psychiatric Association (mimeographed).

Klagsbrun, Samuel C.
1967 "In search of an identity." Archives of General Psychiatry, 16: 266–289.

Lawrence, D. H., and Leon Festinger
1962 Deterrents and Reinforcements: The Psychology of Insufficient Reward. Stanford: University Press.

Light, Donald Jr.
1980 Becoming Psychiatrists: The Professional Transformation of Self. New York: Norton (in press).

Merklin, Lewis, Jr. and Ralph B. Little
1967 "Beginning psychiatric training syndrome." American Journal of Psychiatry, 124: 193–197.

Pasnau, Robert O., and Stephen J. Bayley
1971 "Personality changes in the first year of psychiatric residency training." American Journal of Psychiatry, 128: 79–83.

Reiss, Albert J. Jr.
1975 "Systematic observation surveys of natural social phenomena." In H. Wallace and Laurie A. Broedling (eds.), Perspectives on Attitude Assessment: Surveys and Their Alternatives: 132–154. Washington: Smithsonian Institution.

Russell, A. T., R. O. Pasnau, and Z. C. Taintor
1975 "Emotional problems of residents in psychiatry." American Journal of Psychiatry, 132: 263–267.

Rutter, Michael, Barbara Maughan, Peter Mortimore, and Janet Ouston
1979 Fifteen Thousand Hours: Secondary Schools and Their Effects on Children. Cambridge, MA: Harvard University Press.

Van Maanen, John, and Edgar H. Schein
1979 "Toward a theory of organization socialization." Research on Organization Behavior, 1: 209–264.

Weiss, Robert S.
1966 "Alternative approaches in the study of complex situations." Human Organization, 25: 198–205.

Worby, Cyril M.
1970 "The first-year psychiatric residents and the professional identity crisis." Mental Hygiene, 54: 373–377.

Yarrow, M. R.
1963 "Problems of methods in parent-child research." Child Development, 34: 215–226.

Yarrow, M. R., J. D. Campbell, and R. G. Burton
1964 "Reliability of maternal retrospection: a preliminary report." Family Process, 3: 207–218.

Qualitative Research Techniques in Economics

Michael J. Piore

DISCOVERING QUALITATIVE RESEARCH

I did not plan to do open-ended interviewing and participant observations: I happened into it, in the course of my graduate education, in two ways: in my thesis research and in my work with civil rights and anti-poverty groups. My thesis topic was the effect of automation upon the skill composition of manufacturing jobs. At the time, there was considerable controversy about whether technological change was increasing or decreasing the skill requirements of jobs. An important group of analysts in the debates about national economic policy were arguing that skill requirements were increasing, leaving a residue of workers who had, or might have, been employed by the old techniques but who were unqualified for the new jobs. This growing residue was supposed to be a barrier to reductions in the level of unemployment.

John Dunlop, my thesis advisor, proposed investigating this question by comparing two factories using old and new techniques. The idea was to find a series of cases where an old factory that was being torn down or abandoned, to be replaced by a totally new facility, producing the same product. Engineering designs for the two factories would show the various work stations and the jobs associated with them. A comparison of these manning tables, as they were called, would provide the maximum contrast between old and new technologies and thus would indicate the direction of change for the economy as a whole. The project required exceptional cooperation on the part of the companies whose factories were involved. Dunlop obtained access at the headquarters level. I went to the factories, or in some cases to the engineers designing the plants, to collect the data.

There were, however, several problems with this approach which I had not anticipated. One problem was that the data were available in the expected form in only one company and even there the data were very difficult to interpret without the aid of plant personnel. Elsewhere, the data had to be constructed, and this required a considerable input from a variety of different company and factory officials.

Second, the cooperation of local officials was not forthcoming merely on command from national headquarters; it was necessary to first gain their confidence and interest in the project. For this purpose, I spent a lot of time visiting various local officials, trying to make conversation with them in a way which would seem purposeful enough so as not to be wasting their time, but far enough away from my actual interest so as not to queer the whole project by premature disclosure of the magnitude and degree of confidentiality of what I was about to ask them to do.

At first, I developed an elaborate list of questions for this "preliminary" part of the interview, but I quickly found that the questions had very little to do with the success or failure of the interview. As I learned much later in a write-up of one of the Hawthorne experiments, most people had a story to tell. The interviewees used my questions as an excuse for telling their stories. Since I thought of my initial interview as a means of developing rapport, this did not bother me at first. Indeed, I was glad to be relieved of the burden of keeping the conversation going, and I began to look for ways to get the respondent to do his or her thing. Later, I became interested in using the same interview format to obtain the answers to a specific list of questions, but I was unable to change the interview process. Either I let the respondent tell his or her story, using my questions as an excuse, or else I forced him or her to treat the questions seriously and to give me a codable response to each item. If I took the latter approach, the respondents soon lost interest in the project and began to concentrate on getting through the questionnaire and on to their next appointment. In this process, they often provided misinformation in order to avoid an anticipated follow-up question.

As this process continued, I became increasingly interested in the stories I was being told in the interviews. The stories revealed that the processes of technological change and labor allocation, indeed the basic process of business management, were totally different from the ways in which the original project had been conceived. The manning tables which I had set out to collect were only tangentially related to the manning structure of the plant and the skill composition of jobs — a consequence of the process diverging so radically from what I had envisioned. I would never have understood this if I had focused only on the manning tables; what I would have understood was that there was an "error" between the tables and the data I wanted, and I would have looked for, and found, a correction factor.

Finally, however, the interviews seemed to reveal what the actual process was and, at least in retrospect, what my thesis came to be about was the definition of that actual process, and a comparison between it and the process I had first envisaged.

The actual process was one in which there was no clear distinction between jobs or workers of varying skills. The manning tables were used as only a rough guide to factory layout and cost. The actual manning was arrived at experimentally and evolved over time, through adjustments in which work was first done by design engineers and then gradually transferred to craftsmen who, in turn, taught operators. It was indicative of an informal process of skill development on the job in the process of production or, in the case of new technologies, in the process of technological change. When this process worked well the "skilled" work force was trained without cost by participating in the installation and start-up of the new equipment. Bottlenecks of the kind envisaged in theories of structural unemployment were created by failures of this informal on-the-job training. Such failures were most often social, rather than economic, and were generated by racial or class distinctions which inhibited the necessary contacts between the skilled and unskilled employees.

Civil Rights and Poverty

My experience with open-ended interviews in thesis research was reinforced by work that I did during my graduate
studies with civil rights groups and inner city manpower and
poverty programs. My graduate education coincided with the
rise of the civil rights movement and the development of
the various manpower and poverty programs in the rural
South and the inner city areas of the North. I went through
a series of *crises de conscience,* periodically, thinking of
dropping out of graduate school for a career as an organizer
and social agitator. I tried to resolve these *crises* by offering
my services as an economist to various grass roots organizations and local governmental programs. It was, however, not
so easy to get my services accepted on these terms, and it
became increasingly difficult as Black power and power-to-
the-people came increasingly to dominate the movement.

I tried to solve this problem by finding issues that local
communities were interested in, understanding the
framework in which they viewed these issues, and then
either translating my perspective into their terminology or
adopting their framework in place of my own. I found my
approach to community leaders similar to my approach with
the business executives for my thesis: letting them tell their
story and then trying to abstract from that story their interests and their world view. However useful this approach
actually was in helping the communities with which I was
working, it turned out to be fairly successful in helping me
to pursue my professional education in good conscience.
Ultimately, it also led me to a very different view of the
economics of race and poverty from that of my colleagues
in economics.

Earlier Qualitative Research

While this approach to economic research is not very popular among professional economists today, it is not without
its antecedents, especially in labor economics. Economists in
the 1930s and 1940s who worked with trade unions, with
the wage and price control agencies in World War II, and as
arbitrators and mediators in the collective bargaining process
in the postwar period had experiences that must have been

very similar to mine with civil rights and poverty groups. They could not define the problems and impose their own analytical framework on the search for a solution but were forced instead to accept the problems as defined by the participants and to understand and sometimes to accept as well, the participants' analytical perspective. This was especially true of economists who served as labor arbitrators and mediators, for their ability to play those roles is predicated upon continued acceptability by the parties to labor disputes. There were also a series of formal research studies in this period that examined actual economic decision making using similar qualitative research techniques: studies of price formation by Hall and Hitch, 1939; local labor market studies by Reynolds (1951); Myers and Shulz (1951); Lester (1954); investment decision studies by Heller (1951) and Duesenberry (1958). These studies led several of the authors into intensive theoretical conflicts with the conventional wisdom of the profession. In retrospect, neither the analytical positions nor the evidence advanced in support of them seems to be very solid if taken at face value. I find it possible to understand the intensity of commitment to the unorthodox theories expounded in that period only in terms of a conviction that participants had a view of the world very different from the view ascribed to them by a conventional theory, and that that view had an internal coherence and consistency, however difficult it might be for the observer to abstract and articulate as a theoretical statement. The intensity of this commitment must have emerged through the interviews taken as a whole and not individually as presented in research reports. The capacity to recognize such an alternative, let alone the effort to articulate it, has, however, since disappeared almost completely from economic research. In order to understand why, one has to understand the nature of the discipline as it is now structured.

FORMAL ECONOMIC RESEARCH

Contemporary economics is divided into two branches both of which work from a set of rigorous theoretical propositions. One of these branches, which the profession calls theory, starts from a model of economic man, purposively maximizing a constrained objective function. It is concerned with the outcome of this maximizing process and with the interaction of economic units behaving in this way. That interaction is generally understood to occur through a market.

The other branch of economics is econometrics. It is a theory of statistical inference. It is basically concerned with inferring quantitative estimates for the parameters of behavioral models on the basis of individual observations. Quantitative variables display a certain dispersion. A part of that dispersion is random; another part is systematically introduced by economic behavior. Econometricians are concerned with how to separate out the random dispersion and to attribute the nonrandom variation to the several different variables which are responsible for it. Such attribution is possible only if one starts with a formal behavioral model that identifies the relevant variables and the relationship among them. That model is provided by formal economic theory. Econometric theory could be used to distinguish, at least within certain limits, among alternate theoretical formulations of behavioral models, but it is seldom used in this way and the theoretical foundations of that approach are relatively underdeveloped.

Many of the observations upon which econometric estimation is based are gathered in interviews with individual economic agents, i.e., households and business enterprises. To be useful for econometric purposes, the data must be collected in a random way, and the answers must be quantifiable. Generally, each question is treated as an observation upon a specific variable although occasionally a block of questions is designed to determine the "state" of a unit of observation; for example, the status of employed or unemployed is measured this way.

When open-ended interviews are ridiculed as "impressionistic" and "anecdotal," it is against the standard of econometric theory that they are being judged. The term anecdotal usually implies that the observations are not randomly collected and are not sufficiently numerous to identify a systematic pattern of behavior. The term impressionistic usually implies that the answers are neither quantitative nor quantifiable. Open-ended interviews and participant observation thus clearly do not meet the standards of econometric evidence.

Given the present structure of the discipline, analysis which is not econometrics must be "theory." But, in order to understand what this could imply, one must understand how the concept of theory has evolved in recent years. The core of economic theory is the notion of the maximization of some objective function subject to a series of constraints. The household is assumed to maximize utility; the business enterprise is assumed to maximize profits. There is no generally accepted objective for other units but the approach to modeling their behavior follows these lines: political units, for example, are assumed to maximize either power, votes, or the tax base.

When theory fails in some important way to track reality — and most developments in economics seem to be stimulated by a failure of this sort — the remedy is sought in three basic ways. One has been to develop in a deeper, more fundamental way the implications of the basic maximizing model or of market interactions among maximizing agents. The second has been to place the action within the constraints upon maximizing behavior and to explain differences in behavior among economic units or in a given economic unit over time, by changes in those constraints. The third has been to question the basic maximizing assumptions themselves or to bolster those with supplementary behavioral assumptions drawn from outside the discipline.

The greatest blow to standard economic analysis was the Depression of the 1930s. This most dramatic economic event was incomprehensible in terms of standard economic models. The attempt which followed to formulate an understanding of economic behavior was dominated by the latter two of these approaches. The developments in economic theory in the immediate postwar decades involved an exploration both of alternative behavioral assumptions and of the specific nature of behavior constraints imposed by institutions, technology, law, and broader social structure. The work of that period which resembled the interviews that I conducted for my thesis was conceived in these terms. Most of the labor and industrial organization economists working in this period thought of what they were doing as a relatively mundane effort to identify specific technological or institutional constraints. A number of them, however, saw this work as a more fundamental contribution to behavioral theory. Simon (1958) interviewed firms about their decision-making processes and drew from these interviews a "new" theory of business behavior. Duesenberry (1967) developed a consumption theory out of psychoanalytic theory. And Lester (1946) used his work to open a debate with Machlup (1946) that challenged the behavioral assumptions of standard theory.

An important, possibly essential, component of the intellectual framework in which this exploration took place was Keynesian economics. Keynes provided the analytical framework in terms of which the Depression was ultimately understood. That analytical framework built rather heavily upon behavioral assumptions and constraints drawn from outside the basic maximizing framework. The issue of exactly how these assumptions were to be interpreted, it may be noted, was never fully resolved, but an important component was the distinction between the long and the short run. Keynes seemed to argue that the conventional model would explain only the long run. The space for alternatives was opened up by the remark "in the long run, we are all dead."

The difficulty with these approaches is that neither the alternative behavioral assumptions nor the technological and institutional constraints, which were introduced into the standard models, had any coherent intellectual underpinnings. They appeared, relative to the standard economic model, to be ad hoc. One "found out" what the technical constraints or institutional characteristics were. There was no coherent theory of technology or of institutions. In the beginning, one might have expected the exploration of these constraints to lead to such a theory but, as time went on and it did not do so, the approach became increasingly unsatisfactory. The introduction of alternative behavioral assumptions may have seemed more promising in this regard since it was in principle possible to ground those assumptions in some other social science, or better yet natural science. But in the event, the promise proved elusive. No discipline provided the breadth and cohesion which economists had been led by their initial maximizing models to expect from a theory. To explain behavior with axiomatic assumptions one had to draw several different "other" theories, which at best had no obvious relationship to each other and were, at worst, conflicting. Thus, the attempt to provide an alternative theory came to seem equally as ad hoc as the identification of specific technological and institutional constraints.

The attempt to borrow from other disciplines proved disappointing in another respect as well. Conventional economics is a very big story about the nature of the socioeconomic system. New stories that emerged from alternative models were either confused or trivial.

Gradually in the 1960s and overwhelmingly in the 1970s, the profession abandoned the notion that understanding is to be expanded either by modifying the basic behavioral assumptions or by an exploration of the nature of the constraints, and has returned to the first approach, i.e., an attempt to explore in a deeper and more meaningful way the basic maximizing model. Current research is focused rather heavily upon two aspects of that model — information and uncertainty. Paradoxically, however, it may be precisely in these terms that it is easiest to understand the limits of conventional economic theory and to identify exactly how it is that open-ended interviewing might permit us to overcome these limits.

QUALITATIVE RESEARCH AND LIMITED INFORMATION

Most economic theories tend to view information as consisting of discrete bits and pieces, which can be thought of as the values of quantitative variables. The problem of information is, in this way, converted into the problem of the estimation of the values of the parameters of an econometric model. And, indeed, limited information and uncertainty in economics generally means lack of information about the precise value of a given set of variables. Either one does not know what the value of a variable is or the value has a random component and cannot be known with certainty.

This conception of the problem, however, obscures a prior step in the epistemological process, identifying the variables that are worth estimating in the first place. Econometrics avoids this step by drawing upon economic theory. But economic theory also skips this step! It attributes to the economic actors a prior knowledge about how the world is structured and what the values of the relevant variables in that structure actually are. When one examines the issue, however, it is not at all clear how the actors acquire the knowledge that economists attribute to them; if that knowledge could in fact be abstracted from their own experience and, if not, how their experience would in fact lead them to conceptualize the decision-making problems which they face. For example, economists generally assume that economic actors examine the relative prices of all substitute resources before making a decision. But if relative prices are constant over a long period of time, it would be unnecessary to do this in order to make an optimal economic decision. It would in fact be a waste of time to do so, and for this reason suboptimal. Suppose businessmen did not bother to examine relative prices and then the prices of some important sets of inputs, such as energy sources, began to shift. How would economic agents learn about the shift if they were not accustomed to examine price? Once they did learn, how would they separate out permanent shifts from random variation? How would they estimate the new values of relative prices? Would they assume that relative prices were now variable or that the relationship among relative prices had simply changed once and for all and a new but stable relationship had emerged? These questions do not have a standard answer in economic theory. They arise at all only if one does not assume that one knows the structure in terms of which economic agents see the world.

Open-ended interviews and participant observation may be interpreted as instruments for answering these types of questions. They are ways of discovering how economic participants think about the world. They are means, in other words, of identifying the model of that portion of the socioeconomic world which the participants themselves use in making decisions. The conventional interpretation is captured in what at MIT is called Robert Hall's Law: You can never believe the answer to a direct question about behavior, or more crudely, "businessmen always lie." This interpretation, however, suggests that this law misses the point: what interviews can reveal is not a set of specific answers to specific questions, individual bits and pieces of information. What they reveal are *patterns* of responses. Each answer, whether true or false, is a piece of that pattern. Individual responses cannot be interpreted in isolation. But the responses grouped together, and taken as a whole, are clues to the mental processes of the economic participants. This has been difficult for economists to recognize because these mental processes constitute the answers to problems which the discipline has thought to be already resolved. But if current work on uncertainty and limited information is pursued, the need for answers of this kind must eventually be recognized.

While an interpretation of this kind suggests what open-ended interviewing is about and how it fits into the discipline of economics, it is not complete. In particular, it does not explain how one identifies the *structures* or models which the interviews reveal. My own work in this regard has been largely based upon hunch and intuition. It has proved viable not so much because I have been able to use my fieldwork to sustain in any scientific way the "theories" I have abstracted from it but because these theories have led to policy conclusions which have currency. That currency comes from the fact that they are derived from the models which people actually use in thinking about the processes that the proposed policies are designed to influence and thus the proposals seem particularly plausible to them. But however important such plausibility is in making the research approach viable, it does not *validate* either the policies or the models used to derive them. The world may well not operate in a way which is intuitively plausible to any single participant. How does one know from interviews what the relationship between the participants' view and the actual operation of a given socioeconomic system is? Other social science disciplines have moved relatively far in exploring this question; the epistemological issues are central to structural and developmental psychology. It is not possible in a paper of this kind to explore the implications of this work for economic theory. But it may be useful to develop one distinction simply to illustrate how this kind of understanding helps.

If one interprets the open-ended interviewing as a way of identifying structure of thought, then any particular interview may indicate three distinct types of structures. First, the interviews may reveal a model, or more broadly, understanding, which the respondent has of socioeconomic reality that actually reflects that reality itself (or, more precisely, it may be the way the economist wishes to model that reality). Second, the interviews may reveal how the participant views reality, and hence, may be a clue as to how to model that participant's own behavior, but it may not be a true causal model. Third, the interview may reveal that the participant's model is unstable: it may suggest, in other words, genuine confusion on the participant's part.

Most of what I have uncovered through interviews are models that I have used as direct reflection of reality. My favorite example of this was an understanding of the public assistance system which I developed through an interview with a militant welfare recipient. I was confronted with this woman in an interview situation but at a complete loss as to how to begin, so I asked her what she had learned through her experience in the movement. She replied immediately, "That America is all fucked-up." Startled and feeling, if anything, more at a loss, I asked limply, "Didn't you know that before?"

It turned out that in organizing for the welfare rights movement, this woman had gone door to door in the housing project where she lived and met, for the first time, other women who like her were on public assistance. She had been profoundly shocked (and truly radicalized) by the depth of poverty and degradation which she discovered among these women, as shocked and radicalized, it would appear, as middle class college women were by the same organizing experience. What this reveals about the structure of the welfare system would take a whole paper to develop. Two points may be underscored here: (1) the way the system is structured vertically so that social relationships run from the client to the social worker (who represents control, authority) and never horizontally among clients and (2) the extremely uneven distribution of income among people ostensibly falling under the same system of eligibility rules and the tendency of the system to reward exactly the same character traits as those rewarded by the labor market.

It is a little more difficult to illustrate the case where the structure model of the respondent is a poor indicator of actual social structure in which he or she is acting. Obviously this cannot be inferred from only one respondent's interview. An interview with the welfare recipient before she discovered that America was "all fucked-up" would have revealed a view of the public assistance system which was in fact very partial but not to what degree. Competitive theory in economics *assumes* that businessmen have a view that is partial in this sense, that businessmen accept prices as a given and have absolutely no notion of how their own actions affect the market. But the only businessmen I ever met who had this model of one of the markets in which they operated were shrimp packers in Louisiana who called a broker in New Orleans every morning to find out what price to pay for fresh shrimp. Another case is that of factories where there is a strong commitment to customary wage differentials among jobs. Workers in these factories have an attachment to past practice and custom which implies a commitment to wages *as an end in themselves*. This contrasts to the role that wages play in economic theory as a *means* for the individual of obtaining income and for the society of labor allocation. It also contrasts with the view of managers in the same factory who see the role of wages somewhat as economic theory does. I am convinced — although I would have difficulty proving it — that the difference between the manager's and the worker's views derives from the different perspectives of these two types of participants on the system in which they are operating. Managers are able to see the operation of the competitive market forces which govern wage variation and, hence, they can meaningfully understand wage determination in these terms. Workers are not in a position to observe the working of a market and the only sense they can make out of wage movement is in terms of past practice and custom. The *actual* determinants of wage movements are probably captured by neither model. The fact that workers believe in customs does indicate a certain stability in wage relationships over time. That stability may — indeed probably does — reflect stability in certain underlying market conditions. But workers not only *think* that custom governs wages: they also exert collective pressures to *make* it so. Their model of the process becomes a causal factor in wage determination (although it is not necessarily the determining factor).

A final example of inference from interviews is suggested by a conversation which I had with my local hardware merchant during the first bout of double digit inflation after the 1973 oil embargo. He was extremely upset because some of his customers had complained that he was price gouging by charging different prices for the same product. He insisted his pricing was indeed fair: he was using a fixed mark-up but the prices varied from one shipment to another, and in a rapid inflation he often sold from two different shipments on the same day. The case is interesting because of an old debate in economic theory about whether businessmen use mark-up rules and if so whether those rules are consistent with the conventional assumption of profit maximizing. An observation that one might have made was that, in contrast to the conventional profit maximizing model, the man indeed was using a mark-up pricing rule. But the real message of the interview was one of upset and confusion: whatever pricing model the man had was about to change. The new pricing system might have been one which maximized profits in some narrow sense but the more important criterion, in the man's mind, was something the old economic debate does not admit at all: that the rule be perceived as fair by his customers. To understand what such a pricing rule might be, however, one would have had to interview the customers. Although I did a little inspection, my self-interview was not very revealing.

REFERENCES

Duesenberry, James S.
1958 Business Cycles and Economic Growth. New York: McGraw Hill.
1967 Income Savings and the Theory of Consumer Behavior. New York: Oxford University Press.

Hall, R. L., and C. J. Hitch
1939 "Price theory and business behavior." Oxford Economic Papers, 2: 12.

Heller, Walter W.
1951 "The Anatomy of investment decisions." Harvard Business Review, 29: 95–103.

Lester, Richard A.
1946 "Shortcomings of marginal analysis for wage-employment problems." American Economic Review, 36: 63–82.

1954 Hiring Practices and Labor Competition. Princeton, NJ: Princeton University Press.

Machlup, Fritz
1946 "Marginal analysis and empirical research." American Economic Review, 36: 519–554.

Myers, Charles, and George Shulz
1951 The Dynamics of a Labor Market. New York: Prentice-Hall.

Reynolds, Lloyd
1951 The Structure of Labor Markets, Wages and Labor Mobility in Theory and Practice. New York: Harper.

Simon, Herbert A., and James G. March
1958 Organizations. New York: Wiley.

On Studying Organizational Cultures

Andrew M. Pettigrew

This paper is representative of my long-term research interests in the longitudinal-processual study of organizations, a
perspective I feel is neglected. The longitudinal-processual
approach to the study of organizations recognizes that an
organization or any other social system may profitably be
explored as a continuing system with a past, a present, and
a future. Sound theory must, therefore, take into account
the history and the future of a system and relate them to
the present. What are advocated here are not mere methodological niceties. They have a fundamental impact on the
kinds of research problems that become open for investigation, the possibilities of making certain kinds of conceptual
developments, and the choice of language systems with
which these concepts are expressed. A longitudinal-
processual analysis is more likely to be interested in language systems of *becoming* than of *being,* of processes of
structural elaboration rather than the precise description of
structural form, of mechanisms that create, maintain, and
dissolve systems of power (Pettigrew, 1973) rather than just
attempt to codify distributions of power at one point in time.

BACKGROUND

This paper offers a brief and necessarily speculative look at
some of the concepts and processes associated with the
creation of organizational cultures and, therefore, with the
birth of organizations. Although no strong reference will be
made to the data here, the frame of reference chosen for
the paper has been influenced by the empirical study of a
private British boarding school. The school was founded by

an individual with a strong and quite idiosyncratic personality who had a definite vision of what kind of organizational structures, mechanisms, people, and processes could realize his vision.

The data collection began in 1972 with a before, during, and after analysis of the impact of a major structural change on certain aspects of the structure, functioning, and climate of relationships in the school. The change began in September 1972. Two sets of interviews and questionnaires were administered to staff and pupils during the spring of 1973 and 1974.

The cross-sectional and processual analyses have been complemented with a historical analysis of the birth and evolution of the school from 1934 to 1972. This retrospective analysis is based on long interviews with former masters, governors, and pupils who were at the school from the 1930s, until 1972. These interview data have been supplemented with documentary sources, including private papers, speeches, administrative documents, and other archival material. A number of unobtrusive measures have been and are being developed from these data.

Social Dramas as a Research Focus

The overall design of the research is anchored around the study of a set of social dramas (Turner, 1957) and the relative routine that intersperses them. The point of studying a sequence of social dramas longitudinally is that they provide a transparent look at the growth, evolution, transformation, and, conceivably, decay of an organization over time. The dramas in the school were the points of leadership succession as the school changed from headmaster to headmaster and as it made a major structural change in 1972 that altered its population. Each of these dramas was sufficiently engaging of the minds and actions of the people in the school to be regarded as critical events. It should be clear, therefore, that it is not just the researcher's judgment which pinpoints the social dramas. The sequence of dramas, which gives a form to the order of the research design, is shown in Figure 1.

In terms of a general analysis of social process and the particular concern with unravelling the dynamics of the evo-

1934 Birth of the School	Drama 1 1953 Founding Headmaster Retires	Drama 2 1958 Headmaster 2 Retires	Drama 3 1968 Headmaster 3 Retires	Drama 4 1972 Structural Change	1975 End Point of Data Collection
	Retrospective Data Collection			Real Time Data Collection	

Figure 1   Longitudinal research design

lution of an organization, this kind of design has a number of potential advantages:

1. Each drama provides a clear point of data collection, an important practical consideration in such an extended stream of time, events, people, and processes.

2. Each drama can act as an in-depth case study within the overall case study and thereby provide a dramatic glimpse into the current workings of the social system.

3. The longitudinal study of a sequence of dramas allows varying readings to be taken of the development of the organization, of the impact of one drama on successive and even consequent dramas, and of the kinds of mechanisms that lead to, accentuate, and regulate the impact of each drama.

4. As the point about mechanisms of transformation implies, only dramas can provide consequence and meaning in relation to routines. The quality and analytical impact of the study of the dramas can only be as good as the researcher's understanding of the relative routines with which each drama is interspersed. In this sense the routines provide the contextual backdrop for the foreground drama and the researcher becomes interested in the interactive effect between context and foreground and the mechanisms and processes of transformation from routine to drama to new routine and further drama.

5. Examining the dramas affords the opportunity to study continuous processes.[1] In the school study the focus on continuous process relates to questions of organizational goals, their emergence and transformation, and to changes in systems of beliefs, power relationships, and culture.

DESCRIBING ORGANIZATIONAL CULTURES: KEY CONCEPTS

One of the benefits of a research design built around the analysis of a sequence of social dramas is the possibility it affords to study the emergence and development of organizational cultures. Using the example of the school study, I will discuss how purpose, commitment, and order are generated in an organization both through the feelings and actions of its founder and through the amalgam of beliefs, ideology, language, ritual, and myth we collapse into the label of organizational culture.

I have another objective: to encourage the use of some concepts which have developed in sociology and anthropology. These concepts are directly relevant to the concern in the field of organizational behavior as to how purpose, commitment, and order are created in the early life of an organization. In the context of the action frame of reference for the study of organizations (Silverman, 1970), those concepts reveal man as a creator of symbols, languages, beliefs, visions, ideologies, and myths, in effect, man as a *creator* and *manager* of *meaning*.

Yet before I discuss the importance of the symbolic in the study of organizations, I shall briefly discuss some aspects of the literature on entrepreneurs, followed by sections on symbolism and its role in the creation of purpose, and on identity and meaning in a newly established organization, and a discussion of how the problem of commitment was handled by an entrepreneur in the school.

Entrepreneurs

To define entrepreneurs is difficult for it is one of those terms used so regularly by the general public as well as in more specific and yet differing ways by social scientists that one wonders if it has any discriminatory power left at all. The tendency to attribute highly symbolic value to the word entrepreneur is starkly visible in one of the most often quoted research studies in the field by Collins and Moore (1970). In the introduction to their book (p. 2), they justify their research on entrepreneurs and the process of founding an organization partly to provide systematic knowledge to allow "the free world to stay free." Elsewhere entrepreneurs are portrayed as heroes. Boswell (1972: 70), while asking the researcher to be wary of the romanticization often associated with founding entrepreneurs, presents a fairly heroic picture of entrepreneurship: "His course is determined by fiats of various key outsiders on the one hand and his own supply of persistence, guts, and ability on the other."

This concern with the courage, persistence, and ability of entrepreneurs is reflected in a more refined way in the established research literature that constructs psychological profiles of the entrepreneur. McClelland (1961) and his associates have built up an impressive, though controversial set of instruments and data around the theme of achievement motivation. The aim is to tease out the psychological characteristics that differentiate entrepreneurs from nonentrepreneurs and therefore to work toward specifying some of the prerequisites for the emergence of entrepreneurship. The kinds of conclusions drawn from this research are that entrepreneurs in high-performing firms tend to have high needs for achievement and moderate needs for power while entrepreneurs in low-performing firms tend to have low needs for achievement and either high or low needs for power (Roberts, 1968; Wainer and Rubin, 1969). This work and the less ambitious research by Schrage (1965) on veridical perception, by Hornaday and Bunker (1970) examining the deprivation of entrepreneurs in their early years, and by Stanworth and Curran (1973) on entrepreneurs as socially marginal people, have made a useful contribution toward probing into the psychology of entrepreneurs. What each of these studies lacks, however, is any real attempt to examine the relationships between the entrepreneur and his organization. Apart from some vague references to leadership style, this research literature does not deal with the interdependencies and reciprocities between the entrepreneur and his staff or how some of the crucial problems of organizational functioning such as those associated with purpose, commitment, and order are handled by the entrepreneur.

If we move away from considering (in isolation) the personal characteristics of entrepreneurs toward an analysis of the *person* in his context, the problem of entrepreneurship may be stated in a specifically interactive fashion. I assume here that the essential problem of entrepreneurship is the translation of individual drive into collective purpose and commitment. With this viewpoint the focus is not what makes the entrepreneur but rather what does the entrepreneur make.

Although it is conventional to equate entrepreneurship with the taking of financial risks in the context of business enterprises, this seems an unnecessarily limited institutional context within which to use the term entrepreneur. Many of those who create new institutions outside the business sector and who are often referred to by the terms founders and innovators, have to deal with many of the same organizational, managerial, and personal challenges as those faced by business entrepreneurs. For the purposes of this paper the term entrepreneur will be used to denote any person who takes primary responsibility for mobilizing people and other resources to initiate, give purpose to, build, and manage a new organization.

Symbolism and the Creation of Organizational Cultures

There have been a number of different approaches in the research literature around the theme of the birth, growth, and evolution of organizations. One approach represented by Pugh and his associate, Donaldson (1972), has examined the dimensions of bureaucracy and how they change with organizational size. Another approach found in the works of Boswell (1972), Greiner (1972), and Strauss (1974) looks rather more specifically at the interaction between organizational structuring and functioning and uses characterizations either of phases or crises of development to discuss the evolution of organizations. A third focus in the literature, and the one closest to our present concern, approaches organizational birth and evolution through processes of character formation (Selznick, 1957) and the creation of organizational sagas (Clark, 1972).

Selznick's and Clark's definitions of their terms character and saga are fairly similar. Selznick talks of the embodiment of values in an organizational structure through statements of mission, program of activity, selective recruitment, and socialization, while Clark defines saga as a system of collective understanding of unique accomplishment in a formally established group. Both authors discuss the necessary conditions for the creation of sagas and highlight the importance of an initially strong purpose, conceived and enunciated by a single man or a small group. Clark also emphasizes the importance for saga creation of the setting of an autonomous new organization where there is no established structure or rigid customs and where the leader can build from the top down.

Entrepreneurs may be seen not only as creators of some of the more rational and tangible aspects of organizations such as structures and technologies but also as creators of symbols, ideologies, languages, beliefs, rituals, and myths, aspects of the more cultural and expressive components of organizational life. New organizations thus represent settings where it is possible to study transition processes from no beliefs to new beliefs, from no rules to new rules, from no culture to new culture, and in general terms to observe the translation of ideas into structural and expressive forms.

The Concept of Organizational Culture

In the pursuit of our everyday tasks and objectives, it is all too easy to forget the less rational and instrumental, the more expressive social tissue around us that gives those tasks meaning. Yet in order for people to function within any given setting, they must have a continuing sense of what that reality is all about in order to be acted upon. Culture is the system of such publicly and collectively accepted meanings operating for a given group at a given time. This system of terms, forms, categories, and images interprets a people's own situation to themselves. Indeed what is supposed to be distinctive about man compared with other animals is his capacity to invent and communicate determinants of his own behavior (White, 1949; Cassirer, 1953).

While providing a general sense of orientation, culture treated as a unitary concept in this way lacks analytical bite. A potentially more fruitful approach is to regard culture as the source of a family of concepts. The offsprings of the concept of culture I have in mind are symbol, language, ideology, belief, ritual, and myth. Of these symbol is the most inclusive category not only because language, ritual, and myth are forms of symbolism but because symbolic analysis is a frame of reference, a style of analysis in its own right (Duncan, 1968; Abner Cohen, 1974; Willis, 1975).

The definition of symbol used here is derived from anthropology: "Symbols are objects, acts, relationships, or linguistic formations that stand ambiguously for a multiplicity of meanings, evoke emotions, and impel men to action" (Abner Cohen, 1974: 23). Symbol construction serves as a vehicle for group and organizational conception. As a group[2] or organization at birth represents its situation to itself and to the outside world it emphasizes, distorts, and ignores and thereby attaches names and values to its structure, activities, purposes, and even the physical fabric around it. The symbols that arise out of these processes — the organization's vocabulary, the design of the organization's buildings, the beliefs about the use and distribution of power and privilege, the rituals and myths which legitimate those distributions — have significant functional consequences for the organization.

Another aspect of organizational culture is the system of vocal signs we call language. With its immense variety and complexity, language can typify and stabilize experience and integrate those experiences into a meaningful whole (Berger and Luckman, 1966). These processes of typification are essential features of the process of creating culture in a new organization. But language is not just outside us and given to us as part of our cultural and historical heritage, it is also within us, we create it, and it impels us. Language is also a vehicle for achieving practical effects. Words are part of action. Socially built and maintained, language embodies implicit exhortations and social evaluations. By acquiring the categories of a language, we acquire the structured "ways" of a group, and along with the language, the value implications of those ways. "A vocabulary is not merely a string of words; immanent within it are societal textures — institutional and political coordinates. Back of a vocabulary lie sets of collective action" (Mills, 1972: 62). The study of organizational vocabularies is long overdue. The analysis of their origins and uses and in particular their role in expressing communal values, evoking past experiences, providing seed beds for human action, and legitimating current and evolving distributions of power represent key areas of inquiry in research on the creation and evolution of new organizations.

As mentioned, one of the key attributes of symbols in general and language systems in particular, is their potential for impelling men to action. Ideologies and their component systems of belief are also widely accepted to have such action-impelling qualities. According to Wilson (1973: 91), "An ideology is a set of beliefs about the social world and how it operates, containing statements about the rightness of certain social arrangements and what action would be undertaken in the light of those statements." Ideologies can play a significant role in the processes of organizational creation because they have the potential to link attitude and action. Smelser (1963) describes this as a process of social short circuiting. The link is made between broad, often moral diagnoses of situations and to action at a specific level. The ideology mobilizes consciousness and action by connecting social burdens with general ethical principles. The result is that commitment is provided to perform everyday organizational tasks on the way to some grand scheme of things. But the potency of organizational ideologies will depend not only on the social context in which they function and how they are created and by whom, but also how they are maintained and kept alive. It is here that the final two concepts relevant to this analysis of creating culture play their part.

The concepts of ritual and myth tend to have implicit definitions in everyday use which trivialize their potential value as analytical tools. Ritual, for example, is sometimes understood to be merely repetitive sequences of activity devoid of meaning to the actors in the ritual and myth is often thought of as false belief. Bocock (1974: 37) defines ritual as "the symbolic use of bodily movement and gesture in a social situation to express and articulate meaning." The crucial feature of ritual as a medium of culture creation is the message it contains. But as Beattie (1966) notes, the crucial question about its role is not what does it do but what does it say. What it can say, of course, is that these are the central or pheripheral values, the dominant or marginal people, the highly prized or less important goals and activities of this or that organization. It is partly through ritual that social relationships become stylized, conventionalized, and prescribed. It can create distinctiveness and exclusiveness and fashion order out of delineating the margins which separate the pure from the impure.

Just as ritual may provide a shared experience of belonging and express and reinforce what is valued, so myth also plays its crucial role in the continuous processes of establishing and maintaining what is legitimate and that which is labelled unacceptable in an organizational culture. Percy Cohen (1969: 337) has written that in popular usage the term myth is almost always intended pejoratively: "my beliefs are a strong conviction, yours a dogma, his a myth. Myths, in this view, are erroneous beliefs clung to against an evidence." Cohen defines myths in terms of their internal structure and the functions they perform. Thus they contain a narrative of events often with a sacred quality which explores in dramatic form issues of origin and transformation. In so doing they anchor the present in the past, offer explanations and, therefore, legitimacy for social practices and contain levels of meaning that deal simultaneously with the socially and psychologically significant in any culture.

Leach (1954) and Anthony Cohen (1975) while recognizing that myths have qualities that can reinforce the solidarity and stability of a system also argue that myths can be created and used in the furtherance of sectionalized interests. Leach views myth as a weapon deployed by individuals and ideological groupings to justify public and private stances and affirm wavering or aspiring power positions. Anthony Cohen connects myth even more directly with political processes, suggesting that myths justify and sustain values that underlie political interests, explain, and thereby reconcile the contradictions between professed values and actual behavior and legitimate established leadership systems faced with environmental threats. These value-imparting, justifying, and reconciling qualities of myths are precisely the ones that would suggest that the concept of myth has a powerful analytical role to play in studies of the creation of organizational cultures.

In describing and defining the various forms and functions of symbols, language, ideologies, beliefs, rituals, and myths, it should be recognized that these concepts are to varying degrees interdependent and that there is some convergence in the way they relate to functional problems of integration, control, and commitment. These concepts direct attention toward the mobilization of consciousness and purpose, the codification of meaning, the emergence of normative patterns, the rise and fall of systems of leadership and strategies of legitimization. It is through such mechanisms and processes that culture evolves, and indeed the ever fluctuating state which we describe as an organizational culture then acts as a determinant or constraint on the way further attempts to handle issues of purpose, integration, and commitment are handled. Man creates culture and culture creates man.

THE ENTREPRENEUR IN HIS CONTEXT

Through the focus on the creation of organizational culture, we can more easily come to understand both aspects of the entrepreneur's leadership role and the emerging context which inevitably places bounds on that leadership role. I earlier emphasized the limitations of approaching the study of entrepreneurship entirely through the analysis of personality profiles. The focus on entrepreneurs in terms of sets of needs and abilities tends both to overly emphasize the personal qualities of entrepreneurs and to forget that those qualities have to be mobilized and made effective within a particular institutional context. The leadership component of entrepreneurship, therefore, is not just concerned with the explanation of the individual drive of the entrepreneur in terms of skills and opportunities, but also with the interactive processes between entrepreneurs and their followers and the more general processes through which purpose and commitment are generated and sustained within an organization. Thus the leadership aspect of entrepreneurship is a function of institutional dynamics and leader-follower relations as well as the skillful deployment of personal qualities.

Problems of Commitment

The relationship of leadership to entrepreneurship may be analyzed under the guise of commitment mechanisms. One way to look at commitment is through a cultural approach. Following Kanter (1972) and Buchanan (1974) commitment is defined as the willingness of participants to give energy and loyalty to an organization, to be effectively attached to its goals and values and thereby to the organization for its own sake. The role of commitment mechanisms is partly to disengage the person from some of his preexisting attachments and to redirect his system of language and beliefs and the patterning in his social relationships toward the organization's needs and purposes. In this way, a set of disparate individuals are fashioned into a collective whole.

But to study commitment mechanisms begs the question of commitment to what. In the school "what" was not only the personal qualities of the entrepreneur but also the vision he had for his organization. Visions are not merely the stated purposes of an organization, though they may imply such purpose, but they also are and represent the system of beliefs and language which give the organization texture and coherence. The vision will state the beliefs, perhaps implying a sacredness of quality to them, use a distinctive language to define roles, activities, challenges, and purposes, and in so doing help to create the patterns of meanings and consciousness defined as organizational culture.

Critical to the success of a vision in "consciousness raising" in a new organization will be the credibility of its source and the form and process by which it is communicated. One would expect the potency of a vision to be conditional on the degree of simplicity and complexity with which it is expressed, the extent to which it used rational or formal systems of language as distinct from highly expressive systems of language, and various stylistic considerations. Stylistic components of a vision which may be crucial might include the presence of a dramatically significant series of events, rooting the vision back into history and thus indicating the vision was much more than a fad, and using oppositions and their resolution as ways of boldly conveying messages. Visions with a simple yet ambiguous content, expressed in symbolic language with the appeal of a dialectic style are not only likely to be potent consciousness raisers but also flexible enough to survive and thereby validate events.

If visions are to be used by an entrepreneur as a potent mechanism for directing and influencing others the language contained within the vision is crucial. Visions may contain new and old terminology, sometimes using metaphors and analogies to create fresh meanings. Words can provide energy and raise consciousness. The capacity to use the full power of words — to make words walk — I suspect is one of the unexplored characteristics of successful entrepreneurs.

Pondy (1975) has discussed leadership as "a language game." He noted that language is one of the key tools of social influence and that a leader's effectiveness is likely to be influenced by the language overlap with his followers and by the extent to which a leader can create words that explain and thereby give order to collective experiences. This may be one of the key processes by which identity is given to an organization and therefore to which individuals can commit their emotions and energies.

Commitment may also derive from sacrifice (Kanter, 1968, 1972). Commitment-building processes involve persons detaching themselves from one set of options to go to another. They make sacrifices and investments. In a new organization the sacrifices may be giving up a secure career elsewhere, doing without expected standards of creature comforts and organizational resources and even building the new institution. The investments can be actual financial commitments and the extraordinary amounts of time and energy needed to build an institution. Investment is thus a process of tying a person's present and potential resources to the organization in exchange for a share of the organization's future acclaim and rewards.

These processes involving sacrifice and investment may also necessitate relinquishing or at least partly withdrawing from other relationships and beliefs. Social processes are set in motion whereby the individual actively moves toward building an exclusive world of primary contact and belief and withdraws from the more inclusive patterns that had existed before he joined the new organization. In this way a sense of communion or group consciousness may develop. Once formed, the newly exclusive community can reinforce this identity by various ecological devices. Building walls around the organization may be facilitated by geographical isolation but also by limiting contact from the inside out and the outside in. The school was very geographically isolated and had clear rules and rituals for handling the strangers who entered the organization and for inhibiting contact with the community outside. A new organization can also help to create a sense of exclusiveness and internal commitment through the development of a distinctive organizational vocabulary and idiosyncratic forms of dress. Finally, it may be possible for an organization to create a sense of institutional completeness, a set of beliefs reinforced by behaviors that practically all of life's needs can be at least partially satisfied within its bounds. The distinctive languages, dress, and institutional completeness were all present in the school.

Building commitment can involve action at the entry stage of the organization. The entrepreneur may initially be able to recruit on the basis of prior acquaintance and homogeneity of background. He may continue to recruit in a highly personalized fashion, insisting on seeing all potential employees and using the interview process as an opportunity to display his vision, personal drive, and presence. Once inside the new organization the employee is confronted with the emerging culture through the language, the performance and observation of everyday tasks, the regular contact, and the group rituals. In the school the rituals varied from dramatic public meetings, where organizational deviants were exposed, to the headmaster's breakfast.

In the school, myths also played their part in generating and sustaining commitment and in legitimating the entrepreneur's control over his organization. There were myths about the school's experience of persecution in relation to its social setting, about major victories and significant defeats in its history, and above all about the special qualities possessed by the entrepreneur. Many accounts were given in interviews of his extraordinary powers of empathy for other people.

There have been a number of assumptions in the preceding argument. One has been that employee commitment is a necessary condition for the success of a new organization. A second is that such commitments are not generated automatically out of interaction, but must be earned. Part of the earning will undoubtedly come from the energy and vision of the entrepreneur, from his personalized recruiting and through the language and style with which he communicates his vision. A vision becomes an ideology through the endorsement of the organization. The ideology can impart meaning, demand involvement and behavioral consistency, motivate the performance of routine tasks, and resolve the concerns of its people. Closely interwoven with these processes are the mechanisms of sacrifice and investment, the forms of boundary management and tendencies to institutional completeness, and the potential for community arising out of group rituals, homogeneity of background, and organizational myths.

SUMMARY

The overall purpose of this paper has been to highlight in the language of social process some of the more cultural and expressive aspects of organizational life by introducing and illustrating some concepts widely used in sociology and anthropology but which have not yet been integrated into the theoretical language of organizational behavior. The substantive problem used here to provide a focus for these concepts has been how are organizational cultures created? The problem has been approached through the concepts of symbol, language, ideology, belief, ritual, and myth. These concepts have been defined and some of their functions and analytical interconnections and overlaps distinguished. Attention has been drawn to their value not only in understanding the creation of new cultures, but also in unravelling the related processes by which entrepreneurs give energy, purpose, and commitment to the organizations they are bringing into being.

No suggestion is being made that these concepts are universally applicable across all organizations in differing institutional spheres. The works of Etzioni (1961), Goffman (1961), and Coser (1974) would seem to indicate these concepts are more likely to be useful in certain kinds of organizations than others. Caution is in order, however, before assuming this kind of cultural analysis is only applicable to educational, religious, correctional, or social movement types of organization. The study by Pettigrew and Bumstead (1980) of how variations in organizational culture have affected the impact of organization development activities illustrates the use of the concepts in this paper in business organizations. In addition it is only recently (Pettigrew, 1977) that conceptual developments in the analysis of political processes in organizations have explored processes of legitimation and delegitimation, although there is a strong tradition of using symbolic analysis in political science (Edelman 1964; Graber 1976). More specifically claims are being made that the kinds of analyses made possible by these concepts are potentially useful in understanding the creation of organizational cultures, the leadership components of entrepreneurship, and how the problems of commitment are handled in organizations. This paper has only listed some items on a menu and put some of the items together in some simple dishes; it remains for others to broaden the menu and produce the *cordon bleu* meals.

NOTES

1

Using a similar research design I (1973) studied four capital investment decisions in a single firm over a twelve-year period. In that case, the real time data collection was two years and the retrospective-historical analysis ten years. The dramas were major capital investment decisions and the continuous processes, the study of the ebb and flow of power relationships, and the emergence, transformation, and decline of two occupational groups.

2

See Pettigrew (1975) for examples of symbol construction among groups of specialists in organizations.

REFERENCES

Beattie, John
1966 "Ritual and social change." Man (new series), 1: 60–74.

Berger, Peter L., and Thomas Luckman
1966 The Social Construction of Reality. Harmondsworth, England: Allen Lane; Penguin Press.

Bocock, Robert
1974 Ritual in Industrial Society. London: Allen & Unwin.

Boswell, Jonathon
1972 The Rise and Decline of Small Firms. London: Allen & Unwin.

Buchanan, Bruce
1974 "Building organizational com-

mitment: The socialization of managers in work organizations." Administrative Science Quarterly, 18: 533–546.

Cassirer, Ernst
1953 An Essay on Man. Garden City: Doubleday; Anchor Books.

Clark, Burton R.
1972 "The organizational saga in higher education." Administrative Science Quarterly, 17: 178–184.

Cohen, Abner
1974 Two Dimensional Man: An Essay on the Anthropology of Power and Symbolism in Complex Society. London: Routledge and Kegan Paul.

Cohen, Anthony P.
1975 The Management of Myths: The Politics of Legitimation in a Newfoundland Community. Manchester, England: Manchester University Press.

Cohen, Percy S.
1969 "Theories of myth." Man (new series), 4: 337–353.

Collins, Orvis, and David Moore
1970 The Organization Makers. New York: Meredith.

Coser, Lewis A.
1974 Greedy Institutions. New York: Free Press.

Donaldson, Lex
1972 "Forecasting the future trend of bureaucratisation." London: Graduate School of Business (mimeo).

Duncan, Hugh Dalziel
1968 Symbols in Society. Oxford: University Press.

Edelman, M.
1964 The Symbolic Uses of Politics. Urbana: University of Illinois Press.

Etzioni, Amitai
1961 A Comparative Analysis of Complex Organizations. New York: Free Press.

Goffman, Erving
1961 Asylums. New York: Doubleday; Anchor Books.

Graber, D. A.
1976 Verbal Behavior and Politics. Urbana: University of Illinois Press.

Greiner, Larry E.
1972 "Evolution and revolution as organizations grow." Harvard Business Review, 50: 37–46.

Hill, Michael
1973 A Sociology of Religion. London: Heinemann.

Hornaday, John A., and Charles S. Bunker
1970 "The nature of the entrepreneur." Personnel Psychology, 23: 47–54.

Kanter, Rosabeth Moss
1968 "Commitment and social organization: A study of commitment mechanisms in utopian communities." American Sociological Review, 33: 499-517.

1972 Commitment and Community. Cambridge, MA: Harvard University Press.

Leach, E. R.
1954 Political Systems of Highland Burma. London: Bell.

McClelland, David C.
1961 The Achieving Society. London: Collier Macmillan.

Mill, C. Wright
1972 "Language, logic and culture." In A. Cashdan and E. Crugeon (eds.), Language in Education: A Source Book: 59– 66. London: Routledge and Kegan Paul.

Pettigrew, Andrew M.
1973 The Politics of Organizational Decision Making. London: Tavistock.
1975 "Strategic aspects of the management of specialist activity." Personnel Review, 4: 5–13.
1977 "Strategy formulation as a political process." International Studies of Management and Organization, 7: 78–87.

Pettigrew, Andrew M., and D. C. Bumstead
1980 "Strategies of organization development in differing contexts." In P. A. Clark, J. Guiot, and H. Thirry (eds.), Organizational Change and Development in Europe. London: Wiley.

Pondy, Louis R.
1975 "Leadership is a language game." Working paper, Department of Business Administration, University of Illinois–Urbana.

Roberts, E. B.
1968 "Entrepreneurship and technology — A basic study of innovators." Research Management, 11: 249–266

Schrage, Harry
1965 "The R&D entrepreneur: Profile of success." Harvard Business Review, 43: 56–69.

Selznick, P.
1957 Leadership in Administration. Evanston, IL: Row, Peterson.

Silverman, David
1970 The Theory of Organizations. London: Heinemann.

Smelser, Neil
1963 Theory of Collective Behavior. New York: Free Press.

Stanworth, M. J. K., and J. Curran
1973 Management Motivation in the Smaller Business. London: Gower Press.

Strauss, George
1974 "Adolescence in organization growth." Organizational Dynamics, 2: 3–17.

Turner, V. W.
1957 Schism and Continuity in an African Society. Manchester, England: Manchester University Press.

Wainer, Herbert A., and Irwin M. Rubin
1969 "Motivation of research development entrepreneurs: Determinants of company success." Journal of Applied Psychology, 53: 178–184.

White, L.
1949 The Science of Culture. New York: Grove Press.

Willis, Roy, ed.
1975 The Interpretation of Symbolism. London: Malaby Press.

Wilson, John
1973 Introduction to Social Movements. New York: Basic Books.

An Emerging Strategy of "Direct" Research

Henry Mintzberg

For about eight years now, a group of us at McGill University's Faculty of Management has been researching the process of strategy formation. Defining a strategy as a pattern in a stream of decisions, our central theme has been the contrast between "deliberate" strategies, that is, patterns intended before being realized, and "emergent" strategies, patterns realized despite or in the absence of intentions. Emergent strategies are rather common in organizations, or, more to the point, almost all strategies seem to be in some part at least, emergent. To quote that expression so popular on posters these days, "Life is a journey, not a destination."

In this article I will describe my journey into research, to step back from the stream of decisions concerning my own research since I began a doctoral dissertation in 1966, and to discuss the patterns — the themes or strategies — that appear. In retrospect, some seem more deliberate to me, others more emergent, but in general they appear to represent a blending of the two. The point I wish to make is that these themes form their own strategy of research, one that I would like to contrast with a more conventional strategy of research that seems to have dominated our field.

A word on the data base. I have been involved in three major research projects these past 13 years (and since three do not a sharp pattern make, the title refers to an emerging rather than an emergent strategy). First was my doctoral dissertation, a study of the work of five managers through structured observation (Mintzberg, 1973). Essentially, I watched what each did for a week, and recorded it systematically — in terms of who they worked with, when, where, for how long, and for what purpose. These data were used to induce a set of characteristics and of roles of managerial work. Second, over the course of some years, teams of MBA students were sent out to study local organizations; one assignment was to take a single strategic decision and to describe the steps the organization had gone through from the very first stimulus to the authorization of the final choice. From these reports, we selected the 25 most complete and inferred a structure of the "unstructured" decision process (Mintzberg, Raisinghani, and Théorêt, 1976). Our third project, mentioned in the opening of this paper, involves the study of organizational strategies through the tracing of patterns in streams of decisions over periods of 30 or more years. This is a large project, at the present time involving a number of months of on-site research in each organization. We first spend a good deal of time reading whatever historical documents we can find, in order to develop thorough chronologies of decisions in various strategy areas. Then we switch to interviews to fill in the gaps in the decision chronologies and to probe into the reasons for breaks in the patterns (i.e., for strategic changes). We have so far completed five of these studies (Mintzberg, 1978, reports on the earliest phase of this research), and five more are now underway (in addition to about 15 similar but shorter studies carried out by MBA students as part of their term work). Two other projects, while not based on our own research, form part of the data base of this paper. These are attempts to synthesize the empirical literature in two areas — organizational structuring and power. These efforts have led to two books (Mintzberg, 1979, forthcoming), both revolving around the notion of configurations, or ideal types of many dimensions.

This paper focuses on seven basic themes each of which underlies to a greater or lesser degree these various research activities.

1. The research has been as purely descriptive as we have been able to make it. This hardly seems unusual in organization theory. But most of the work has been concentrated in the policy area, where prescription has been the norm for a long time. Moreover, one could argue that much of the "descriptive" research about organizations has set out to prove some prescription, for example that a participative managerial style is more effective than an autocratic one.

The orientation to as pure a form of description as possible has, I believe, enabled us to raise doubts about a good deal of accepted wisdom: to be able to say that managerial work observed has more to do with interruption, action orientation, and verbal communication than with coordinating and controlling; to say that diagnosis and timing count more in strategic decision making than the choice of an alternative from a given set; to say that strategy formation is better understood as a discontinuous, adaptive process than a formally planned one. The little boy in the Hans Christian Andersen story, who said that the emperor wore no clothes, has always served as a kind of model to me. This is not to imply that our work so exposes the manager; in fact, I believe it clothes him in more elegant garments. It is the literature of management that often emerges as naked, since much of what it says becomes transparent when held up to the scrutiny of descriptive research.

2. The research has relied on simple — in a sense, inelegant — methodologies. The field of organization theory has, I believe, paid dearly for the obsession with rigor in the choice of methodology. Too many of the results have been significant only in the statistical sense of the word. In our work, we have always found that simpler, more direct methodologies have yielded more useful results. Like sitting down in a manager's office and watching what he does. Or tracing the flow of decisions in an organization.

What, for example, is wrong with samples of one? Why should researchers have to apologize for them? Should Piaget apologize for studying his own children, a physicist for splitting only one atom? A doctoral student I know was not allowed to observe managers because of the "problem" of sample size. He was required to measure what managers did through questionnaires, despite ample evidence in the

literature that managers are poor estimators of their own
time allocation (e.g., Burns, 1954; Horne and Lupton, 1965;
Harper, 1968). Was it better to have less valid data that
were statistically significant?

Given that we have one hundred people each prepared to
do a year of research, we should ask ourselves whether we
are better off to have each study 100 organizations, giving
us superficial data on ten thousand, or each study one, giving us in-depth data on one hundred. The choice obviously
depends on what is to be studied. But it should not preclude
the small sample, which has often proved superior.

3. The research has been as purely inductive as possible.
Our doctoral students get a dose of Popper (1968) in their
research methodology course. Popper bypasses induction as
not part of the logic of scientific inquiry, and the students
emerge from the course — like many elsewhere — believing that somehow induction is not a valid part of science. I
stand with Selye (1964) in concluding that, while deduction
certainly is a part of science, it is the less interesting, less
challenging part. It is discovery that attracts me to this business, not the checking out of what we think we already know.

I see two essential steps in inductive research. The first is
detective work, the tracking down of patterns, consisten-
cies. One searches through a phenomenon looking for order, following one lead to another. But the process itself is
not neat.

Even in the nineteenth century, celebrated discoveries were often
achieved enigmatically. Kekuly tortuously arrived at his theory of
the benzene molecule; Davy blundered onto the anesthetic properties of nitrous oxide; Perkin's failure to produce synthetic quinine
circuitously revealed aniline dyes; and Ehrlich tried 606 times before he succeeded in compounding salvarsan in 1910 (Dalton,
1959: 273).

The second step in induction is the *creative leap.* Selye cites
a list of "intellectual immoralities" published by a well-
known physiology department. Number 4 read "Generalizing
beyond one's data." He quotes approvingly a commentator
who asked whether it would not have been more correct to
word Number 4: "Not generalizing beyond one's data"

(1964: 228). The fact is that there would be no interesting hypothesis to test if no one ever generalized beyond his or her data. Every theory requires that creative leap, however small, that breaking away from the expected to describe something new. There is no one-to-one correspondence between data and theory. The data do not generate the theory — only researchers do that — any more than the theory can be *proved* true in terms of the data. All theories are false, because all abstract from data and simplify the world they purport to describe. Our choice, then, is not between true and false theories so much as between more and less useful theories. And usefulness, to repeat, stems from detective work well done, followed by creative leaps in relevant directions.

Call this research "exploratory" if you like, just so long as you do not use the term in a condescending sense: "OK, kid, we'll let you get away with it this time, but don't let us catch you doing it again." No matter what the state of the field, whether it is new or mature, all of its interesting research explores. Indeed, it seems that the more deeply we probe into this field of organizations, the more complex we find it to be, and the more we need to fall back on so-called exploratory, as opposed to "rigorous," research methodologies.

To take one case of good exploration and a small leap, a young doctoral student in France went into the company in that country that was reputed to be most advanced in its long-range planning procedures (in a country that takes its planning dogma very seriously). He was there to document those procedures, the "right" way to plan. But he was a good enough detective to realize quickly that all was not what it seemed on the surface. So he began to poke around. And with small creative leaps he produced some interesting conclusions, for example, that planning really served as a tool by which top management centralized power (Sarrazin, 1977–78). Peripheral vision, poking around in relevant places, a good dose of creativity — that is what makes good research, and always has, in all fields.

Why do we let our doctoral students be guided by mechanical methodologies into banal research? Weick (1974: 487)

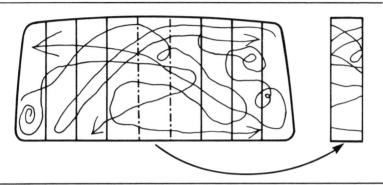

Figure 1   Slicing up the organization

quotes Somerset Maugham: "She plunged into a sea of platitudes, and with the powerful breast stroke of a channel swimmer made her confident way toward the white cliffs of the obvious." Why not, instead, throw them into the sea of complexity, the sea of the big questions, to find out if they can swim at all, if they can collect data as effective detectives, and if they are capable of even small leaps of creativity. If not, perhaps they have chosen the wrong profession.

4. The research has, nevertheless, been systematic in nature. I do not mean to offer license to fish at random in that sea. No matter how small our sample or what our interest, we have always tried to go into organizations with a well-defined focus — to collect specific kinds of data systematically. In one study we wanted to know who contacts the manager, how, for how long, and why; in the second we were interested in the sequence of steps used in making certain key decisions; in the third, we are after chronologies of decision in various strategic areas. Those are the "hard" data of our research, and they have been crucial in all of our studies.

5. The research has measured in real organizational terms. Systematic does not mean detached. Probably the greatest impediment to theory building in the study of organizations has been research that violates the organization, that forces it into abstract categories that have nothing to do with how it functions. My favorite analogy is of an organization rich in flows and processes, as implied in Figure 1, kind of like a marble cake. Then along comes a researcher with a machine much like those used to slice bread. In goes the organization and out come the cross-sectional slices. The researcher then holds up one of them, shown to the right in Figure 1, and tries to figure out what it is he or she is seeing. "Hmmmm . . . what have we here? The amount of control if 4.2, the complexity of environment, 3.6." What does it mean to measure the "amount of control" in an organization, or the "complexity" of its environment? Some of these concepts may be useful in describing organizations in theory, but that does not mean we can plug them into our research holus-bolus as measures. As soon as the researcher insists on forcing the organization into abstract categories — into his terms instead of its own — he is reduced to using perceptual measures, which often distort the reality. The researcher intent on generating a direct measure of amount of control or of complexity of environment can only ask people what they believe, on seven-point scales or the like. He gets answers, all right, ready for the computer; what he does not get is any idea of what he has measured. (What does "amount of control" mean anyway?[1]) The result is sterile description, of organizations as categories of abstract variables instead of flesh-and-blood processes. And theory building becomes impossible. Far from functioning like detectives, "In touching up dead data with false colors, [social scientists] function much like morticians" (Orlans, 1975: 109).

If someone is interested in studying perceptions, then by all means let him study perceptions. But let him not study perceptions if it is control or complexity he is after. There is no doubt that "the perceptions of the chief executive are important in understanding why organizations are structured as they are" (Pfeffer and Leblebici, 1973–74: 273). But that does not justify researchers — these and many others — in drawing conclusions about how the "environment," as opposed to the "perception of the environment," affects structure.

Measuring in real organizational terms means first of all getting out into the field, into real organizations. Questionnaires often won't do. Nor will laboratory simulations, at least not in policy research. The individual or group psychologist can bring the phenomenon he is studying into his laboratory holus-bolus; the *organization* theorist cannot. What is the use of describing a reality that has been invented? The evidence of our research — of interruptions and soft data and information overload — suggests that we do not yet understand enough about organizations to simulate their functioning in the laboratory. It is their inherent complexity and dynamic nature that characterize phenomena such as policy making. Simplification squeezes out the very thing on which the research should focus.

Measuring in real organizational terms means measuring things that really happen in organizations, as they experience them. To draw on our research, it means measuring the proportion of letters sent by customers or the number of new stores opened in a given year. It is the job of the researcher to abstract from the particular to the general, to develop concepts from his measurements in the field. I believe the researcher shirks his responsibility when he expects the manager to do the abstracting, to decide how complex is the environment (or even what complexity means). Managers do not think about complex environments; they think about new discoveries in plastics, about the problems of getting the R&D people to work with those in marketing, about how a proposed piece of legislation will affect sales.

My favorite anecdote in this regard concerns Peter Travis, an Australian and one of the world's great potters. He was approached by a researcher who wanted to study the creative process. The researcher proposed to elicit protocols from Travis as he worked. They tried that, but got nowhere. Travis felt he could not verbalize about the creative process; he had to demonstrate it visually. So he proposed to make a bowl on his wheel, then another, then another, and continue until he had a thousand pots. He might make ten alike and then vary the rim on the eleventh. By the twentieth he might modify the shape, and by the one-hundredth he might not feel like making bowls at all but instead decide to form bottles. One form would lead to another so that by the one-thousandth pot Travis would have a visual record of the creative process. The researcher could then come in and describe it. (Travis apparently really intends to carry out his side of the bargain. The best part of the story is that Travis, in recounting, thought that his proposal was so "obvious." One thousand pots. "How else would you study creativity?" It seems that we need creative minds to study creativity. And complex minds to study complexity. Too bad Peter Travis didn't choose to become a management researcher. But then again, which doctoral program would have let him in?)

6. The research, in its intensive nature, has ensured that systematic data are supported by anecdotal data. More and more we feel the need to be on site, and to be there long enough to be able to understand what is going on. (We began with a week and are now spending months and even years.) For while systematic data create the foundation for our theories, it is the anecdotal data that enable us to do the building. Theory building seems to require rich description, the richness that comes from anecdote. We uncover all kinds of relationships in our "hard" data, but it is only through the use of this "soft" data that we are able to "explain" them, and explanation is, or course, the purpose of research. I believe that the researcher who never goes near the water, who collects quantitative data from a distance without anecdote to support them, will always have difficulty explaining interesting relationships (although he may uncover them). Perhaps this has something to do with how our minds work. Those creative leaps seem to come from our subconscious mental processes, our intuition (e.g., Hadamard, 1949). And intuition apparently requires the "sense" of things — how they feel, smell, "seem." We need to be "in touch." Increasingly in our research, we are impressed by the importance of phenomena that cannot be measured — by the impact of an organization's history and its ideology on its current strategy, by the role that personality and intuition play in decision making. To miss this in research is to miss the very lifeblood of the organization. And missed it is in research, that by its very design, precludes the collection of anecdotal information.

7. The research has sought to synthesize, to integrate diverse elements into configurations of ideal or pure types. Organizations intermingle a great many elements in their functioning. Researchers who focus on two variables at a time — who catch what someone has called "the economists' plague": holding all other things constant — seem to cloud issues almost as often as they clarify them. Consider the unending debates about size and administrative ratio or bureaucracy and centralization. Literally, the more that has been published, the more confused the issues have become (and I apologize for this bivariate hypothesis). We shall never have closure so long as we pretend that other things can be held constant. We live in a world of dynamic systems. (A colleague of mine claims that everything in the world correlates with everything else at 0.3.) Organizations also experience all kinds of lags and discontinuities. For example, because structural change often follows strategic change (Chandler, 1962; Stopford and Wells, 1972; Rumelt, 1974), it is somewhat a matter of luck whether a two-variable cross-sectional study manages to capture the structure that reflects today's situation — which it typically measures — or yesterday's, which it typically does not. And the presence of discontinuities (e.g., Woodward, 1965, about structure as a function of technology; Klatzky, 1970, about A/P as a function of size) plays havoc with these conventional approaches.

We can also question whether the human brain prefers to think in terms of continuous and bivariate relationships, or searches for another kind of order, characterized by clusters or configurations, ideal or pure types. We seem to put diverse elements together into various envelopes. The word "democracy," for example, seems to be captured less by some scale of freedom than by a configuration of elements — a free press, due process, elected officials, and so on. Likewise I believe that we prefer to understand our organizations in terms of pure types — configurations of many elements.

But to generate those configurations, I have more faith in typologies than taxonomies, if I understand correctly how these terms are used. In other words, while I believe we need empirical data to generate our categories — systematic data reinforced by a good deal of anecdote — I do not expect them to come from mechanical data reduction techniques. It is pattern recognition we are after, in the form of those creative leaps, and I believe that human, not electronic, brains are most capable of achieving those leaps.

To conclude, these seven characteristics underlie the research we have been doing these past 13 years. Together they seem to form their own configuration: research based on description and induction instead of implicit or explicit prescription and deduction; reliance on simple, inelegant, as opposed to "rigorous" methods of data collection; the measurement of many elements in real organizational terms, supported by anecdote, instead of few variables in perceptual terms from a distance; and the synthesis of these elements into clusters, instead of the analysis of pairs of variables as continuous relationships. We might call this strategy, for want of a better term, "direct research."

NOTE

1

A number of studies in management policy have sought correlations of performance and amount of planning — to show that planning pays. But what exactly is the definition of planning in the context of actual strategy formation? The answer to that question requires intensive research on decision-making processes, as in the research in France cited earlier, not a few measures on questionnaires or the counting up of a bunch of formal documents that management may never look at.

REFERENCES

Burns, Tom
1954 "The directions of activity and communication in a departmental executive group." Human Relations, 7: 73–97.

Chandler, Alfred D.
1962 Strategy and Structure. Cambridge, MA: MIT Press.

Dalton, M.
1959 Men Who Manage. New York: Wiley.

Hadamard, J. S.
1949 Psychology of Invention in the Mathematical Field. Princeton: Princeton University Press.

Harper, W. K.
1968 Executive Time: A Corporation's Most Valuable, Scarce and Irrecoverable Resource. DBA thesis, Graduate School of Business Administration, Harvard University.

Horne, J. H., and T. Lupton
1965 "The work activities of 'middle' managers — an exploratory study." Journal of Management Studies, 2: 14–33.

Klatzky, S. P.
1970 "Relationship of organizational size to complexity and coordination." Administrative Science Quarterly, 15: 428–438.

Mintzberg, Henry
1973 The Nature of Managerial Work. New York: Harper & Row.
1978 "Patterns in strategy formation." Management Science, 24: 934–948.
1979 The Structuring of Organizations. Englewood Cliffs, NJ: Prentice-Hall.
1983 Power in and Around Organizations. Englewood Cliffs, NJ: Prentice-Hall.

Mintzberg, Henry, Duru Raisinghani, and André Théorêt
1976 "The structure of 'unstructured' decision processes." Administrative Science Quarterly, 21: 246–275.

Orlans, H.
1975 "Neutrality and advocacy in policy research." Policy Sciences, 6: 107–119.

Pfeffer, Jeffrey, and Huseyin Leblebici
1973–74 "The effect of competition on some dimensions of organizational structure." Social Forces, 52: 268–279.

Popper, K. R.
1968 The Logic of Scientific Discovery. New York: Harper & Row.

Rumelt, R. P.
1974 Strategy, Structure, and Economic Performance. Boston: Division of Research, Graduate School of Business Administration, Harvard University.

Sarrazin, J.
1977-78 "Decentralized planning in a large French company: An interpretative study." International Studies of Management and Organization, 7: 37–59.

Selye, Hans
1964 From Dream to Discovery: On Being a Scientist. New York: McGraw-Hill.

Stopford, J. M., and L. T. Wells
1972 Managing the Multinational Enterprise: Organization of the Firm and Ownership of the Subsidiaries. New York: Basic Books.

Weick, Karl E.
1974 "Amendments to organizational theorizing." Academy of Management Journal, 17: 487–502.

Woodward, Joan
1965 Industrial Organization: Theory and Practice. London: Oxford University Press.

Qualitative Data as an Attractive Nuisance: The Problem of Analysis

Matthew B. Miles

The legal doctrine of an "attractive nuisance" is simply illustrated by what happens if you abandon a car in your back yard: if neighboring children come eagerly to play in it, you are liable for their injuries. Qualitative data collected during the study of organizations fit this illustration well: there are many reasons why more and more researchers are currently seeking such data, and there are many ways they can get hurt — or at least fail to achieve their purposes, and just as most children think that driving is easy, so many researchers somehow think that qualitative data present few problematic methodological issues.

Qualitative data are attractive for many reasons: they are rich, full, earthy, holistic, "real"; their face validity seems unimpeachable; they preserve chronological flow where that is important, and suffer minimally from retrospective distortion; and they, in principle, offer a far more precise way to assess causality in organizational affairs than arcane efforts like cross-lagged correlations (after all, intensive fieldwork contains dozens of "waves" of data collection, not just two or three). Furthermore, their collection requires minimal front-end instrumentation. Qualitative data also have attractive qualities for their producers and consumers; they lend themselves to the production of serendipitous findings and the adumbration of unforeseen theoretical leaps; they tend to reduce a researcher's trained incapacity, bias, narrowness, and arrogance; and their results, reported in forms ranging from case studies to vignettes, have a quality of "undeniability" (Smith, 1978) that lends punch to research reports. Finally, there are many reasons to believe that qualitative data can very usefully be played off against quantitative information from the same organizational setting (Sieber, 1973) to produce more powerful analyses than either sort of information could have produced alone.

But qualitative data have serious weaknesses and problems as well. Collecting and analyzing the data is a highly labor-intensive operation, often generating much stress, even for top-quality research staff. Qualitative fieldwork is traditionally demanding even for the lone fieldworker, accountable only to the data and his or her discipline; when several fieldworkers' efforts must be coordinated, as is more and more typically the case, much energy is required to make data systematically "comparable." Qualitative data tend to overload the researcher badly at almost every point: the sheer range of phenomena to be observed, the recorded volume of notes, the time required for write-up, coding, and analysis can all become overwhelming. But the most serious and central difficulty in the use of qualitative data is that methods of analysis are not well formulated. For quantitative data, there are clear conventions the researcher can use. But the analyst faced with a bank of qualitative data has very few guidelines for protection against self-delusion, let alone the presentation of "unreliable" or "invalid" conclusions to scientific or policy-making audiences. How can we be sure that an "earthy," "undeniable," "serendipitous" finding is not, in fact, *wrong?*

This article addresses the issues and problems in analysis of qualitative data, through a review of experiences in a four-year project that relied centrally on such data. Called the Project on Social Architecture in Education, it focused on the processes involved in the creation of innovative organizations.[1] The organizations were public schools — three elementary and three secondary. We examined closely how people went about the long process of envisioning the new organization, staffing it, dealing with the political surroundings, designing the organization's structures, core technologies, and environmental linkages, bringing the actual organization into being, and stabilizing it over the first years of its life. Much of what is written about "organization de-

sign" (e.g., Burack and Negandhi, 1977; Kilmann, 1977;
Pfeffer, 1978) is conceptually abstract, with little relation to
the actual process of organizational creation, so intensive
qualitative data collection was indicated.

THE SOCIAL ARCHITECTURE PROJECT

Conceptualization

Beginning with Glaser and Strauss (1967), much has been
written about developing "grounded theory," "being open to
what the site has to tell us," and slowly evolving a coherent
framework rather than "imposing" one from the start. But
the need to develop grounded theory usually exists in tension with the need for clarity and focus; research projects
that pretend to come to the study with no assumptions
usually encounter much difficulty. We believed — and still
do — that a rough working frame needs to be in place near
the beginning of fieldwork. Of course it will change. The risk
is *not* that of "imposing" a self-blinding framework, but that
an incoherent, bulky, irrelevant, meaningless set of observations may be produced, which no one can (or even wants to)
make sense of. Thus, we chose the strategy of developing
explicit preliminary frameworks quite early; even so, we revised them repeatedly over the life of the project.

Our effort to develop a coherent conceptual framework for
the project began in 1974 with a series of "concept papers"
developed by staff members on such topics as school-
community relations, consulting behavior, leader and core-
group member behavior, political processes in new-school
development, alternative planning models, and social architecture generally. A preliminary general accounting-
scheme framework posited a "core group" of planners and
implementers, making decisions that bore on the internal
properties of the new school and its political environment,
based in part on goals and "desired system properties" of
the organization that was being created. Prior analyses of
schools as organizations (Bidwell, 1965; Miles, 1967) were
drawn on.

Beginning in 1975, we revised and extended the general
framework through several means: a work conference on
problems of consultation in new systems; a series of staff

seminars built around the earlier concept paper topics; the production of several convention papers (e.g., Gold, 1976; Miles, 1967a; Sullivan and Kironde, 1976) and the fact that in parallel with the research, a materials developer joined the research staff to create practical "learning materials" drawn from the study (Taylor, 1978) for future use by new-school planners. The production of a series of survey instruments for teachers, parents and students, to assess "the state of the system" in two of our sites, caused substantial shifts.

More generally, the demands of continuing fieldwork in six sites forced us to simplify, select, and collapse a very large collection of categories into a more focused, winnowed-down, and coherent set of variables. New variables also appeared: we learned far more than we had dreamed of in our original "rational-designer" model about political maneuvering, environmental buffering, decision dilemmas, and coping styles. Additionally, six sites and three fieldworkers provided useful comparative perspectives: a common conceptual language began to emerge during shared discussion and analysis of site events; cross-visits helped to make corrections for conceptual bias.

A final formal framework was generated from a series of propositions during 1977; it outlined a series of "key dilemmas" (such as whether to choose familiar or innovative design components, whether to utilize external expertise or rely on internal resources, and whether to approach the political environment proactively or maintain a buffering stance). These dilemmas, which had been clearly visible in the fieldwork, were seen in the framework as deriving from generic aspects of the organizational creation task, such as its novelty, task complexity, and uncertainty (cf. Stinchcombe, 1965); they infused a series of "primary tasks" including political stabilization, knowledge utilization, vision development, social-architectural design, actualization of the design, and stabilization. Skills of developing legitimacy and investment, meta-planning, obtaining resources, acting reflexively, and decision making were seen as determining the outcomes of dilemmas and work on primary tasks.

The important thing to note is that even with a starting framework, conceptual development occurred almost continuously for the first three years of the project; not until the production of case studies began in 1977 was there a firm stabilization. The process was arduous and often stressful; but increasingly productive, informed as it was by analysis of site data.

The Data Base

Each of our six sites was visited weekly by a fieldworker, for a half or full day, and was often phoned as well. Senior project staff also visited sites from time to time. Field contacts lasted for periods ranging from two to nearly three years. The corpus of field notes ran to several thousand pages per site.

Direct observation and informal interviewing were supplemented by document collection, a few formal retrospective interviews on the history of planning, a brief questionnaire on espoused goals for the new schools, and one to two waves of survey questionnaires administered to teachers, administrators, parents, and students after the schools opened.

We should note here some problems of time cost. There is no easy way to record qualitative data other than through running notes. But raw notes ordinarily mean little or nothing to anyone other than the fieldworker and need to be converted into write-ups. It takes almost as much time for a fieldworker to type notes as the time of the original contact, even for a fieldworker who is also a good typist. Dictated write-ups, much the easier for the fieldworker, typically take a good transcriber a similar or longer amount of time. For example, an all-day contact usually resulted in 60–90 minutes of tape, which took the fieldworker 2–2½ hours to produce, and a secretary 6–8 hours to transcribe, and the fieldworker another hour to review and correct. These figures cannot be reduced very much without losing many of the direct quotes, earthy data, etc. which make ethnographic data so useful, and introducing systematic inattention and biases in the interests of "simplicity."

Since data recording and transformation are defined as essential, they tend to drive out data reduction, analysis, and conceptualization. Fieldworkers characteristically ran late on write-ups. They ran even later on data reduction, coding, and analysis. Being at the site typically took priority: the fear was of "missing" something crucial. But the more such "crucial" events were attended, the further behind data transformation, reduction, and coding fell. We usually had write-up backlogs of 2–3 contacts, and coding backlogs of anywhere from 15–30 contacts.

Under these circumstances, data analysis becomes somewhat meaningless, and fieldworkers get progressively less interested in doing it. Instead of really understanding and thinking about the site, the fieldworker risks being run by the site. And the richer and fuller the contacts with the site, the more reluctant the fieldworker is to miss a new and crucial site event.

Write-up delays can also cause problems in the quality of reported data: much is forgotten, oversimplified, or reinterpreted in the light of more recent contacts.

Data Analysis

It is fair to say that by the best of current standards, analysis of qualitative data is a mysterious, half-formulated art. We detail our experience here to warn, and perhaps to enlighten others.

Data reduction. How can write-ups be rendered less prolix, and their main issues and themes extracted as fieldwork goes forward? There is a strong need to establish meaning in a systematic way. Data reduction is a form of preliminary analysis, which refines, iterates, and revises frameworks, suggests new leads for further data collection, and makes data more available for final assembly into case studies and cross-site analyses.

Our project used several methods. At the beginning we developed an elaborate coding scheme, with over one hundred categories for key actors ("planner," "principal"), for planning and implementation processes ("energy mobilization," "resource allocation"), and for aspects of the new organization being planned ("governance," "budget," "reward system"). The fieldworker applied these codes in the margins of the write-ups. As we got deeper into the sites, this scheme was finally elaborated into 202 categories. Fieldworkers, including the coding specialist, hated the job. It fell far behind. The aim of the coding scheme was to permit systematic analysis "later." Coded excerpts from the write-ups were put on 5 x 7 file cards to provide quick retrieval of all excerpts dealing with a particular code, such as "resource allocation."

The number of categories and what had become the meaninglessness of the coding task led us after a few more months to condense our 202 codes into 26 major "themes," such as "planning adaptiveness" or "commitment." The fieldworker reread the write-up, gave a rating on each theme (high, medium, low, uncertain), and filled out two forms that summarized and coded key or salient points in the field contact, identified decisions made, and asked for hypotheses or explanations.

A lone fieldworker usually manages all this in a much less systematic, more intuitive way. But the question of coding reliability and validity remained, and the fact that we were trying to generate good knowledge across six different sites, with three different fieldworkers, had pushed us into an effort that we came to call "the bureaucratization of fieldwork": how to systematize, regularize, and coordinate the work of observation, recording, and analysis.

But the system, finally, did not work in the sense in which it was intended. Fieldworkers tended to become increasingly "the authorities" on their sites, and increasingly driven and absorbed by them. And though they shared in the quest for a common intellectual framework, they were often the first to protest that their sites were in some important respects unique. So the project director's demands and plans for systematic coding and formal continuing analysis were in fact resisted, and were eventually abandoned. The coding stopped, and the cards were not used for analysis. Since the project's outcomes rested centrally on the continued high quality of data collected by fieldworkers, the director felt he could not alienate them by continuing to press demands they were unwilling to meet.

There was, however, a genuine residue of the extended efforts at coding. The arguments and clarifications they required were successful in generating a common language of concepts, which found their way into the general framework, and guided further data analysis in less-formal modes.

Experiments with Informal Data Analysis

Concerned about formulating clearer guidelines for qualitative data analysis, we also approached the problem empirically. The strategy was that of producing *site summaries.* Some of these were the straightforward, mirror-like reports we fed back as part of our contracts with sites, which had a minimum of inference and analysis. Others, for research staff use, were more interpretive and attempted to integrate what we thought we knew about each of our sites as of 1975 in reports that ran from 40 to 50 pages.

We also learned that much analysis was going on in the mind of the fieldworker. Each one developed a fairly rich set of working hypotheses about what was going on in his or her site, along with a fairly retrievable store of specific anecdotes and incidents supporting the hypotheses. But without interaction with colleagues, the hypotheses went unchallenged and usually untested, and the anecdotes remembered were only those in support of the hypotheses.

We developed the idea of *site updates,* which were regular addenda to the site summaries. The fieldworker ordinarily met with one other staff member who knew the site, to summarize recent developments and to give his or her interpretations of what was happening.

This mode was further extended to the *site analysis meeting;* here the primary fieldworker met every few weeks with the rest of the staff to review updates, identify major themes in the site, propose explanations, entertain alternative (or unpopular) explanations, and identify new data that needed to be collected. A site analysis recording form was used to keep notes of the discussions.

These informal methods, less obsessive and atomized than the coding efforts, actively engaged staff in conceptualization and felt quite productive. The interaction provided some assurance against self-delusion, but just how much remained unclear.

Use of Quantitative Data

We had been committed from the start to integrating quantitative and qualitative data, along the lines suggested by Sieber (1973), and did find the strategy fruitful. In one method, which we invented and labelled "goal-system state analysis," selected goals for the new organization were extracted from questionnaire and fieldwork data, and the analyst sought quantitative and qualitative evidence that the goals had been achieved, revised, or abandoned in the actualized organization of the new school, and generated possible explanations. Other quantitative-qualitative linkages were simpler: for example, two principals in the same district with radically differing implementation success in their new schools were shown to differ substantially on the Social Support scale developed by Gross and Herriott (1965). For example, 72 percent of Principal A's teachers said he (always) "displayed integrity in behavior," while only 16 percent of Principal B's said so. In the fieldwork we had already noticed that several teachers in B's school were reluctant to say much to the fieldworker because "it might get back to George,"; rumors and mistrust were present. More elegantly, we had enough survey data to conduct path analyses (Galanter, 1978) to test our fieldworkers' beliefs about "support systems" in the two schools.

Formal Approaches to Qualitative Data Analysis

We could not escape the suspicion that others did not know much more than we about the arcane process of making valid sense of large amounts of qualitative information. Sieber (1976a), a staff member, reviewed the state of the art as described in seven well-respected texts on field methods (Glaser and Strauss, 1967; Filstead, 1970; Glaser, 1972; Runkel and McGrath, 1972; Schatzman and Strauss, 1973; Bogdan and Taylor, 1975; Smith, 1975). He found that most of the texts largely ignored the problem of analysis, typically devoting not more than 5 to 10 percent of their pages to it:

Methodologists obviously prefer to spend more time on such matters as gaining access, interviewing, choosing informants, handling reciprocities, and so on, rather than on the intellectual work of analysis (p. 1).

His other conclusions, not more optimistic, were: (1) there was little suggestion in the texts as to how analysis modes might vary according to varying purposes of fieldwork (e.g., generating theory, testing hypotheses, evaluating a program); (2) few guidelines were suggested as to when particular analytical approaches might be employed, or why; (3) the texts tended to confuse and blur concepts of reliability, validity, generalizability, and analysis. Elsewhere Sieber (1976b: 1) pointed out that the quantitative view of reliability (inter-observer, inter-respondent, inter-instrument, or intra-respondent over time) is in many respects inapplicable in qualitative data collection:

Certain kinds of reliability must be intentionally violated in order to gain a depth of understanding about the situation (i.e., the observer's behavior must change from subject to subject, unique questions must be asked of different subjects . . . there is an inherent conflict between validity and reliability — the former is what fieldwork is specially qualified to gain, and increased emphasis on reliability will only undermine that unique function.[2]

Sieber went on, however, to extract what advice he could, suggesting that good analysis, as described in the texts, generally involved something like the following:

Intertwining of analysis and data collection. We have already reviewed how this proceeded in our project, and most text authors stressed it.

Formulating classes of phenomena. This is essentially a categorizing process, subsuming observations under "progressively more abstract concepts." An example from our study is "legitimacy" (the right to plan a new organization, as accorded by the environment).

Identifying themes. Here the process is one of making linkages between concepts, noting regularities which have aroused the researcher's curiosity, and perhaps specifying "if-then" hypotheses. For example, we noted a puzzling and recurrent pattern of wandering circular discussion in one organizational planning group, and finally began speculating that it was a consequence of weak legitimacy.

Provisional testing of hypotheses. Here, as with quantitative data, the analyst looks for concomitant variation, tries to rule out spurious or confounding factors, assesses conditions making for greater or lesser concomitant variation, looks for intervening variables, and so on. In the example, a possible factor that might have caused the circular discussion was lack of group process skills. This could be ruled out when one noted that a process consultant had supplied assistance to the group, but with little or no effect; the circular discussions (and the weak legitimacy) continued.

Sieber's work led to the production of a set of "rules of thumb" (Miles, 1976b) for qualitative analysis, including such items as:

Consider the validity of any particular generalization. Is there supporting evidence from elsewhere in the data? Does it hold true for several different people, roles, groups, or occasions? Is there any *negative* evidence?

Given a generalization, make a prediction. What *else* would be true if this generalization were true? Then go look at the "else" to see if it is there or not.

Test propositions: does Y always go with Z, and is it reasonable to think that it causes Z? Are certain conditions necessary for Y to cause Z? Sufficient?

Look at extreme-bias cases: if even the most self-interested role or group gives an explanation which fits yours, though it's against their interest or bias, then the conclusion is stronger.

Since Sieber's analysis, some additional thoughtful work has appeared, including Smith's (1978) overview, Glaser's (1978) set of practical guidelines for the "constant comparative" method, and Dawson's (1979) overview of validity issues.

Case Study Production

Though these (and our other) rules of thumb seemed reasonable and desirable, and reduced anticipatory analysis anxiety a good deal, we found that the actual process of analysis during case-writing was essentially intuitive, primitive, and unmanageable in any rational sense. As we have noted, the data cards were not used, and fieldworkers and analysts (usually, but not always, the same person) read through the write-ups and interim analyses, selected data, and arranged the information using a chronologically-organized case outline derived from the general conceptual framework of the study. While one can remember occasional use of the "rules of thumb" (e.g., a pause to search for negative evidence), the analysis process is more memorable for its moments of sheer despair in the face of the mass of data, alternating with moments of achieved clarity, soon followed by second-guessing skepticism ("Would someone else come to the same conclusion?").

The final cases had a strong ring of truth, as well as being fascinating accounts. They had been discussed and cross-checked among the staff, and read and critiqued by the site personnel. But one suspects that cognitive dissonance may have been at work as well: an analysis which has taken 45 days of hard labor, and another 20 for the revision *must* be right. But loving that for which one has suffered is not the soundest basis for confidence in findings.

Validation through Feedback to Sites

We decided to give semifinal drafts to personnel from our sites, inviting them to correct errors of fact, and supply alternative interpretations to those we had made. We learned several things. First, there is no possibility of real anonymity inside the site. Even with pseudonyms, everyone *in* the case knew exactly who was who. Second, some people felt vulnerable. Information not previously known to others had been fed into the system. The vulnerability was justified because jobs and careers could be affected. Third, not surprisingly, there was much self-aggrandizing and self-protective response. (In 3 of 6 sites, we were threatened with suit by one person or another.) In all sites there was "rewriting of history" by individuals to present themselves more favorably. These problems were stronger and deeper the more the case used the unique aspects of qualitative data (its richness, complexity, detail, serendipitousness). People almost never objected to a survey result (76 percent responded in such and such a way), but they almost always objected to direct quotes or specific characterizations of their behavior, if they thought them unflattering or damaging.

Cases usually required a considerable amount of revision to take account of the factual errors, the defensive responses, and the genuinely alternative interpretations. The turn-around time for the whole process was usually a minimum of two months, and longer when we started with the most vulnerable people — teachers — before proceeding to less vulnerable ones — principals, central office staff.

Cross-Site Analysis

One of the major reasons for doing a multi-site study is that idiosyncratic aspects of the sites can be seen in perspective, and self-delusion about conclusions is less likely. The problem is that no well-developed set of methods for doing cross-site analysis exists.

A look at several recent efforts at cross-site analysis (Hyde, 1977; Miles, Fullan, and Taylor, 1978; Herriott and Gross, 1979) suggests only that one should have a reasonably clear conceptual framework in mind and that some form of cross-validation or checking of generalizations, using alternate data sources, is desirable. Beyond this, the methods used in these studies are simply not particularly explicit, though the results sound plausible and fruitful.

In this study, we proceeded primitively, by focusing on the "primary tasks" drawn from our general conceptual framework, and reviewing the case studies, particularly the analysis sections, for themes and generalizations that seemed plausible.

But even when generalizations swam into view, the complexity of cross-site comparison (and the problem that the same behavior may have different meanings in two different contexts) often seemed quite unmanageable. A brief exhibit may be useful: In what way are leaders' roles in new organizations connected to the process of more or less stable institutionalization?

In nearly all of our schools, the principal or director became central as implementation and institutionalization proceeded. Appelbaum's Harold Lassiter exerted more and more influence; Arts Coop's David Steinhoff became more and more isolated and decision-responsible; Lincoln Acres' Ellis Brown more and more abrogated the collegial plan the teachers and he had supposedly opted for. Westgate 3's George Rieger maintained steady centrality from the beginning. Only Westgate 2's Ed Pallacino seemed to be less central, allowing for the development of a strong collegial support system — but even he claimed to have been "responsible" for setting it up: "I was behind it all." And though Brown's successor, Alberta Bard, encouraged collegial decision making in the second year at Lincoln Acres, it was clear that her presence was an immensely calming and stabilizing force. Table 1 compares these six leaders. It shows that the centrality of these leaders did not stem from a comparable style, and displays their differences on five major dimensions and on institutionalization.

Table 1   Leader Styles and Institutionalization

	Task emphasis	Socio-emotional support	Pro-activeness	Collaborativeness	Predictability	Institutionalization
Westgate 2 (Ed Pallacino)	H	H	L	M	H	M+
Westgate 3 (George Rieger)	H	L	H	L	M	M
Lincoln Acres (Ellis Brown)	H	L	L	L	L	L
Lincoln Acres (Alberta Bard)	H	H	H	H	H	H
Appelbaum (Harold Lassiter)	H	L	H	L	H	H
Arts Coop (David Steinhoff)	H	L	H	M	M	H

H= high; L= low; M= medium

As a small experiment, the reader may wish to consider what conclusions he or she would draw from this array. Our conclusions emphasized the importance of predictability and the fact that task emphasis predicts nothing; a closer look at the two Westgate principals also suggested the importance of support and collaborativeness as well, since they apparently succeeded in overriding the otherwise important dimension of proactiveness (quiet, passive Ed Pallacino achieved more institutionalization in the same district than low-supportive, low-collaborative George Rieger).

But these conclusions are surely tempered by deeper and wider knowledge of the site than readers have. An excellent example appears in the Arts Coop case. Though Steinhoff gave little support, and was only moderately predictable and collaborative, he nevertheless achieved rapid and enduring institutionalization. So he contradicts the theory. But other knowledge of Arts Coop by the analyst includes the fact that Arts Coop, more than any other site, had a clear and compelling vision driving the planning and implementation. So the theory about leaders' roles holds only when visions are cloudy. Is such an analysis believable, replicable? We simply do not know, at the present state of the art.[3] If anything, the art of cross-site analysis is even less well-formulated than within-site analysis.

ISSUES IN TEAM RESEARCH

We have already alluded to the problems encountered when our project tried to systematize and bureaucratize fieldwork across multiple sites and among multiple workers. There are several unresolved issues here; it is clear that the social psychology of research projects complicates and deepens the formidable issues of qualitative data analysis we have been outlining.

First, should projects be organized collegially or hierarchically? The former gains "ownership" but runs the risk of conceptual mushiness, and the latter is crisper but may easily produce the "hired hand" syndrome, with resultant problems of data validity. Second, should coding and analysis be separated from data collection? Glaser (1978) says resoundingly no, since fieldworkers generate all the implicit hypotheses that are worth anything anyway. But such differentiation was workable in our project, has been historically useful in quantitative studies, and should not be ruled out. Third, what are possible conceptual and organizational solutions to the steady tension between the unique, contextually specific nature of single sites, and the need to make sense across a number of sites? Must we trade close-up descriptive validity for accurate but "thin" generalization?

Many more problems have been named here than have been solved, in the belief that the attractive aspects of qualitative research are real, and that the nuisances can be reduced by thoughtful methodological inquiry — most centrally into the problem of analysis and how it can be carried out in ways that deserve the name of science. Without more such inquiry, qualitative research on organizations cannot be expected to transcend story-telling, and we will be stuck with the limitations of numbers.

NOTES

1

Many of the methodological themes noted here appeared in the project's final report (Miles et al., 1978, Part II, Research Methods). I am grateful to the Huron Institute (Cambridge, Massachusetts) for the opportunity to extend these ideas at a staff seminar held in June 1979. The reader with strong substantive interests should consult the complete report or Miles (1979) for a precis.

2

Guba (1979) has also stressed that qualitative research should perhaps be seen as "auditable," "confirmable," and "cred-

itable" rather than as "reliable" and "valid" in the usual sense.

3

This form of semi-quantified cross-site analysis may well be inappropriate. Robert Stake and others at the Huron Institute seminar who tried this exercise pointed out that the display supplies the "worst of both worlds," not drawing on the richness of qualitative data in context, nor including clearly valid quantitative results. In a sense, it would be far more sensible to display the differential causal *network* of the five independent variables and the outcome, for each of the sites, and then make cross-site conclusions.

REFERENCES

Bidwell, Charles E.
1965 "The school as a formal organization." In James G. March (ed.), Handbook of Organizations: 972–1022. Chicago: Rand McNally.

Bogdan, Robert, and Steven J. Taylor
1975 Introduction to Qualitative Research Methods. New York: Wiley.

Burack, Elmer H., and Anant R. Negandhi
1977 Organizational Design: Theoretical Perspectives and Empirical Findings. Kent, OH: Kent State University Press.

Dawson, Judith
1979 "The validity of qualitative research." Paper presented to American Educational Research Association meeting, San Francisco.

Filstead, William J.
1970 Qualitative Methodology. Chicago: Rand McNally.

Galanter, Wynne
1978 Elementary School Staff Support System Effects on Program Implementation and Job Satisfaction. Doctoral dissertation, School of Education, Fordham University.

Glaser, Barney G.
1978 Theoretical Sensitivity: Advances in the Methodology of Grounded Theory. Mill Valley, CA: Sociology Press.

Glaser, Barney G., and Anselm L. Strauss
1967 The Discovery of Grounded Theory: Strategies for Qualitative Research. Chicago: Aldine.

Glazer, Myron
1972 The Research Adventure-Promise and Problems of Field Work. New York: Random House.

Gold, Barry A.
1976 "The bureaucratization of a planned non-bureaucratic school." Paper presented to American Educational Research Association meeting, San Francisco.

Gross, Neal, and Robert E. Herriott
1965 Staff Leadership in Public Schools: A Sociological Inquiry. New York: Wiley.

Guba, Egon G.
1979 "Investigative journalism as a metaphor for educational evaluation." Paper written for Northwest Regional Educational Laboratory, Portland, Oregon.

Herriott, Robert E., and Neal Gross
1979 The Dynamics of Planned Educational Change. San Francisco: McCutchan.

Hyde, Arthur
1977 Capacities for Solving Problems: Problems and Problem-Solving Methods of School Principals. Chicago: Center for New Schools.

Kilmann, Ralph H.
1977 Social Systems Design. Amsterdam: Elsevier North-Holland.

Miles, Matthew B.
1967 "Some properties of schools as social systems." In Goodwin Watson (ed.), Change in School Systems: 1–29.

Washington: National Training Laboratories.

1976a "Thinking about how to do it: Alternative models for planning and implementation of new schools." Paper presented to American Educational Research Association meeting, San Francisco.

1976b "Quantitative analysis: Some possible rules of thumb." Project on Social Architecture in Education (memorandum). New York: Center for Policy Research.

1979 "Creating new school programs: The dilemmas of 'social architecture.'" New York University Education Quarterly (in press).

Miles, Matthew B., Michael Fullan, and Gib Taylor
1978 OD in Schools: The State of the Art. Part III. Case studies. New York: Center for Policy Research, and Toronto: Ontario Institute for Studies in Education.

Miles, Matthew B., Ellen Sullivan, Barry A. Gold, Beverly Lay Taylor, Sam D. Sieber, and David E. Wilder
1978 Designing and Starting Innovative Schools: A Field Study of Social Architecture in Education. Final Report. New York: Center for Policy Research.

Pfeffer, Jeffrey
1978 Organizational Design. Arlington Heights, IL: AHM Publishing.

Runkel, Philip J., and Joseph E. McGrath
1972 Research on Human Behavior. New York: Holt, Rinehart, Winston.

Schatzman, Leonard, and Anselm I. Strauss
1973 Field Research. Englewood Cliffs, NJ: Prentice-Hall.

Sieber, Sam D.
1973 "The integration of fieldwork and survey methods." American Journal of Sociology, 78: 1335–1359.

1976a "A synopsis and critique of guidelines for qualitative analysis contained in selected textbooks." Project on Social Architecture in Education. New York: Center for Policy Research.

1976b Project on Social Architecture in Education (memorandum). New York: Center for Policy Research.

Smith, H. W.
1975 Strategies of Social Research. Englewood Cliffs, NJ: Prentice-Hall.

Smith, Louis M.
1978 "An evolving logic of participant observation, educational ethnography, and other case studies." In L. Shulman (ed.), Review of Research in Education. Chicago: Peacock Press.

Stinchcombe, Arthur L.
1965 "Social structure and organizations." In James G. March (ed.), Handbook of Organizations: 142–193. Chicago: Rand McNally.

Sullivan, Ellen W., and E. Wamboi Kironde
1976 "Circumvention and cooptation in the planning of new schools." Paper presented to American Educational Research Association meeting, San Francisco.

Taylor, Beverly Lay
1978 Mapping New Schools. New York: Center for Policy Research.

Mixing Qualitative and Quantitative Methods: Triangulation in Action

Todd D. Jick

There is a distinct tradition in the literature on social science research methods that advocates the use of multiple methods. This form of research strategy is usually described as one of convergent methodology, multimethod/multitrait (Campbell and Fiske, 1959), convergent validation or, what has been called "triangulation" (Webb et al., 1966). These various notions share the conception that qualitative and quantitative methods should be viewed as complementary rather than as rival camps. In fact, most textbooks underscore the desirability of mixing methods given the strengths and weaknesses found in single method designs.

Yet those who most strongly advocate triangulation (e.g., Webb et al., 1966; Smith, 1975; Denzin, 1978) fail to indicate how this prescribed triangulation is actually performed and accomplished. Graduate training usually prepares us to use one method or another as appropriate and preferred, but not to combine methods effectively. And even those who use multiple methods do not generally explain their "technique" in sufficient detail to indicate exactly how convergent data are collected and interpreted.

WHAT IS TRIANGULATION?

Triangulation is broadly defined by Denzin (1978: 291) as "the combination of methodologies in the study of the

Author's Note: I am indebted to Dafna Izraeli for helpful comments and criticisms of an earlier version of this paper.

same phenomenon." The triangulation metaphor is from navigation and military strategy that use multiple reference points to locate an object's exact position (Smith, 1975: 273). Given basic principles of geometry, multiple viewpoints allow for greater accuracy. Similarly, organizational researchers can improve the accuracy of their judgments by collecting different kinds of data bearing on the same phenomenon.

In the social sciences, the use of triangulation can be traced back to Campbell and Fiske[1] (1959) who developed the idea of "multiple operationism." They argued that more than one method should be used in the validation process to ensure that the variance reflected that of the trait and not of the method. Thus, the convergence or agreement between two methods ". . . enhances our belief that the results are valid and not a methodological artifact" (Bouchard, 1976: 268).

This kind of triangulation is labeled by Denzin (1978: 302) as the "between (or across) methods" type, and represents the most popular use of triangulation. It is largely a vehicle for cross validation when two or more distinct methods are found to be congruent and yield comparable data. For organizational researchers, this would involve the use of multiple methods to examine the same dimension of a research problem. For example, the effectiveness of a leader may be studied by interviewing the leader, observing his or her behavior, and evaluating performance records. The focus always remains that of the leader's effectiveness but the mode of data collection varies. Multiple and independent measures, if they reach the same conclusions, provide a more certain portrayal of the leadership phenomenon.

Triangulation can have other meanings and uses as well. There is the "within-method" kind (Denzin, 1978: 301) which uses multiple techniques within a given method to collect and interpret data. For quantitative methods such as survey research, this can take the form of multiple scales or indices focused on the same construct. For qualitative methods such as participant observation, this can be reflected in "multiple comparison groups" (Glaser and Strauss, 1965: 7) to develop more confidence in the emergent theory. In short, "within-method" triangulation essentially involves cross-checking for internal consistency or reliability while "between-method" triangulation tests the degree of external validity.

Blending and integrating a variety of data and methods, as triangulation demands, may be seen on a continuum that ranges from simple to complex designs (Figure 1). Scaling, that is, the quantification of qualitative measures, would be at the simple end. Smith (1975: 273) concluded that scaling is only a "primitive triangulatory device." It does not effectively force a mix of independent methods, neither does it reflect fundamentally diverse observations nor varieties of triangulated data. Another primitive form of triangulation often found in organizational research is the parenthetical, even somewhat patronizing, use of field observations to strengthen statistical results. For example, a hypothetical study of job satisfaction among employees might revolve around a significant chi-square result demonstrating deep discontent. To support the results, it might be noted that a strike occurred earlier that year. But, we are likely not informed about the intensity, dynamics, meaning, and aftermath of the strike. Thus, important qualitative data had been insufficiently integrated with quantitative findings.

A somewhat more sophisticated triangulation design, already discussed, would be the "within-methods" strategy for testing reliability. The limitations of this approach lie in the use of only one method. As Denzin noted (1978: 301–302), "observers delude themselves into believing that five different variations of the same method generate five distinct varieties of triangulated data. But the flaws that arise using one method remain . . . ." Next in the continuum is the conventional form, the "between methods" approach designed for convergent validation. The use of complementary methods is generally thought to lead to more valid results, as noted. It is currently the archetype of triangulation strategies.

Scaling	Reliability	Convergent Validation	Holistic (or Contextual) Description
Simple Design			Complex Design

Figure 1   A continuum of triangulation design

Triangulation, however, can be something other than scaling, reliability, and convergent validation. It can also capture a more complete, *holistic,* and contextual portrayal of the unit(s) under study. That is, beyond the analysis of overlapping variance, the use of multiple measures may also uncover some unique variance which otherwise may have been neglected by single methods. It is here that qualitative methods, in particular, can play an especially prominent role by eliciting data and suggesting conclusions to which other methods would be blind. Elements of the context are illuminated. In this sense, triangulation may be used not only to examine the same phenomenon from multiple perspectives but also to enrich our understanding by allowing for new or deeper dimensions to emerge.

In all the various triangulation designs one basic assumption is buried. The effectiveness of triangulation rests on the premise that the weaknesses in each single method will be compensated by the counter-balancing strengths of another. That is, it is assumed that multiple and independent measures do not share the same weaknesses or potential for bias (Rohner, 1977: 134). Although it has always been observed that each method has assets and liabilities, triangulation purports to exploit the assets and neutralize, rather than compound, the liabilities.

Perhaps the most prevalent attempts to use triangulation have been reflected in efforts to integrate fieldwork and survey methods. The viability and necessity of such linkages have been advocated by various social scientists (e.g., Vidich and Shapiro, 1955; Reiss, 1968; McCall and Simmons, 1969; Spindler, 1970; Diesing, 1971; Sieber, 1973). They all argue that quantitative methods can make important contributions to fieldwork, and vice versa.

Thus, researchers using qualitative methodology are encouraged to systematize observations, to utilize sampling techniques, and to develop quantifiable schemes for coding complex data sets. As Vidich and Shapiro (1955: 31) wrote, "Without the survey data, the observer could only make reasonable guesses about his area of ignorance in the effort to reduce bias." Survey research may also contribute to greater confidence in the generalizability of results.

Conversely, quantitative-oriented researchers are encouraged to exploit "the potentialities of social observation" (Reiss, 1968: 360). Among other assets, field methods can contribute to survey analysis with respect to the validation of results, the interpretation of statistical relationships, and the clarification of puzzling findings (Sieber, 1973: 1345). Thus, informants can be utilized during the course of quantitative research (Campbell, 1955) and "holistic interpretation" (i.e., context variables) can be used to shed light on quantitative data (Diesing, 1971: 171). More implicitly, the very selection of a research site is typically a function of qualitative data as is the process of building and pretesting a survey instrument.

Diesing (1971: 5) boldly concluded that the variety of combinations is so great that survey research and fieldwork are better viewed as two ends of a continuum rather than as two distinct kinds of methods. Yet, research designs that extensively integrate both fieldwork (e.g., participant observation) and survey research are rare. Moreover, journals tend to specialize by methodology thus encouraging purity of method.

Fortunately, there are some exceptions to be found. Some particularly good examples of combining methods include LaPiere's (1934) seminal investigation of the relationship between attitudes and behavior, Reiss' study of police and citizen transactions (1968: 355), Sales' (1973) study of authoritarianism, Van Maanen's (1975) data on police socialization, and the studies described in, or modeled after, Webb et al. (1966). Furthermore, it is probable that the triangulation approach is embedded in many doctoral theses that, when packaged into articles, tend to highlight only the quantitative methods. Thus the triangulation model is not new. However, this model of research and its advantages have not been appreciated. In this respect, it would be helpful to articulate and describe its usage.

AN ILLUSTRATION OF HOW TRIANGULATION WORKS

The triangulation strategy was used in a study I conducted on the effects of a merger on employees (Jick, 1979). Early interviews suggested that employees were intensely anxious in this state of flux, especially concerning their job security. One focus of the research was to document and examine the sources and symptoms of anxiety, the individuals experiencing it and its impact on the functioning of the newly merging organization.

How have anxiety and its dynamics in an organization been measured? Marshall and Cooper (1979: 86) noted, for example, that there is no one generally agreed way of measuring stress manifestations. On the basis of past research, there are several alternative techniques one could use: (a) Ask the person directly, (b) Ask the person indirectly (e.g., projective tests), (c) Ask someone who interacts with the person, and (d) Observe systematically the person's behavior or (e) Measure physiological symptoms. Predictably, each of these strategies has both strengths and weaknesses. Most of the limitations revolve around the likelihood of high demand characteristics and considerable obstacles in the measurement process.

Given high demand characteristics in the study of anxiety and the potential pitfalls in each method, the most appropriate research strategy was deemed to be triangulation. No single method was sufficient and thus a design evolved that utilized a combination of methods. Data were collected over a period of 14 months which incorporated multiple viewpoints and approaches: both feelings and behaviors, direct and indirect reports, obtrusive and unobtrusive observation. Methods were wide-ranging enough to tap a variety of anxiety dimensions.

The research "package" used in the investigation of the dynamics of anxiety and job insecurity included many standard features. Surveys were distributed to a random sample of employees. They contained a combination of standard and new indices related to stresses and strains. To complement these data, a subsample was selected for the purposes of semistructured, probing interviews. The survey also contained items related to the symptoms of anxiety as well as projective measures. These were developed to be indirect, nonthreatening techniques. In addition to self-reports, interviews were conducted with supervisors and coworkers to record their observations of employees' anxiety.

Another set of methods, somewhat less conventional, proved to be especially fruitful. Predominantly qualitative in nature, they were based on unobtrusive and nonparticipant observation as well as archival materials. For example, one of the merging organizations housed an archives library, which contained a variety of files, books, and organization memorabilia from its 100-year history. It also contained a comprehensive set of newspaper clippings that cited the organization and the merger, as well as a broad variety of internal memos to employees. This was indeed a rich data source.

The development of unobtrusive measures tends to be far more unorthodox and innovative than most research methods. Perhaps the most instructive unobtrusive measure in this case was a kind of anxiety "thermometer." The idea emerged because of certain fortuitous circumstances in that a further research opportunity was found in the archives. The archivist mentioned that employees were frequently using the files. When asked why, he said that they came to compare recent news reports and memos (regarding the organization's future) with past pronouncements. Since recent information tended to be ambiguous, if not contradictory, the files provided an opportunity to review materials systematically. Most employees were apparently seeking information to relieve their anxiety about the uncertain shape of things to come.

Hence these visits to the archives were treated as expressions of employee anxiety, a thermometer of anxiety level in the organization. The search for information seemed to represent an attempt to reduce uncertainty. It was hypothesized that the more people who visited the archives to use the files, the higher the anxiety level. Thus emerged an effort to track the pattern of visits. The archivist consented to record the number of archive users along with some supplementary data on the visitors such as age, work location, and the amount of time spent at the files.

The pattern of archive usage was then compared with data culled from ongoing interviews, the cross-sectional survey, and other unobtrusive techniques. These other measures also tracked anxiety-related behavior, as for example, (a) archival data on turnover and absenteeism trends and (b) a content analysis of rumors, news stories, and hospital events reflecting the flow of "shocks" to which employees were subjected.

It should be underscored that the quantitative results were used largely to supplement the qualitative data, rather than the reverse which is far more common in organizational research. The surveys became more meaningful when interpreted in light of critical qualitative information just as other statistics were most useful when compared with content analyses or interview results. Triangulation, in this respect, can lead to a prominent role for qualitative evidence (just as it also should assure a continuing role for quantitative data).

PUTTING IT ALL TOGETHER: IS THERE CONVERGENCE?

These various techniques and instruments generated a rather rich and comprehensive picture of anxiety and job insecurity (Greenhalgh and Jick, 1979; Jick, 1979). Self-reports, interviews, and coworker observations reflected a range of perceptions — some qualitatively described while others quantitatively represented. In turn, behavioral and objective data collected through archival sources and unobtrusive measures complemented the other data.

It is a delicate exercise to decide whether or not results have converged. In theory, a multiple confirmation of findings may appear routine. If there is congruence, it presumably is apparent. In practice, though, there are few guidelines for systematically ordering eclectic data in order to determine congruence or validity. For example, should all components of a multimethod approach be weighted equally, that is, is all the evidence equally useful? If not, then it is not clear on what basis the data should be weighted, aside from personal preference. Given the differing nature of multimethod results, the determination is likely to be subjective. While statistical tests can be applied to a particular method, there are no formal tests to discriminate between methods to judge their applicability. The concept of "significant differences" when applied to qualitatively judged differences does not readily compare with the statistical tests which also demonstrate "significant differences."

The various methods together produced largely consistent and convergent results. Archival and interview data indicated a strong relation between high turnover rates and job insecurity/anxiety while survey data showed a parallel relation between expressed propensity to leave and job insecurity.[2] These findings were formed on the basis of telephone interviews with employees who quit, personal interviews with their former supervisors, significant correlations found in survey data with a large random sample of employees, and the clear pattern seen between lay-off rumors reported in news stories and turnover statistics. Not only were the within-methods comparisons consistent, but there was also consistency in between-methods comparisons. Thus, the sociometric charting results of archive visits were congruent with the expressed anxiety reported in surveys and interviews. Both sets of results confirmed which events tended to be most anxiety producing and under what conditions anxiety was reduced. Thus, different measures of the same construct were shown to yield similar results (Phillips, 1971: 19).

There were also some surprises and discrepancies in the multimethod results which led to unexpected findings. When different measures yield dissimilar results, they demand that the researcher reconcile the differences somehow. In fact, divergence can often turn out to be an opportunity for enriching the explanation.

For example, in my study, those most stressed (according to surveys of self-reports) were least likely to visit the archive's news files (according to sociometric data), *contrary* to what was hypothesized. That is, while the survey showed that the group reporting the most anxiety were the least educated and least professionally mobile in terms of job skills, these low-skilled employees were underrepresented at the archive's library. One method produced results which predicted manifestations of anxiety but a second method failed to confirm the prediction. However, further interviews and observations — still other qualitative methods — helped to reconcile the disagreement by suggesting that the poorly educated employees tended to rely more on oral communication (e.g., close informal grapevines) than written documents. This interpretation resulted then from the divergent

findings based on sociometric data, nonparticipant observations at work and outside work, and open-ended interviewing.

In seeking explanations for divergent results, the researcher
may uncover unexpected results or unseen contextual factors. In one instance, interview data helped to suggest a
relation between job insecurity/anxiety and certain attitudinal
symptoms. Survey results, however, indicated that while
employees at the site of the central organization were less
insecure in their jobs than employees at the satellite site the
magnitude of symptoms was the reverse. That is, the "vic-
tors" reported more symptoms than the "vanquished." But
further interviewing and an analysis of field notes showed
that the more severe symptoms reflected unique sources of
anxiety at the central organization. Fieldwork and survey results were thus compatible as a variety of previously uncon-
sidered contextual factors were brought to light.

The process of compiling research material based on multimethods is useful whether there is convergence or not.
Where there is convergence, confidence in the results
grows considerably. Findings are no longer attributable to a
method artifact. However, where divergent results emerge,
alternative, and likely more complex, explanations are generated. In my investigation of anxiety, triangulation allowed for
more confident interpretations, for both testing and developing hypotheses, and for more unpredicted and context-
related findings.

Overall, the triangulating investigator is left to search for a
logical pattern in mixed-method results. His or her claim to
validity rests on a judgment, or as Weiss (1968: 349) calls it,
"a capacity to organize materials within a plausible
framework." One begins to view the researcher as builder
and creator, piecing together many pieces of a complex puz-
zle into a coherent whole. It is in this respect that the firsthand knowledge drawn from qualitative methods can become critical. While one can rely on certain scientific conventions (e.g., scaling, control groups, etc.) for maximizing
the credibility of one's findings, the researcher using triangulation is likely to rely still more on a "feel" of the situation.
This intuition and firsthand knowledge drawn from the multiple vantage points is centrally reflected in the interpretation
process. Glaser and Strauss' (1965: 8) observation about

fieldworkers summarizes this point of how triangulated investigations seem to be crystallized:

> The fieldworker knows that he knows, not only because he's been there in the field and because of his careful verifications of hypotheses, but because "in his bones" he feels the worth of his final analysis.

THE "QUALITY" IN TRIANGULATION

Triangulation provides researchers with several important opportunities. First it allows researchers to be more confident of their results. This is the overall strength of the multimethod design. Triangulation can play many other constructive roles as well. It can stimulate the creation of inventive methods, new ways of capturing a problem to balance with conventional data-collection methods. In my study, this was illustrated by the development of an anxiety "thermometer," which unobtrusively measured changes in anxiety level.

Triangulation may also help to uncover the deviant or off-quadrant dimension of a phenomenon. Different viewpoints are likely to produce some elements which do not fit a theory or model. Thus, old theories are refashioned or new theories developed. Moreover, as was pointed out, divergent results from multimethods can lead to an enriched explanation of the research problem.

The use of multimethods can also lead to a synthesis or integration of theories. In this sense, methodological triangulation closely parallels theoretical triangulation (Denzin, 1978: 295); that is, efforts to bring diverse theories to bear on a common problem (e.g., LeVine and Campbell, 1972; Marris, 1975). Finally, triangulation may also serve as the critical test, by virtue of its comprehensiveness, for competing theories.

A thread linking all of these benefits is the important part played by qualitative methods in triangulation. The researcher is likely to sustain a profitable closeness to the situation which allows greater sensitivity to the multiple sources of data. Qualitative data and analysis function as the glue that cements the interpretation of multimethod results. In one respect, qualitative data are used as the critical counterpoint to quantitative methods. In another respect, the analysis benefits from the perceptions drawn from personal experiences and firsthand observations. Thus enters the artful researcher who uses the qualitative data to enrich and brighten the portrait. Finally, the convergent approach utilizes qualitative methods to illuminate "behavior in context" (Cronbach, 1975) where situational factors play a prominent role. In sum, triangulation, which prominently involves qualitative methods, can potentially generate what anthropologists call "holistic work" or "thick description." As Weiss concluded, "Qualitative data are apt to be superior to quantitative data in density of information, vividness, and clarity of meaning — characteristics more important in holistic work, than precision and reproducibility" (1968: 344–345).

The triangulation strategy is not without some shortcomings. First of all, replication is exceedingly difficult. Replication has been largely absent from most organizational research, but it is usually considered to be a necessary step in scientific progress. Replicating a mixed-methods package, including idiosyncratic techniques, is a nearly impossible task and not likely to become a popular exercise. Qualitative methods, in particular, are problematic to replicate. Second, while it may be rather obvious, multimethods are of no use with the "wrong" question. If the research is not clearly focused theoretically or conceptually, all the methods in the world will not produce a satisfactory outcome. Similarly, triangulation should not be used to legitimate a dominant, personally preferred method. That is, if either quantitative or qualitative methods become mere window dressing for the other, then the design is inadequate or biased. Each method should be represented in a significant way. This does however raise the question of whether the various instruments may be viewed as equally sensitive to the phenomenon being studied. One method may, in fact, be stronger or more appropriate but this needs to be carefully justified and made explicit. Otherwise, the purpose of triangulation is subverted.

Triangulation is a strategy that may not be suitable for all research purposes. Various constraints (e.g., time costs) may prevent its effective use. Nevertheless, triangulation has vital strengths and encourages productive research. It heightens qualitative methods to their deserved prominence and, at the same time, demonstrates that quantitative methods can and should be utilized in complementary fashion. Above all, triangulation demands creativity from its user — ingenuity in collecting data and insightful interpretation of data. It responds to a foreboding observation suggested by one sociologist (Phillips, 1971: 175):

We simply cannot afford to continue to engage in the same kinds of sterile, unproductive, unimaginative investigations which have long characterized most . . . research.

In this sense, triangulation is not an end in itself and not simply a fine-tuning of our research instruments. Rather, it can stimulate us to better define and analyze problems in organizational research.

NOTES

1

Webb et al. (1963: 3) list other sources from the 1950s, but Campbell and Fiske's article is most often cited elsewhere in the literature.

2

For specific results and data tables, see Jick (1979).

REFERENCES

Becker, Howard S., and Blanche Geer
1957 "Participant observation and interviewing: A comparison." Human Organization, 16: 28–32.

Bouchard, Thomas J., Jr.
1976 "Unobtrusive measures: An inventory of uses." Sociological Methods and Research, 4: 267–300.

Campbell, Donald T.
1955 "The informant in quantitative research." American Journal of Sociology, 60: 339–342.

Campbell, Donald T., and D. W. Fiske
1959 "Convergent and discriminant validation by the multitrait-multimethod matrix." Psychological Bulletin, 56: 81–105.

Cronbach, Lee J.
1975 "Beyond the two disciplines of scientific psychology."

American Psychologist, 30: 116–127.

Denzin, Norman K.
1978 The Research Act, 2d ed. New York: McGraw-Hill.

Diesing, Paul
1971 Patterns of Discovery in the Social Sciences. Chicago: Aldine-Atherton.

Glaser, Barney G., and Anselm L. Strauss
1965 "Discovery of substantive theory: A basic strategy underlying qualitative research." American Behavioral Scientist, 8: 5–12.

Greenhalgh, Leonard, and Todd D. Jick
1979 "The relationship between job security and turnover and its differential effects on employee quality level." Paper presented to Academy of Management conference, Atlanta, Georgia.

Jick, Todd D.
1979 Process and Impacts of a Merger: Individual and Organizational Perspectives. Doctoral dissertation, New York State School of Industrial and Labor Relations, Cornell University.

LaPiere, R. T.
1934 "Attitudes vs. actions." Social Forces, 13: 230–237.

LeVine, R. A., and D. T. Campbell
1972 Ethnocentrism, Theories of Conflict, Ethnic Attitudes, and Group Behavior. New York: Wiley.

Marris, Peter
1975 Loss and Change. Garden City: Anchor Books-Doubleday.

Marshall, Judi, and Cary Cooper
1979 "Work experiences of middle and senior managers: The pressures and satisfactions." Management International Review, 19: 81–96.

McCall, George J., and J. L. Simmons, eds.
1969 Issues in Participant Observation: A Text and Reader. Reading, MA: Addison-Wesley.

Phillips, Derek L.
1971 Knowledge from What?: Theories and Methods in Social Research. Chicago: Rand McNally.

Reiss, Albert J.
1968 "Stuff and nonsense about social surveys and observation." In Howard Becker, Blanche Geer, David Riesman, and Robert Weiss (eds.), Institutions and the Person: 351–367. Chicago: Aldine.

Rohner, Ronald P.
1977 "Advantages of the comparative method of anthropology."

Behavior Science Research, 12: 117–144.

Sales, Stephen M.
1973 "Threat as a factor in authoritarianism: An analysis of archival data." Journal of Personality and Social Psychology, 28: 44–57.

Sieber, Sam D.
1973 "The integration of fieldwork and survey methods." American Journal of Sociology, 78: 1335–1359.

Smith, H. W.
1975 Strategies of Social Research: The Methodological Imagination. Englewood Cliffs, NJ: Prentice Hall.

Spindler, George D., ed.
1970 Being an Anthropologist. New York: Holt, Rinehart and Winston.

Van Maanen, John
1975 "Police socialization: A longitudinal examination of job attitudes in an urban police department." Administrative Science Quarterly, 20: 207–228.

Vidich, Arthur J., and Gilbert Shapiro
1955 "A comparison of participant observation and survey data." American Sociological Review, 20: 28–33.

Webb, Eugene J., Donald T. Campbell, Richard D. Schwartz, and Lee Sechrest
1966 Unobtrusive Measures: Nonreactive Research in the Social Sciences. Chicago: Rand McNally.

Weiss, Robert S.
1968 "Issues in holistic research." In Howard S. Becker, Blanche Geer, David Riesman, and Robert Weiss (eds.), Institutions and the Person: 342–350. Chicago: Aldine.

Applying the Logic of Sample Surveys to Qualitative Case Studies: The Case Cluster Method

Charles C. McClintock
Diane Brannon
Steven Maynard-Moody

The differences between case study and sample survey strategies in the analysis of organizations reflect a broader distinction in the social sciences between qualitative and quantitative methods. While there are underlying similarities in logic — for example, both approaches recognize the need to control for threats to internal validity — it is the differences of method that are often emphasized (cf. Fienberg, 1977: 50). Qualitative methods are described as "thick" (Geertz, 1973: 6), "deep" (Sieber, 1973), and "holistic" (Rist, 1977: 44). By contrast quantitative approaches can be characterized as "thin" (Geertz, 1973: 6), "narrow" (Rist, 1977: 47), but generalizable (Sieber, 1973). These distinctions often extend to fundamental epistemological differences resulting in the mutual denial of validity to the data of the other approach. Without disputing that the differences in outlook and method are real, Zelditch's (1962: 567) question remains provoking: "What do you do if you prefer data that are real, deep, *and* hard . . .?"

Authors' Note: We are grateful to Joe Frances, Raymond G. Hunt, Ray C. Rist, and the anonymous *ASQ* reviewers for the constructive criticisms of the earlier drafts of this paper.

One answer is to invent research designs that incorporate qualitative and quantitative strategies (cf. Yin and Heald, 1975), or as Warwick (1975: 187) has put it, ". . . to wed the qualitative and historically attuned case study with representative coverage and quantification." This is the spirit of the present analysis and is a message that has been sounded by others concerned with methodological advance in the social sciences (Cronbach, 1975; Proshansky, 1976).

In the sample survey, standardized measurement and sampling procedures are intended to (1) enhance the reliability of observation; (2) facilitate replication studies; and (3) permit statistical analysis of data and generalizations to larger populations. The goals of the qualitative case study are (1) to capture the frame of reference and definition of the situation of a given informant or participant and thus to avoid instrumentation artifacts of standardized measurement procedures, (2) to permit detailed examination of organizational process, (3) and to elucidate those factors peculiar to the case that may allow greater understanding of causality.[1]

Although each approach has advantages, the purpose of this paper is to describe how the logic and the method of survey research can improve qualitative case studies. There is no intention to diminish the significance of the case study method, and it would be just as valid to emphasize the means by which qualitative case studies could improve sample surveys of organizations (Myers, 1977; Stake, 1978). In fact, the method that we describe incorporates both strategies, and relies heavily on the use of informants, documents, and observational techniques — procedures that are commonly associated with case studies of organizations. It walks a line between the atheoretical encyclopedic case study and the standardized sample survey. It resembles each of these approaches to research as well as the middle ground methods that are theory-building, semistructured, informant-based inquiries of organizations. Yet it can be differentiated from traditional approaches because it incorporates the *potential* for moving back and forth between them. It forces the researcher to acknowledge methodological tradeoffs (Weick, 1979: 35) but creates opportunities to produce thick *and* generalizable analyses.

OVERVIEW OF THE METHOD

The method essentially involves three features: (1) the definition, enumeration, and sampling of units of analysis within the case study that are theoretically meaningful and represent the phenomenology of informants; (2) stratified sampling of data sources based on theoretical grounds and on features of the case, crossed with a stratified sampling of units of analysis; and (3) the optional creation of a quantitative data set consisting of standardized codes for variables pertaining to each unit of analysis. Qualitative analyses are possible both for the entire case and at the level of the unit of analysis and, indeed, are strengthened by the use of different data sources for each unit of analysis. By forcing different perspectives on the same phenomenon the researcher will need to qualitatively portray divergent images that might emerge from each perspective.

Because the single case is treated as a cluster of heterogeneous units of analysis the term case cluster is used to designate this method. The rationale for describing the case as a cluster of units of analysis will be described in a later section.

Degrees of Freedom in the Case Study

Most pertinent to the development of the case cluster method is Campbell's (1975) discussion of how to create "degrees of freedom" in qualitative case studies.[2] In sharp contrast to his earlier treatment of the "one-shot case study" design (Campbell and Stanley, 1966: 6–7), Campbell argues for capitalizing on the richness of detail within a single case by looking for multiple implications of the theoretical ideas being tested. In this manner the single case becomes a set of diverse manifestations of theory. Each manifestation, rather than each case, can be thought of as a unit of analysis in which a particular effect might be present.

When looked at in the aggregate the single case has more observations than variables. This creates sufficient degrees of freedom for the statistical testing of hypotheses. Essentially Campbell is proposing that the researcher sample situations or other attributes of a system within a single case. It is therefore possible to apply some of the rigors of sampling theory, and if desired, quantified measurement to studies in which the case (that is, the organization) is still the overarching subject of interest. Such a method in no way restricts the use of data collection techniques that are common in case studies such as participant observation, interviewing informants, and archival analysis, though it does require systematic, documented, and replicable procedures.

Sampling, Quantification, and Units of Analysis

We extend Campbell's proposal in three significant ways. Most obvious is the use of survey sampling procedures and the optional addition of quantified measurement and multivariate statistical techniques to qualitative approaches for the analysis of data. Perhaps a more complex extension involves proposing a definition for units of analysis that corresponds to Campbell's idea of examining multiple implications of a theory within a single case. The key to defining units of analysis is theoretical guidance and phenomenological integrity for those informants who are providing observations.[3] Although units of analysis are typically defined as individuals, groups, or organizations, they could be almost any activity, process, feature, or dimension of organizational behavior. Even commonly accepted units of analysis such as individuals represent arbitrary divisions. It would often make more theoretical sense to view individuals as clusters of skills, motivations, tasks, interdependencies, and the like, and to representatively sample these attributes instead of the persons in which they may be unevenly distributed.

The trick is to arrive at a definition of units of analysis that is stable enough to sample and that lends itself to the possible application of standardized codes. The units of analysis that were used in our research were called planning events, choice situations, and tasks. The case cluster method requires informants to assist in the enumeration of a sampling frame, a procedure analogous to snowball sampling (Coleman, 1958–1959). This encourages the identification of units of analysis that represent informal activities as well as those that are formally designated as instances of the unit's definition. The researcher, however, maintains control over the definition and selection of units of analysis.

THREE EXAMPLES OF THE CASE CLUSTER METHOD

Planning Study

The first study using the case cluster method analyzed approaches to planning in public sector organizations (McClintock, 1978). It was different in two ways from the more refined uses of the method in the other studies. First, it was a completely qualitative study, largely because of its hypothesis-generating purposes and because the research team could not agree on a standard set of codes for all units of analysis. Secondly, it was not done on a single case and thus departs to some degree from the discussion so far. It represents, however, the sampling strategies and unit of analysis definition of the case cluster method. We will focus on the second phase of the study which involved the study of planning events in public sector human service organizations in eight states. A stratified sample of agencies, informants, and units of analysis was based on a theoretical model of organizational planning and on the structure of the human service planning and delivery system. While states and selected bureaucracies within them were the cases, the units of analysis were planning events. Planning events were enumerated based on formal designation and with the assistance of informants who identified processes that functionally served as planning events (e.g., budgeting procedures).

Choice Behavior Study

The central purpose of the Choice Behavior Study (Brannon, 1979) was to test the generalizability of the decision-making theories of Cohen, March, and Olsen (1972) and March and Olsen (1976) to a public welfare agency. Data were gathered through informant interviews, participant observation, and archival analyses. Informants were stratified by functional unit within the agency and they, in turn, assisted in enumerating units of analysis, called choice situations, in a stratification of settings.

Task Analysis Study

The previous two studies were concerned with organizational processes that were mainly interorganizational and interpersonal in nature. The Task Analysis Study (McClintock,

1979) took a more intrapersonal focus in an effort to understand variations in tasks in terms of their complexity and predictability. While there was a methodological purpose to the study in terms of developing generalizable procedures for multidimensionally measuring uncertainty in tasks, the research was a case study of a single organization, a university, focusing on patterns of loose and tight coupling (Weick, 1976) and modes of evaluation and organizational learning (Dornbusch and Scott, 1975; Hedberg, 1981). A stratified sample of informants based on job classification was followed by a stratified enumeration of tasks based on complexity and predictability. Tasks were the units of analysis.

The order of presentation for the case cluster method is somewhat arbitrary. While one would not enter the field without a definition for the boundaries of units of analysis, it is likely that such definitions would be altered through interactions with informants, since informants play an active role in identifying and selecting units of analysis. Likewise, if one intends to quantify variables the initial codes will evolve (although one would want to minimize this). The highly interactive nature of these processes distinguishes the case cluster method from the standard sample survey.

THREE FEATURES OF THE CASE CLUSTER METHOD

1. Defining, Enumerating, and Sampling Units of Analysis.

Advocates of qualitative research willingly sacrifice breadth for depth. Participant observation, in-depth interviewing, and repeated contacts with informants give researchers intimate knowledge of the social forces they are studying. This intimacy informs the selection of significant and representative features but it can be time consuming and restricts attention to a small number of cases. The extreme situation where there is only a single case is especially troublesome. Inferential statistical procedures require that the number of cases studied be equal to or greater than the number of variables that are being tested. While most qualitative researchers would claim to be unconcerned with statistical inferences, a more important problem is that a small N provides a tenuous foundation for generalizations. Single examples do not illustrate patterns (Bateson, 1979: 27–30). Finally, and perhaps most importantly, where there is a single data source with an N of 1, the effects of measurement and of the features of the case are confounded. Thus, it is necessary to develop multiple cases and use multiple data sources or methods of observation, following the multitrait-multimethod logic of Campbell and Fiske (1959), in order to reduce threats to internal validity.

Theory-based units of analysis. Despite these methodological problems, a single case study is desirable for many reasons such as opportunity, unusual events, cost limitations, needs for hypothesis development, and so on. On the other hand, in addition to methodological problems, there are theoretical and practical reasons why it may make little sense to use the entire case or individuals within the case as units of analysis in studying organizations. Several of the major streams of organizational theory describe organizations as heterogeneous aggregates of something: of decisions (March and Simon, 1958), technological processes (Woodward, 1965), functional subsystems (Katz and Kahn, 1966), patterns of loose and tight coupling (Weick, 1976), and organization-environment interactions (Aldrich, 1979). Such dimensions of organizational behavior provide the analytic framework for many case studies and may better serve as units of analysis if they are recognized and operationalized before the data are collected rather than as ex-post facto analytic guides.

This is one distinguishing feature of the case cluster method. The researcher brings to the case study a clearly articulated, although not immutable, analytic framework. This contrasts sharply with Lofland's (1976: 64) advocacy for studying social situations without any preconceived definitions. We disagree with this approach because it does not provide generalizable bases for intercase comparisons and because one cannot get a sense of the relative frequency of events. Our concern is similar to Weick's (1976) about the need to understand what is not happening as well as what is obvious. Only with preconceived expectations can non-events be identified. Moreover, regardless of one's epistemological preferences, perception is itself a prestructured and organizing process (Neisser, 1976). It is impossible to enter a situation without a theory of some sort, and the case cluster method formalizes this process in its search for relevant units of analysis, multiple data sources, and common variables.

On the practical side, using individuals as units of analysis may not be a solution to an N of 1, either because the case contains too few individuals (e.g., a small R&D unit; Hunt, 1970) or too many (e.g., a large public bureaucracy; Warwick, 1975). In the first instance the researcher needs a unit of analysis that is more numerous than staff size (e.g., opportunities for innovation in the R&D unit) in order to thoroughly understand the case and to test hypotheses. In the latter case the requirement is for a unit of analysis that is less numerous than staff size (e.g., organizational planning processes) for manageability of the research.

The case as a cluster of units of analysis. The problem in the single case study is how to identify and sample a reasonable number of theoretically meaningful units of analysis within the case. Accomplishing this task will strengthen case studies in three ways. First, it allows one to treat the case as a cluster of dimensions of interest. The term cluster is borrowed from sampling theory. Cluster sampling is a procedure in which the units of analysis are selected first in groups rather than individually. There may be several stages of clustering and stratification before the final selection of units of analysis, as in the Task Analysis Study.

In case studies involving a single organization one tries to select a case with maximum within-case variance and as little between-case variance as possible. This is an extreme form of cluster sampling in which the researcher relies on the single cluster for generalizations to a larger population. Ideally the single case constitutes a complete miniature of the population, though this would be very unusual in practice. Still, if the researcher can demonstrate that heterogenity in the cluster is similar to that in the population then generalizations are more secure. For example, Rist's (1970) study of stereotyping in the classroom would have been strengthened with evidence showing the similarity of the case to other schools in terms of characteristics of students, teachers, class procedures, social structure, and so on (Fienberg, 1977). Treating the case as a cluster and quantitatively measuring its relevant dimensions allow one to systematically compare it with other cases, and therefore to address the external validity problems that are common to the single case study design (Stake, 1978: 7).[4]

A second benefit that derives from formally sampling units of analysis within a case cluster, is the possibility for cross-stratification with different data sources in order to sort out the effects of measurement or perspective. For example, in the Planning Study we factorially crossed types of informants with types of planning events.

Finally, by creating formal and replicable sampling designs the researcher is in a good position to create quantitative data sets if so desired. Quantification within the case is not feasible where standardized units of analysis have not been identified.

Units of analysis in the Planning Study. The definition of units of analysis in the Planning Study, planning events, reflected a desire to be able to describe planning processes, products or traces of those processes, and the contextual features of the entire planning event. It was soon discovered that limiting the focus only to planning that yielded formal plans as products would not result in a sample of units that truly reflected planning activities. For example, many planning processes were often tied closely to program management or budget preparation and plans per se were not intended as products. At the same time it was necessary to have some tangible output from the planning process that could serve as the basis for analysis and evaluation of successful planning.

The operational definition of planning stated that it was any activity directed to the preparation of information and decision alternatives for policy development, resource allocation, and program operation for specified human services to a defined population over some span of time. Such a definition led to analysis of an often diffuse set of processes that merged with management, budgetary, and service delivery functions. While this made interviewing and analysis more challenging, it resulted in a more valid representation of the activities that informants called planning, and allowed us to more accurately examine the links between planning and related organizational processes.[5]

Units of analysis in the Choice Behavior Study. The units of analysis in the Choice Behavior Study, choice situations, were defined as circumstances in which the potential for a decision existed. Three dimensions of situations identified by Lofland (1976) provided the definitional guidelines for the units of analysis: the human population, the space inhabited, and the time occupied. First, choice situations were limited to those activities that involved the population of direct service workers, supervisory staff, and administrators in the performance of their work. Situations as small as encounters between two people and as large as organization-wide were considered. Secondly, in terms of organizational space, the choices had to be program-relevant rather than task-specific; for example, a decision to record a client interview now or later was not included, whereas a decision about what action to take as a result of the interview, which was in the realm of organizational policy interpretation, was included. Finally, the choice situations studied could occupy any amount of time within the duration of the research. If it was anticipated that the issue would not be "deactivated" (that is, terminated but not necessarily resolved; March and Olsen, 1976) during this time, the choice situation was excluded since it would not have been possible to observe the outcome.

A choice situation included the time from when an issue or problem was articulated, verbally or in writing, until at least temporary deactivation was observed, or in other words, the dependent variable was scored. It should be noted that although some choices were continuously reactivated, for purposes of this study, choice situations included only the time span between the first observable articulation of the issue and the first observable deactivation. It was also assumed that a choice situation involved at least two competing values, though these may not have been clearly articulated. These criteria were similar to those Steinbruner (1974) used to identify complex decisions in his case study analysis of NATO negotiations.

Units of analysis in the Task Analysis Study. In the Task Analysis Study several guidelines were provided on the definition of the unit of analysis. First, tasks were identified by informants in terms of what they customarily defined as a task. The focus was on the activities and behavior, not goals or larger purposes, that informants considered as separable tasks. The questions centered around four topic areas having to do with uncertainty about task inputs, transformation processes, outputs, and feedback/evaluation processes.

Secondly, informants were guided by having the researcher identify upper and lower limits of specificity. It was explained that the researchers were not interested in tasks at a level so broad that specific questions about how the task was performed could not be meaningfully answered. Thus, for example, the task of "doing research" was too general. A specific research project was more reasonable. At the other end of the spectrum, a definition of task that was so narrow that one could not cover the range of factors described above in any detail was not useful. Thus, the task of making coffee was too limited although maintaining office supplies was acceptable. Examples of other units of analysis are budgeting, typing, chairing a meeting, writing articles, repairing equipment, doing payroll, and making policy decisions.

2. Stratified Sampling of Data Sources

Informant interviews, participant observation, and archival analysis are the primary sources of data in qualitative research. The problem is how to apply replicable procedures for selecting data sources that simultaneously satisfy methodological, theoretical, and practical criteria. Sampling strategies should also provide for the stratified allocation of different data sources and/or observational methods across units of analysis within the case. We will concentrate on ways of sampling informants, since the research in which the case cluster method has been tried has relied mainly, though not exclusively, on this source of data.

The virtues of using informants in case studies of organizations are that they can think in terms of the organization as a whole as well as various settings within it, they can be used to keep researchers in continuous contact with the setting, and, assuming certain levels of motivations and articulateness, small numbers of them can be used repeatedly to gather data about a broad range of events (Scott, 1965; Seidler, 1974: 816–817). These advantages do not, however, eliminate two of the fundamental methodological problems in using informants. It is important to select informants who are knowledgeable and to know if what informants say is accurate (Hyman, Levine, and Wright, 1967: 12). The problem is not that bias exists but how to control it in the research design. Salamone (1977: 121) argues that even lies, when identified as such, are useful sources of information: "Lies, in short, are a form of communication, not its negation." Moreover lies, incomplete perceptions, and ulterior motives are not random features of a setting, and it is possible to strategically select informants who represent desired variation in perspective.

Procedures for controlling bias rely on an interplay of methodological and theoretical guidance and center around replicable sampling methods. These methods are not incompatible with qualitative case studies, but they are seldom used or highlighted as significant methodological guides (Scott, 1965: 286–296). There are at least two sources of informant bias in studies of organizations that can be controlled through sampling and statistical procedures; proximity to events (Barker, 1968: 49–52) and position in the organizational structure (Seidler, 1974).

Sample designs for selecting informants would normally use nonprobability procedures due to the nature of the informant role and the often small number of individuals who qualify for that role. Such designs, referred to as dimensional (Arnold, 1970), strategic (Hunt, 1970), or purposive (Warwick and Lininger, 1975) samples, ensure better representation across dimensions of theoretical or applied interest to the researcher. While they are nonprobability samples, they are to be distinguished from haphazard sampling. They rely on systematic and replicable selection procedures that depend on theoretical expectations about sources of bias in the sample. For example, Seidler (1974) presented a method for correcting the biases of informants that involved stratified sampling and the creation of error variables. Based on

theories of power and conflict in organizations, he anticipated that factors such as position in the hierarchy, age, and
political orientation would affect informants' protectiveness
of church officials in describing the amount of dissent in the
church. The sample of informants was then stratified according to position, and bias scores were created for statistical analysis. Similar procedures could be based on proximity
of the informant to the event studied.

In the case cluster method these sampling ideas are extended by proposing a full or partial factorial sampling design
that incorporates stratified sampling of informants (or other
data sources) crossed with stratified sampling of units of
analysis. Hunt (1970) discusses the practical benefits of having a respondent provide data on multiple units of analysis in
organizational studies where staff size is too small to yield
sufficient degrees of freedom for statistical analysis. To do
this one must create units of analysis that represent attributes or roles of the respondents, or settings and processes
in the organization. Since each respondent provides data on
multiple units of analysis, the role becomes more like that of
an informant. When informants are strategically sampled to
represent specific categories of perspective and this stratum
is crossed with a stratum of categories of units of analysis,
one begins to approximate a multimethod-multitrait design
(Campbell and Fiske, 1959).[6]

The Planning Study Design. An example of this design
from the Planning Study is shown in Figure 1. Informants
were defined in terms of their roles vis-à-vis the practice of
planning. The three categories of informants were: (1) planners whose primary work involved the preparation of planning outputs; (2) managers who requested and/or consumed
the products of planning; and (3) externals who were not
part of the direct planner-manager relationship, but who observed and occasionally interacted with it. Some individuals
provided information from several roles if they were qualified. The units of analysis — planning events — were defined so as to reflect the spectrum of activities and products
that could legitimately be called planning. An informant
might provide observations on several categories of planning
events. A unit of analysis might have observations from
several informants.

UNITS OF ANALYSIS

Type of Planning Event*

Type of Informant	Cross Domain	Client Group	Department Wide	Program	Special Issue
Planners					
Managers					
Externals					

Figure 1 Stratified sampling design for informants and planning events in the Planning Study

*Within some of the categories of type of Planning Event a further stratification was performed to reflect variation across specific functional areas (e.g., health, welfare, employment) and client groups (e.g., elderly, developmentally disabled).

UNITS OF ANALYSIS
Type of Choice Situation

Type of Informant	Managerial	Service Delivery
Income Maintenance		
Services		
Administration		

Figure 2 Stratified sampling design for informants and choice situations

163

If this study had been quantitative, the presence of multiple observations on single units of analysis would create complications where discrepant judgments were given. One could treat the data quantitatively in several ways by creating parallel variables for different categories of informant or other data source, by having the researcher exercise a judgment in resolving differences, or by creating new variables that reflected the presence of discrepancies which could then be introduced as control factors in the analysis.

On the other hand, the presence of discrepancies signals a point of merger between quantitative and qualitative analysis. If single codes were used in the quantitative data set, the variance from different observational sources could be reflected qualitatively. By encouraging the researcher to gather multiple measurements on each unit of analysis, the case cluster method provides specific points of intertwining between quantitative and qualitative approaches.

The Choice Behavior Study design. In the Choice Behavior Study informants were stratified by functional unit within the agency; income maintenance, services, and administration (Figure 2). They were primarily supervisory personnel who were asked to assist in identifying units of analysis — choice situations — in two major settings, managerial and service delivery activities.

In addition to interview information from at least one informant on each choice situation, the researcher collected observation and archival data on some of the units of analysis. While the researcher synthesized these data sources into a single code for each variable, the multiple data sources created the occasion for qualitative analysis in order to fully represent the richness of the evidence.

The Task Analysis Study design. The Task Analysis Study used a two-stage stratified cluster sampling design that required different selection procedures at each stage. Individual employees were selected from the staff directory of the university and then grouped into strata that consisted of four job categories (Figure 3). Each selected employee described various tasks that he or she performed on the job, and as in the previous two studies, only motivated and ar-

UNITS OF ANALYSIS

Type of Task

Type of Informant		Simple	Complex
Administrative	Predictable (P)	1	2
	Unpredictable (U)	3	4
Faculty	P		
	U		
Nonfaculty Professional	P		
	U		
Clerical/Maintenance	P		
	U		

Figure 3 Stratified sampling design for informants and task clusters

ticulate informants were chosen. It was expected that job category would be correlated with the key variables of interest in the study, the types of uncertainty associated with tasks. This design made possible comparisons among job categories, the factors that influenced complexity and predictability, and the distribution of task uncertainty throughout the organization.

The second stage of sampling involved the enumeration and selection of tasks. Each informant was viewed as someone who could comment on a cluster of tasks. Informants were asked to identify the range of tasks associated with their jobs. The interviewer then explained the concepts of complexity and predictability and had the informant sort the tasks into groups representing the four combinations of these bilevel factors. A task was selected from each group based on the interviewer's judgment of its applicability to the content of data collection. The informant also exercised some discretion in cases where the motivation to discuss certain tasks varied. Finally, a subset of the sample was selected for collecting observation data. The combination of stratified sampling and judgmental selection highlights the interplay of quantitative and qualitative methods.

3. Creating Quantitative Data Sets

A problem with qualitative methods in general, and case studies in particular, is the limitations that are placed on the possibilities for statistical analysis, replication, and secondary analysis of the data. One could implement the case cluster method without quantifying data and still have a set of systematic and replicable procedures which are essential to the scientific method. If desired, however, the addition of quantified codes could result in the application of statistical procedures for assisting in the process of causal inference. Like the purely quantitative investigator, ". . . when push comes to shove [qualitative researchers] wish to make proper inferences from data" (Fienberg, 1977: 51). The use of multivariate statistics for categorical variables (e.g., Bishop, Fienberg, and Holland, 1975) could be of substantial benefit to the qualitative case study that employed the case cluster method.

The term secondary analysis has several meanings each of which poses difficulties in qualitative case studies. Secondary analysis may consist of the reanalysis of data sets within a single organization, for example Parsons' (1974) reinterpretation of the Hawthorne effect studies. Reanalysis of qualitative data is a more complex and costly process due to the inability to engage in data reduction and to the difficulties of organizing and manipulating the information in order to test alternative explanations for the findings, or of even validating what the findings were (Becker, 1958). The case cluster method, because of its sampling and potential quantification procedures alleviates this problem.

Another strategy for secondary analysis involves merging all or parts of quantitative data sets from different studies that center around a relatively well-defined topic. Light and Smith (1971) and Hyman (1972) have elaborated a series of secondary analysis designs for this circumstance. Lazar and Darlington's (1978) longitudinal study of 14 early childhood intervention programs is a good example of this type of secondary analysis. Had each of the original investigations been a qualitative case study, then merging their data and collecting similar data at a later point in time would have been impossible. On the other hand, the absence of rich qualitative descriptions of the organizational features of the intervention programs made it difficult to explain some of the anomalies of the quantitative analyses. This suggests that research on single cases that incorporates a combination of qualitative and quantitative approaches would be optimal for secondary analysis and direct comparison with other cases. Since the case cluster method involves procedures for sampling data sources and units of analysis it is a conceptually straightforward subsequent task to create quantitative codes for variables, assuming sufficient consensus on their meaning.

Table 1 summarizes the features of the case cluster method, the issues they address, and the examples from the three studies.

COMPARISONS WITH OTHER METHODS

Case Studies
Some case studies explore special events such as the birth (Redman, 1973) and death (Hall, 1976) of organizations, or, to take a much less public event, the fate of an effort to

Table 1 Summary of Case Cluster Method and Its Applications

Feature:	Issue Addressed	Planning Study	Choice Behavior Study	Task Analysis Survey
1. Defining, sampling, enumerating and units of analysis	a. Theoretically meaningful units b. Methodological problem of $N=1$ for inference from data c. Practical problem of adequate yet manageable number of units of analysis	a. Planning events were interdivisional and interorganizational b. $N>p$ ($p=$number of variables) c. Decreased number by not defining individuals as units of analysis. Made a multisetting case study feasible	a. Choice situations, not decision makers, provided best theoretical fit b. $N>p$ c. Sample size determined by analysis requirements and resources available	a. Tasks, not positions or subunits, were units of interest for measuring uncertainty b. $N>p$ c. Staff size too large for manageable data collection

	Column 1	Column 2	Column 3	Column 4
2. Stratified sampling of data sources crossed with units of analysis	a. The selection of knowledgeable informants b. Define and control data source bias	a. Informants sampled by role; planners, managers, and externals b. Multiple informants from different perspectives per planning events, document analysis	a. Informants sampled by job: administrators and service providers b. Multiple informants per choice situation, observations, document analysis	a. Informants sampled by job; administration, faculty, technical nonfaculty, and secretarial/maintenance b. Measured between and within informant effects, sample of observations
3. Quantitative data sets	a. Statistical analysis b. Secondary analysis	a. Not used b. Qualitative data set	a. Able to use multivariate statistics b. Mixed data set. Judgments are reinforced by quantitative measures of uncertainty. Also judgments were carefully defined so that replication is possible	a. Able to use multivariate statistics b. Mixed data set. Standardized interviews and questionnaires supported by structured observation

debureaucratize a public sector organization (Warwick, 1975). The case cluster method is distinguished in different ways from each of these studies. In contrast to Redman's story of the Congressional origins of the National Health Service Corps, the case cluster method requires the use of theory for a priori definition of a slice of the action (that is, units of analysis and data sources) that will be systematically examined and compared with other organizational births.

While the case cluster method could be applied to longitudinal designs such as Hall's study of the *Saturday Evening Post,* it would differ from this study by using informants or other data sources that would be strategically selected to provide alternative perspectives on the process of decline and birth. If data were quantified then multiple data sets could be generated, organized by perspective, and contrasted with each other to assess multiple models of the *Post's* decision-making processes. The result would be a thicker description perhaps at the expense of as much longitudinal data.

The case cluster method could be applied to Warwick's study without a great deal of change in the way his results were presented, but with the addition of more systematic comparisons and a sharper sense of external validity. The central purpose of Warwick's analysis of the State Department was to explain how bureaucratic forms were created and sustained in a public sector organization through an examination of forces internal and external to his single case. The methodology consisted of an examination of critical settings in which the seeds of vertical and horizontal differentiation were nourished by such factors as political pressure from Congress, technological and product uncertainties in the tasks of the State Department, personalities of Department personnel, historical patterns of career opportunities and status within the Foreign Service, and so on. By recasting this case study as a set of systematic observations across units of analysis, that one might label "bureaucratic seedbeds," the case cluster method emerges. It is a short conceptual leap to see how these units could have a standardized set of questions applied to them. Each question, or combination thereof, would constitute a potential explanation or predictor for the central dependent variable of interest, bureaucratic growth.

Particular data sources, such as a type of informant or set of documents, might be used to provide information on several units of analysis to which they could speak. In fact, it is likely that Warwick followed such a procedure although there is no evidence in his book that he applied the logic of sampling theory to selection of informants and other data sources, or to the selection of settings (i.e., units of analysis) in which to observe the effects of forces that produce bureaucratic forms of organization.

Sample Surveys

The major distinctions between the case cluster method and sample surveys of organizations are in the definition of units of analysis and the treatment of data from different classes of informants. Typically a respondent survey asks the individual to report on events and conditions in general within some boundary such as the organization, the workgroup, or a time frame (e.g., Lawrence and Lorsch, 1967; Comstock and Scott, 1977). Individuals or their aggregated forms are the units of analysis. One potential problem with this approach is that respondents are more likely to give overly-rationalized descriptions and to focus on the events that typically receive attention rather than on elusive but important phenomena that are not normally the topic of conversation. Thus, if the important theoretical concepts are not individuals or structural units, and we would argue that they often are not, then one needs to seek units of analysis that represent the events, attributes, and activities of theoretical interest, and to focus multiple perspectives on these units.

Aggregating the responses of individuals into subunit or organizational scores, whether weighted or not, is an attempt to average perceptions and resolve discrepancies. This aggregating process is contrary to the philosophy behind the case cluster method. We propose exploiting the differences in data provided by different classes of informant or other data sources. While the researcher may make summary judgments for purposes of quantification or final interpretation, there is an explicit attempt to contrast different perspectives on each unit of analysis. The qualitative portrayal of different perspectives is one way of creating context for the case and for comparing it to other cases in which particular perspectives can be identified (Cronbach, 1975).

Finally, the case cluster method is to be distinguished from simple time-sampling procedures. Units of analysis are defined in terms of multiple attributes that might include time but would also stress location, activity, function, and so on. Sampling could be done without considering time at all.

The case survey method proposed by Yin and Heald (1975) comes closer operationally to the case cluster approach. The case survey is a way of quantifying and aggregating findings of conceptually related but methodologically separate case studies. It incorporates the use of an analyst-observer who codes data in standardized formats based on informant interviews and document analysis. In some ways it faces the same problems as the case cluster method, in particular the sometimes ambiguous definitions of the boundaries for units of analysis. Thus deciding which events, individuals, and observations to include within a single case may be problematic. Where multiple sources of evidence are used, there is also the potential problem of conflicting or ambiguous answers on a given variable. While this may require procedures for improving the reliability of measurement there are instances in which resolving differences would violate validity requirements. The remedy then involves the qualitative exploration of the varying findings on a single variable, the creation of confidence variables or elimination of the unit of analysis from the sample.

The central purpose of the case survey method is to aggregate across cases. Each case is a separate unit of analysis. In this sense there is a significant difference from the case cluster method. Where the researcher's focus is on a single case, however defined, the case survey method is not appropriate, but the case cluster method would be.

Strategies for Analysis and Methodological Tradeoffs

The case cluster method is a hybrid that can be used to steer a research project among the three goals of generalizability, accuracy, and simplicity. Weick (1979: 35–42) argues that a given research strategy can only achieve two of the three goals at a time and therefore must face methodological tradeoffs. Case studies and laboratory experiments are relatively simple and accurate but they are not generalizable. Sample surveys may be general and simple (in the sense of standardized questions) but they lose nuance and accuracy by collapsing different frames of reference.

In general, Weick is correct about the necessity of acknowledging tradeoffs. However, the case cluster method combines features of both case studies and sample surveys, thus it is possible to achieve various combinations of generalizability, accuracy, and simplicity within a single study rather than a series of studies by shifting the strategy or focus of analysis. One could qualitatively speculate on the case by reviewing the perceptions of informants who had different perspectives. On the other hand, by collecting comparable data on a set of units of analysis within the case it would be possible to quantitatively describe and compare it to other cases. One would have moved from a thick and accurate analysis to a thin but generalizable description within the same study. In this sense the case cluster method presents a contingency approach for organizational research that can be tuned to the conditions and ambiguities of a research setting.

PROBLEMS AND PROSPECTS IN THE CASE CLUSTER METHOD

The case cluster method is in a formative stage of development and there is potential for refinement and extension of it both conceptually and operationally. In studying single organizations it may be a more satisfactory approach to hypothesis testing in terms of the theoretical adequacy of the units of analysis and the cost effectiveness of data analysis.

There are three central difficulties in using the case cluster approach. The problem of setting boundaries for units of analysis is critical and is similar in some ways to Weick's (1976) discussion of identifying the elements in studies of loose coupling in organizations. The researcher must exercise some discretion in rejecting units that are too narrow or too broad in range for the purposes of the study. The best guidance to use in this process is to examine the fit between the features of the potential unit of analysis and the kinds of questions or observations that one intends to use. It

is necessary within upper and lower bounds to allow informants latitude for definition in order to maximize phenomenological integrity. Units of analysis may differ on dimensions of scope of activities, duration, number of participants,
and so on, but they will be tied together by the fact that
they have identifiable boundaries, they are within the same
case, and that a common set of questions or codes is
applied to them. Longitudinal studies pose a special problem
since units of analysis may disappear over time. This was
noted often in the Planning Study, and in the Choice Behavior Study it was expected that choice situations would dissolve (perhaps to reappear) after some form of decision outcome was observed. The problem of sample attrition is en-
demic to all forms of research, however, and can best be
dealt with by having formal sampling procedures that allow
one to gauge the resultant bias.

The case cluster method deliberately violates the requirement of some statistical tests that observations on units of
analysis be independent. Certainly this is a feature of any
measurement procedure in which the same observer, interviewer, or experimenter records observations, standardized
or not, across a set of units of analysis or time periods. In
sample surveys of individuals it is expected that members of
families, social groups, neighborhoods, cities, regions, and
so on will have higher correlations among them than with
individuals outside those groupings. While the problem is
real it is mainly a matter of degree when the case cluster
method is compared with standard sample survey or experimental designs.

The strength of the case cluster method lies in the potential
for creating units of analysis that are based on theory and
that have meaning for the actors and observers of the case.
In addition, while preserving the distinctive features of the
case it employs replicable sampling and, if desired, quantitative measurement procedures to complement qualitative
analysis. For these reasons it is a promising method for
improving qualitative studies of organizations.

NOTES

1

This last distinction is blurred by the application of experimental design to sample surveys. Such designs reflect a special concern with internal validity, albeit one that employs different tactics than the qualitative case study.

2

Discussions of this problem in different research contexts may be found in Zelditch (1962: 567) and Fienberg (1977: 53–54).

3

This idea is similar to Bronfenbrenner's (1977) definition of "ecological validity" in which there is concordance between the meanings ascribed to a situation by the researcher and the subjects in the study.

4

In case studies where there are two or more organizations one normally stratifies first and then selects one case cluster from each stratum. This is done when it is obvious that some variables of central interest to the study cannot be fully rep-

resented in a single case. The researcher would then stratify the selection of cases along the dimensions of theoretical interest. Common examples would include the following: public-private, service-manufacturing, young-old, large-small.

5

It is interesting to note that organizations would have been no less difficult to define as units of analysis in this study. This was due to the fact that planning was often interdivisional and interorganizational in nature, thus it was unrealistic to identify a process of planning as representing organization X and not organization Y.

6

This design treats informants who represent different perspectives as different measurement methods. In one sense this is incorrect since informant interviewing is the method. To fully operationalize the multimethod approach one would need to stratify again across such data sources as archival analysis, participant observation, interviewing, questionnaires, and so on.

REFERENCES

Aldrich, Howard E.
1979 Organizations and Environments. Englewood Cliffs, NJ: Prentice-Hall.

Arnold, David O.
1970 "Dimensional sampling: An approach for studying a small number of cases." American Sociologist, 5: 147–150.

Barker, Roger
1968 Ecological Psychology. Stanford, CA: Stanford University Press.

Bateson, Gregory
1979 Mind and Nature. New York: Dutton.

Becker, Howard
1958 "Problems of inference and proof in participant observation." American Sociological Review, 23: 652–660.

Bishop, Y. M. M., S. E. Fienberg, and P. W. Holland
1975 Discrete Multivariate Analysis. New York: McGraw-Hill.

Brannon, Diane
1979 "Choice behavior in a public welfare agency." Unpublished manuscript, Department of Human Service Studies, Cornell University.

Bronfenbrenner, Urie
1977 "Toward an experimental ecology of human development." American Psychologist, 32: 513–531.

Campbell, Donald T.
1975 "'Degrees of freedom' and the case study." Comparative Political Studies, 8: 178–193.

Campbell, Donald T., and Donald W. Fiske
1959 "Convergent and discriminant validation by the multitrait-multimethod matrix." Psychological Bulletin, 56: 81–105.

Campbell, Donald T., and Julian C. Stanley
1966 Experimental and Quasi Experimental Designs for Research. Chicago: Rand McNally.

Cohen, Michael D., James G. March, and Johan P. Olsen
1972 "A garbage can model of organizational choice." Administrative Science Quarterly, 17: 1–25.

Coleman, James S.
1958– "Relational analysis: The
1959   study of social structure with survey methods." Human Organization, 17: 28–36.

Comstock, Donald E., and W. Richard Scott
1977 "Technology and the structure of subunits: Distinguishing individual and work group effects." Administrative Science Quarterly, 22: 177–202.

Cronbach, Lee
1975 "Beyond the two disciplines of scientific psychology." American Psychologist, 30: 116–127.

Dornbusch, Sanford M., and W. Richard Scott
1975 Evaluation and the Exercise of Authority. San Francisco: Jossey-Bass.

Fienberg, Stephen E.
1977 "The collection and analysis of ethnographic data in educational research." Anthropology and Education Quarterly, 8: 50–57.

Geertz, Clifford
1973 The Interpretations of Cultures. New York: Basic Books.

Hall, Roger I.
1976 "A system pathology of an organization: The rise and fall of the old Saturday Evening Post." Administrative Science Quarterly, 21: 185–211.

Hedberg, Bo
1981 "How organizations learn and unlearn." In Paul C. Nystrom and William H. Starbuck (eds.), Handbook of Organizational Design, vol. 1. New York: Oxford University Press.

Hunt, Raymond G.
1970 "Strategic selection: A purposive sampling design for small numbers research, program evaluation, and management." Buffalo, NY: Survey Research Center, State University of New York–Buffalo.

Hyman, Herbert
1972 Secondary Analysis of Sample Surveys. New York: Wiley.

Hyman, Herbert, Gene Levine, and Charles Wright
1967 "Studying expert informants by survey methods: A cross-national inquiry." Public Opinion Quarterly, 31: 9–26.

Katz, Daniel, and Robert Kahn
1966 Social Psychology of Organizations. New York: Wiley.

Lawrence, Paul R., and Jay W. Lorsch
1967 Organization and Environment. Cambridge, MA: Harvard University Press.

Lazar, Irving, and Richard Darlington
1978 "Lasting effects after preschool." Final report, Department of Human Service Studies, Cornell University.

Light, Richard, and Paul Smith
1971 "Accumulating evidence." Harvard Educational Review, 41: 429–471.

Lofland, John
1976 Doing Social Life. New York: Wiley.

March, James G., and Johan P. Olsen
1976 Ambiguity and Choice in Organizations. Bergen, Norway: Universitetsforlaget.

March, James G., and Herbert A. Simon
1958 Organizations. New York: Wiley.

McClintock, Charles C.
1978 "Evaluation of human services planning at state and local levels." Journal of Human Services Abstracts, 3: 26.
1979 "Patterns of uncertainty and organizational learning." Unpublished manuscript, Department of Human Service Studies, Cornell University.

Myers, Vincent
1977 "Toward a synthesis of ethnographic and survey methods." Human Organization, 36: 244–251.

Neisser, Ulric
1976 Cognition and Reality: Principles and Implications of Cognitive Psychology. San Francisco: Freeman.

Parsons, H. M.
1974 "What happened at Hawthorne?" Science, 183: 922–932.

Proshansky, Harold M.
1976 "Environmental psychology and the real world." American Psychologist, 31: 303–310.

Redman, Eric
1973 The Dance of Legislation. New York: Simon and Schuster.

Rist, Ray
1970 "Student social class and teacher expectations: The self-fulfilling prophecy in ghetto education." Harvard Educational Review, 40: 411–451.
1977 "On the relations among educational research paradigms: From disdain to detente." Anthropology and Education, 8: 42–49.

Salamone, Frank
1977 "The methodological significance of the lying informant." Anthropological Quarterly, 50: 117–124.

Scott, W. Richard
1965 "Field methods in the study of organizations." In James G. March (ed.), Handbook of Organizations: 261–304. Chicago: Rand McNally.

Seidler, John
1974 "On using informants: A technique for collecting quantitative data and controlling measurement error in organization analysis." American Sociological Review, 39: 816–831.

Sieber, Sam
1973 "The integration of field work and survey methods." American Journal of Sociology, 78: 1335–1359.

Stake, Robert E.
1978 "The case study method in social inquiry." Educational Researcher, 7: 5–8.

Steinbruner, John D.
1974 The Cybernetic Theory of Decision. Princeton: Princeton University Press.

Warwick, Donald P.
1975 A Theory of Public Bureaucracy: Politics, Personality, and Organization in the State Department. Cambridge, MA: Harvard University Press.

Warwick, Donald P., and Charles A. Lininger
1975 The Sample Survey: Theory and Practice. New York: McGraw-Hill.

Weick, Karl E.
1976 "Educational organizations as loosely coupled systems." Administrative Science Quarterly, 21: 1–19.
1979 The Social Psychology of Organizing, 2d ed. Reading, MA: Addison-Wesley.

Woodward, Joan
1965 Industrial Organization: Theory and Practice. London: Oxford University Press.

Yin, Robert K., and Karen A. Heald
1975 "Using the case survey method to analyze policy studies." Administrative Science Quarterly, 20: 371–381.

Zelditch, Morris
1962 "Some methodological problems of field studies." American Journal of Sociology, 67: 566–576.

Quantitative versus Qualitative: Environmental Assessment in Organizational Studies

H. Kirk Downey
R. Duane Ireland

Questions concerning the gathering, interpretation, and evaluation of data in any research are problematic. Organizational research is no exception. This article addresses the basic issue of the place of "qualitative" data in assessing environments.

A PRESUPPOSITION

The most relevant of the presuppositions that determine one's research perspective is that methodological issues must always be answered within the context of a particular research setting. That is to say, methodologies are neither appropriate nor inappropriate until they are applied to a specific research problem. This perspective treats methodologies as tools of inquiry; each inquiry requires careful selection of the proper tools. Having the wrong tool for the task may be no better than having no tools at all, a notion best summarized by Kaplan's (1964: 214) warning: "Too often, we ask how to measure something without raising the question of what we would do with the measurement if we had it." Thus, both *qualitative* data and *quantitative* data have their place in organizational research. The pertinent questions concern the "where's" and "when's" within a specific research context.

THE PRESENT CONTEXT

The topic of using qualitative data to assess an organization's environment has become increasingly important to organizational research. On the assumption that the editorial policy of *Administrative Science Quarterly* reflects major issues in organizational research, we inferred that the assessment of an organization's environment is a significant research issue. In preparing this article, we surveyed past issues of *ASQ* and found 27 articles that dealt directly with conceptualization and/or measurement of an organization's environment.

Organizational researchers have for some time sought to utilize the environment-organization-effectiveness "paradigm" to understand organizational phenomena. Almost from the outset, they found themselves uncomfortable with their methodologies for tapping the important aspects of environments. Early attempts (Merton, 1957; Gross and McEachern, 1958) sought to specify an environment by describing its elements. Later, Dill (1962) suggested that such a full specification was not possible for modern complex organizations. He suggested the environment be treated and/or analyzed in terms of its effects upon the organization. This generally has been interpreted in terms of such concepts as environmental uncertainty and environmental complexity. Dill's suggestion has been a catalyst for some of the most important organizational research in the past 25 years. It also, however, has planted the seed for some of the biggest controversies. As examples, should perceptual measures be used to operationalize environmental attributes? What "objective" measures should be used? Do individual differences (personality, etc.) influence? Why is it that perceived environmental uncertainty scores do not correlate with price volatility, etc.?

The literature is filled with these questions and controversies. A few examples, however, will illustrate the problem. A study (Downey, Hellriegel, and Slocum, 1975) that dealt with perceived uncertainty suggested that quantitative perceptual measures were important because organizational decision makers operate in "enacted" environments (Weick, 1969). This statement and others like it induced at least one reader (Tinker, 1976: 507) to label the work an "absurd confusion [which] stems from a kind of goal displacement in environmental research over a number of years." Tinker went on to characterize research in organizational studies as suffering from the "poverty of empiricism" (p. 508). Apparently, he believed that more qualitative approaches to environmental assessment would result in a "richness of nonempiricism."

Tinker is not the only critic of current quantitative environment-assessment techniques. Writers have attacked quantitative perceptual measures of uncertainty because they do not correlate sufficiently with certain quantitative measures of environmental attributes. For example, Tosi, Aldag, and Storey (1973) demonstrated that Lawrence and Lorsch's uncertainty scales are not associated with several selected, quantitatively measured environmental attributes. Questions from Tosi, Aldag, and Storey and others like them, however, seem to lead to a desire for more, if not better, empiricism in the assessment of organizations' environments. This is opposite of Tinker's viewpoint.

More recently, Rousseau (1979) and Stewart (1979) engaged in a similar discussion regarding the use of perceptual data in the measurement of job characteristics. This discussion, although not directly involving the environment, reinforces the notion that the use of qualitative data to study organizations is a controversial issue.

This controversy is at least partially fueled by a false dilemma. The real choices that have to be made by researchers regarding qualitative data can only be made intelligently if they are made from real alternatives.

A DILEMMA

In the environmental literature, discussions usually focus on choosing between so-called "objective" and "subjective" measures. "Objective" in these discussions usually refers to the tabulations of objects or events in an organization's environment. The measures are preferably gathered from archival sources. Examples of such measures might be the number of firms in an industry, the number of government regulations specific to a firm's industry, etc. Conversely, "subjective" usually is applied to any measure that seeks somehow to tap participant's perceptions of their organizations' environments. The most widely recognized of the so-called subjective measures is perceived environmental uncertainty.

Given these labels it is not too surprising that researchers would show a decided preference for "objective" measures. While this preference may not stop them from using "subjective" measures, it does tend to influence their future research goals. Rightly or wrongly, current research norms attach high value to anything that can be labeled objective. This preference should be expected since objectivity is the presumed goal of scientific inquiry.

This objective-subjective categorization has had, however, at least two dysfunctional effects on organizational research. First, it has tended, a priori, to push research away from qualitative data when they might be useful for assessing some environmental dimensions. The objective-subjective dilemma has equated objectivity, and thus scientific inquiry, with quantification. As a result, qualitative assessments have been avoided by researchers because of an understandable desire not to appear "unscientific."

Second, the objective-subjective categorization has equated subjective measures with measurement of perceptions. The defining of all measures of perceptions as subjective is based on a confusion over *whose* subjectivity is involved. The objectivity that is desired in scientific inquiry refers to objectivity on the part of the researcher. Subjective behavior on the part of those being studied, however, may well be a legitimate topic for scientific inquiry.

When qualitative measures are equated with subjectivity, subjectivity is ascribed to the *assessor*. When the measurement of perceptions is equated with subjectivity, subjectivity is ascribed to the *assessee*. Stated differently, subjectivity can apply to the way something is measured, or it can apply to the object being measured. For example, Duncan (1972) utilized a highly structured interview form to measure decision makers' perceived environmental uncertainty. In contrast to Duncan, Kimberly (1975) utilized a highly unstructured examination of his organizations' histories to measure environmental constraints. That examination led him to choose the date of founding as the primary historical determinant of environmental constraints. If only the objective-subjective dimensions were to be used, Duncan's work would have to be described as concerning objective measurement of a subjective phenomenon. Kimberly's work, on the other hand, would have to be described as concerning a subjective measurement of an objective phenomenon. Current usage of the objective-subjective categorization to describe the assessment of an organization's environment, however, fails to distinguish properly between these two attempts at assessment.

AN ALTERNATIVE APPROACH

Attempts to assess the environment in organizational studies can be better understood if they are examined using two dimensions. The first dimension concerns *what* is being measured, the second concerns *how*. The first concerns conceptualization, the second concerns operationalization. The first distinguishes between conceptualizing the environment: (1) in terms of the participant's interpretations of the environment or (2) in terms of environmental attributes. The second distinguishes between operationalizing the concepts (1) with quantitative variables or (2) with qualitative variables. (These dimensions are shown in Figure 1.)

It is important to note that these dimensions allow us to distinguish between quantitatively measured perceptions (participants' interpretations) and qualitatively measured perceptions. This distinction is not possible with an objective-subjective unidimensional view of environmental assessments. Likewise, it becomes possible to distinguish between quantitative and qualitative approaches to specifying environmental attributes that do not rely on participants' interpretations.

PAST RESEARCH

As reflected in Figure 1, the suggested dimensions of environmental assessments result in four categories of research, each of which is discussed below.[1]

CONCEPTUALIZATION

	Participant Interpretation	Environmental Attributes
Quantitative	CATEGORY I Lawrence and Lorsch (1967)* Duncan (1972) Osborn and Hunt (1974) Downey, Hellriegel, and Slocum (1975)* Kochan (1975) Nebecker (1975) Pennings (1975) Leifer and Huber (1977) Tushman (1977) Whetten (1978)	CATEGORY III Lawrence and Lorsch (1967)* Pfeffer and Leblebici (1973) Tosi, Aldag, and Storey (1973) Baldridge and Burnham (1975) Downey, Hellriegel, and Slocum (1975)* Kochan (1975)* Pennings (1975)* Staw and Szwajkowski (1975) DuBick (1978)
	Lynton (1969)** Jurkovich (1974)*,**	Hickson et al. (1971)** Jurkovich (1974)*,**
Qualitative	CATEGORY II Lawrence and Lorsch (1967)	CATEGORY IV Hinings et al. (1974)* Hirsch (1975) Kimberly (1975) Sebring (1977) Blau and McKinley (1979)

(left vertical axis label: OPERATIONALIZATION)

*The designs of these research studies include multiple methodologies in terms of the operationalization and conceptualization dimensions and, thus, are included in more than one category.
**These studies are not empirical. Nonetheless, they are included to suggest various methodologies that could be utilized in conducting environmental assessments.

Figure 1   A categorization of research studies that used environmental assessments

Category I: Quantitative-Participant Interpretations

Duncan's (1972) work with perceived environmental uncertainty well illustrates this category. Duncan conceptualized his assessment of the organization's environment with actor's interpretations of three subdimensions which were purported to describe decision makers' perceptions of their decision settings (i.e., ability to assign probabilities, etc.). He operationalized this concept with a highly quantified measure based on highly structured interviews. Previous descriptions of Duncan's work, using the objective-subjective dimension, classify his assessments as subjective. It can be argued that the respondents must make subjective judgments, but there is nothing subjective about his form of measurement. The scheme suggested here avoids this dilemma.

Likewise, Pennings (1975) conceptualized his assessment of the organization's environment with *both* participants' interpretations and environmental attributes. That portion that dealt with participants' interpretations was measured using structured questionnaires which attempted to tap environmental instability, uncertainty, and the like.

Category II: Qualitative-Participant Interpretations

Lawrence and Lorsch's (1967) original work, as reported in *ASQ,* is the only example which was found in our literature review that fits this category. They conceptualized organizations' environments with participants' interpretations of subenvironments and proceeded to operationalize those concepts with qualitative judgments based on interviews with top executives in each of their subject organizations.

Category III: Quantitative-Environmental Attributes

Works in this category can be illustrated using Pfeffer and Leblebici's (1973) research on executive recruitment. They conceptualized the environment without reference to participants' interpretations. Specifically, they classified environments according to a large set of environmental attributes, including the number of organizations in a given industry, average debt-to-equity ratio in an industry, etc. They operationalized this conceptualization by collecting data from quantitative sources such as census reports and *Moody's Industrial Manual.*

Similarly, part of Pennings' (1975) work can be considered in this category because he used company records and census information to operationalize environmental attributes.

Examples of these attributes are customer characteristics and investment patterns in the industry.

Category IV: Qualitative-Environmental Attributes

Hirsch's (1975) work, concerning organizational effectiveness, is a good example of research in this category. Hirsch sought to conceptualize environments by such attributes as patent and copyright statutes, and control of distribution prices. He chose to operationalize these conceptualizations qualitatively by attending trade meetings and conducting unstructured interviews.

Similarly, Sebring (1977), in a case analysis, conceptualized his organizations' environments by the degree to which they were required to respond to state political processes. He sought to operationalize this environmental attribute through a personal review of the organizations' budgetary procedures.

FUTURE RESEARCH

The question of what is the role of qualitative approaches in assessing organizations' environments can now be considered in terms of the two specific conceptualizations of environments, participants' interpretations and environmental attributes.

Figure 1 shows that the majority of the research concerning participants' interpretations of environments has been operationalized using quantitative approaches. These operationalizations appear to be appropriate for two reasons. First, the theories underlying these works treat participants' interpretations as having one of only a small number of dimensions. For example, perceived uncertainty is seldom conceptualized as containing more than three or four subdimensions. Concepts with few subdimensions usually are easier to quantitatively operationalize than are concepts with many subdimensions. Second, operationalizing participants' interpretations makes it possible for the researcher to draw upon the well-established literature in psychometric analysis. This literature makes both the use of existing instruments and the development of new ones relatively easy tasks.

Thus, qualitative approaches to the assessment of participants' interpretations would most likely not be efficient in terms of either utilizing resources or eliminating observer bias.

Assessing environments in terms of their attributes, however, may be a much more fruitful area for qualitative approaches. Organizational theories that deal directly with environmental attributes seldom are able to delineate specifically which attributes are important. Usually these theories are unable even to determine how many attributes might be relevant in specific situations. As a result, it is conceivable that the organizational researcher could be confronted with a potentially infinite number of attributes to operationalize. Additionally, no established literature has been developed that deals with the mechanics of measuring environmental attributes. That is, there is no adequately developed environmental counterpart of psychometric theory.

Thus, it appears that qualitative approaches might be very useful and appropriate when assessing environments without regard to participants' interpretations. This implies that past attempts at quantification of environmental attributes may have been premature because certain questions remain. How is a researcher to decide what attributes should be specified? How are those attributes to be measured? Would it not be better to be able to meaningfully assess an organization's environment qualitatively than to assess a few, perhaps irrelevant, attributes of that environment with highly precise, quantitative methods?

An example of what might have been a premature attempt at quantification of the assessment of environmental attributes is helpful in understanding this analysis. Downey, Hellriegel, and Slocum (1975) attempted to develop quantitative measures of several specific environmental attributes[2]: (1) the degree of concentration in the industry; (2) variation in prices; and (3) volatility of sales. Supposedly, these three highly "quantified" measures were to assess the environment. The study would probably have come closer to its goal had it qualitatively approached the assessment of the organizations' environments. As it was, however, the authors were left with highly precise measures of attributes that might have been totally irrelevant. Why those three attributes? What theory suggests that concentration, price variation, and sales volatility capture the essence of an organization's environment? Were the authors premature in their attempt to assess the environment by quantification of a few environmental attributes? Very possibly so!

SUMMARY

In this article we have sought to demonstrate that qualitative methods have a potentially important role to play in at least one part of organizational studies. This role has, however, been hidden because measurements of organizations' environments usually have been categorized as either objective or subjective. The two-dimensional model in Figure 1 makes the potential role of qualitative methods clearer. The model indicates that qualitative methods and data are likely to be most useful in the assessment of environmental attributes, and are less likely to be appropriate where participants' interpretations of environments are to be measured.

Finally, there is no reason to believe that environmental assessment is the only area where qualitative methods might be useful in organizational studies. These other areas, however, should be explored in terms of *what* is being measured before they are judged appropriate for any type of operationalization, whether it be qualitative or quantitative.

NOTES

1

The specific works discussed are chosen only for their clarity of illustration. Their discussion does not imply any superiority to others in the category.

2

They used the variables as criteria in the validity testing of quantitative-actor interpretation type variables.

REFERENCES

Baldridge, J. Victor, and Robert A. Burnham
1975 "Organizational innovation: Individual, organizational, and environmental impacts." Administrative Science Quarterly, 20: 165–176.

Blau, Judith R., and William McKinley
1979 "Ideas, complexity, and innovation." Administrative Science Quarterly, 24: 200–219.

Dill, William R.
1962 "The impact of environment on organizational development." In S. Mailack and E. Van Ness (eds.), Concepts and Issues in Administrative Behavior: 29–48. Englewood Cliffs, NJ: Prentice-Hall.

Downey, H. Kirk, Don Hellriegel, and John W. Slocum, Jr.
1975 "Environmental uncertainty: The construct and its application." Administrative Science Quarterly, 20: 613–629.

DuBick, Michael A.
1978 "The organizational structure of newspapers in relation to their metropolitan environments." Administrative Science Quarterly, 23: 418–433.

Duncan, Robert B.
1972 "Characteristics of organizational environments and perceived environmental uncertainty." Administrative Science Quarterly, 17: 313–327.

Gross, N., W. Mason, and A. McEachern
1958 Explorations in Role Analysis: Studies of the School Superintendency Role. New York: Wiley.

Hickson, D. J., C. R. Hinings, C. A. Lee, R. E. Schneck, and J. M. Pennings
1971 "A strategic contingencies theory of intraorganizational power." Administrative Science Quarterly, 16: 216–229.

Hinings, C. R., D. J. Hickson, J. M. Pennings, and R. E. Schneck
1974 "Structural conditions of intraorganizational power." Administrative Science Quarterly, 19: 22–44.

Hirsch, Paul M.
1975 "Organizational effectiveness and the institutional environment." Administrative Science Quarterly, 20: 327–344.

Jurkovich, Ray
1974 "A core typology of organizational environments." Administrative Science Quarterly, 19: 380–394.

Kaplan, Abraham
1964 Conduct of Inquiry. Scranton, PA: Chandler Press.

Kimberly, John R.
1975 "Environmental constraints and organizational structure: A comparative analysis of rehabilitation organizations." Administrative Science Quarterly, 20: 1–9.

Kochan, Thomas A.
1975 "Determinants of the power of boundary units in an interorganizational bargaining relation." Administrative Science Quarterly, 20: 434–452.

Lawrence, Paul R., and Jay W. Lorsch
1967 "Differentiation and integration in complex organizations." Administrative Science Quarterly, 12: 1–47.

Leifer, Richard, and George P. Huber
1977 "Relations among perceived environmental uncertainty, organization structure, and boundary-spanning behavior." Administrative Science Quarterly, 22: 235–247.

Lynton, Rolf D.
1969 "Linking an innovative subsystem into the system." Administrative Science Quarterly, 14: 398–416.

Merton, R. K.
1957 Social Theory and Social Structure. Glencoe, IL: Free Press.

Nebecker, Delbert M.
1975 "Situational favorability and perceived environmental uncertainty: An integrative approach." Administrative Science Quarterly, 20: 281–294.

Osborn, Richard N., and James G. Hunt
1974 "Environment and organizational effectiveness." Administrative Science Quarterly, 19: 231–246.

Pennings, Johannes M.
1975 "The relevance of the structural-contingency model for organizational effectiveness." Administrative Science Quarterly, 20: 393–410.

Pfeffer, Jeffrey, and Huseyin Leblebici
1973 "Executive recruitment and the development of interfirm organizations." Administrative Science Quarterly, 18: 449–461.

Rousseau, Denise
1979 "Reply to 'reliability or validity?'" Administrative Science Quarterly, 24: 313–314.

Sebring, Robert H.
1977 "The five-million dollar misunderstanding: A perspective on state government-university interorganizational conflicts." Administrative Science Quarterly, 22: 505–523.

Staw, Barry M., and Eugene Szwajkowski
1975 "The scarcity-munificence component of organizational environments and the commission of illegal acts." Administrative Science Quarterly, 20: 345–354.

Stewart, Rosemary G.
1979 "Reliability or validity? A comment on 'Characteristics of departments, positions, and individuals: Contexts for attitudes and behavior'." Administrative Science Quarterly, 24: 312–313.

Tinker, Anthony M.
1976 "A Note on 'Environmental uncertainty' and a suggestion for our editorial function." Administrative Science Quarterly, 21: 506–508.

Tosi, Henry, Ramon Aldag, and Ronald Storey
1973 "On the measurement of the environment: An assessment of the Lawrence and Lorsch environmental uncertainty scale." Administrative Science Quarterly, 18: 27–36.

Tushman, Michael L.
1977 "Special boundary roles in the innovation process." Administrative Science Quarterly, 22: 587–605.

Weick, Karl E.
1969 The Social Psychology of Organizing. Reading, MA: Addison-Wesley.

Whetten, David A.
1978 "Coping with incompatible expectations: An integrated view of role conflict." Administrative Science Quarterly, 23: 254–271.

Field Stimulations for Organizational Behavior Research

Gerald R. Salancik

Recently a woman who was careful with her pennies received a telephone bill for $0.00. Pleased by the tidiness of the company's recordkeeping, she filed the non-bill and went on to pay the rent. Twenty days later she received the message "NOTICE PRIOR TO DISCONNECTION." She presented this paradox to a polite service representative who found her accounts in order and advised her to disregard the notice. She did. A few days later she received another threat. She returned to the company. This time she spoke with a supervisor. He checked her records, reviewed his subordinate's report, commended the woman, apologized for the company, and promised a correction. True to his word, a corrected bill for $0.00 arrived in two days, followed shortly by a disconnection notice. She called again. The supervisor assured her again. He called the next day to confirm all was well. A week of peace was followed by another threat. Beaten but enlightened, the woman wrote a check for $0.00 and mailed it with the computer billing card to the company, which ended the matter.

This woman's experience is recounted to introduce a general methodology for the study of organizational and human behavior. As this woman had done, the method calls for an investigator to interact with an organization in order to stimulate it to act and to infer the organization's nature from its responses. This method of investigation is designed to encourage researchers to uncover the nature of organization

Author's Note: Ideas for this paper originated from talks at the University of Illinois in 1977 and the Academy of Management annual meeting in 1978.

without asking for an accounting on a questionnaire. The approach promises to bring curiosity and fun to research and to sharpen the intellectual powers of those who use it. Mental sharpening comes because the method forces one to think through why organizations like the telephone company behave as they do.

We label this general methodology field stimulation. It is not new, but it belongs to a class of qualitative methodologies in which the respondent determines the character of the response. It differs from some qualitative methodologies by encouraging the investigator to determine the occasion for a response which is, in turn, a measure of the organization's nature and capacity. It has been called by Webb and his associates "contrived observation," to distinguish it from observational studies in which the investigator acts as a passive recorder who avoids provoking or interrupting responses (Webb et al., 1966; Webb and Salancik, 1970). Although "contrived" is an apt description, I prefer the emphasis which "stimulation" places upon the method.

The titillating ring of the phrase field stimulation fits well with our purpose: to tease the field of organizational behavior away from some masturbatory tendencies evident in its research and to recommend that it study organizations by tickling them, tempting them, and perturbing them. Garfinkel (1967), for instance, sent his students into a grocery store to break a silent norm that governed its relationship with clients. And Goodsell (1976) forced post offices to haggle over the price of a stamp. Both learned something that was not evident before their intrusions.

The slightly licentious strategy of field stimulation encompasses a set of research methods rather than any single instrument or form. It is an approach for researching organizations, although it has been used mainly to study individual social behavior in public places. The researcher may play himself or pose in another role. Interventions might vary from the most natural to the most contrived depending upon theoretical needs, the bounds of decency, and the limits of imagination. Thus, one investigator might merely collect and collate the responses stimulated by others, as when a researcher advertises for copies of company replies to product complaint letters. Or another might organize a group of consumers to file lawsuits against a firm in order to examine the firm's reactions.

Behind this recommendation for field stimulation methods are several premises and preconceptions about organizations, about the epistemological significance of data, and about the investigator. We view an organization as a curious organism which is chanced upon or sought out for study much as a peeping ethologist might approach a lizard or a butterfly. We attribute coherence, structure, substance, and a capacity for responding to it, even though initially we may be ignorant of its properties. We view data as Campbell (1965) has and as Brunswik (1934) had before him. The data we collect are assumed to be outcroppings of some underlying process, and are the stuff from which the structures and processes which generated them are inferred. This naive realism notion of data assumes that data have no meaning outside of the theories which link to them.

Our view of the investigator is that of a free and responsible person who acts within the rights and obligations of his moral and legal culture. One implication of this is that an investigator requires no more permission to carry out his investigation than that required of anyone interacting with an organization in other roles. This last assertion is necessary because many investigators arbitrarily restrict their studies of organizational phenomena by the self-imposed requirement that they be permitted to study them.

Field stimulation studies may help to lessen our historical reliance on questionnaire responses from self-selected samples. These dominate our literature about organizational behavior as a handful of recent volumes of *Administrative Science Quarterly* reflects. Thirty-one of 39 empirical articles reported on questionnaire or interview data, five-sixths of which came only from a fraction of the investigators' intended samples.

Such dependence on questionnaires creates several epistemological problems. The most critical is that organizational behavior research is in danger of becoming an autoerotic fantasy. Many understandings accumulated in the field are self-generated images induced by its methodologies. While most methods can potentially only play back an investigator's fantasies, questioning methods most likely will, because they depend heavily on language. Thus in a simple case, when an interviewer asks the question, "Do you have freedom in your job?" he forces a respondent to think as he himself thinks. And the respondent will answer in these same terms. But the investigator may deceive himself when he thinks his respondent's descriptions are anything more than his own words.

To appreciate the power of questions to create their own answers, we had confederates ask their classmates "How's the class going?" about once a week during four two-week periods throughout a semester. The classmates made such unrefined remarks as "Fine," "Not bad," or "The pits," which we coded as positive, neutral, or negative reactions. Responses from one query to the next then were analyzed for similarity, or stability. The proportion of times for which a response was similar from one query to the next are presented in Table 1, based on three inquiries to each of eight students. In one condition (I in Table 1), two persons asked the same respondent about the class. In another (II), one person asked about the course each week. Thus persons were questioned twice as much in I as in II. In a third condition (III), persons were questioned by one person during two periods only. As the data in Table 1 indicate, stability in the students' remarks follows from the number of inquiries about the class rather than the length of experience with it.

Another experiment was conducted to examine how questioning a person can shape his opinion. Since responses were found to be unstable during the beginning weeks of a class, a confederate randomly chose either a negative or a positive reaction to be shaped. When the classmate answered, "How's the class going?" the confederate asked, "Oh really. Why is that?" This procedure was repeated for all positive or negative reactions of the first two weeks of class. The logic of the study is that when students answer the question "Why is that?" they introduce positive and negative aspects of the course into their thoughts from which subsequent attitudes develop. A positive (or negative) attitude was inferred from student responses in the eighth

Table 1   Proportion of Responses That Were Similar From Query
to Query During Selected Weeks of a Semester

Week	I	Conditions II	III
2–3	.44	.31	———
4–5	.72	.50	———
6–7	.88	.75	.46
8	———	———	———
9	———	———	———
10	———	———	———
11–12	.69	.44	.50

Note: Each proportion is based on approximately three responses from eight
students, a variation because of absences from class.

week to the question "How's the class going?" The direction was inferred when three of the last four remarks were
positive or negative. At the end of eight weeks a very stable
positive attitude had developed among the seven persons in
the positive condition and a very stable negative attitude
developed among six of the eight persons in the negative
condition (chi-squared = 5.90, corrected for continuity).

The epistemological error we can make by relying on questionnaires is obvious from these examples. Because we, as
investigators, only ask questions, and the respondents do
the answering, we assume there must be some substance
beyond that which we put there. But we can deceive ourselves in two ways. First, and less serious, we sometimes
forget that the responses we obtain may be created not
only by the structures and processes of the respondent but
also by the nature of our questions. Second, and more serious, is the deception that in order for us to ask a question
we must put the question into words that both the respondent and we will understand. But, because we do so, we
only learn about the things that we already understand.

This heavy reliance on questions as a way of studying organizations comes partly from believing that in order to
study "real" organizations one must see them, get inside
them, and reduce them to human terms through conversation. Questions are the most direct form of gathering infor-

mation from a new acquaintance. To ask someone, "Do you like this town?" and to hear him answer yes is seductive because it sounds as if something was learned. After all, the question was answered.

A second epistemological problem imposed by the questionnaire method is the necessary condition that someone be available to answer the questions, which poses its own problem. To question an organization about the behavior of its members may require permission. Getting such permission can severely limit our knowledge. Van Maanen, for instance, confessed bravely in a footnote to his study of police departments (1975) that he contacted 20 police departments until he found one that would cooperate with him. This single permission however extended him an invitation only to ask individuals within the department to fill out his questionnaires. The study had five waves of data collection, and only about 57 percent of the policemen made themselves available for the final wave. Although Van Maanen's study was more carefully done than many, it boggles the mind to fathom what our knowledge of organizations must contain when sampling restrictions like these operate as unintended designers of our research.

Our reliance on other people's cooperation selects the knowledge we gather. Participation in surveys frequently can be modeled from psychological and political involvement (Salancik, 1966). People respond to surveys which they feel will contribute to desired policies or which enable them to indulge in reflection about their favorite interests.

Permissions are also severe political gatekeepers. One can assume that to get permission to enter an organization, one must be reasonably agreeable to the host. The knowledge we thus generate may be only that for which permissions will be granted. To illustrate this, we asked firms to fill out a short questionnaire, inquiring about nothing more than the name of the organization, its sales, size, and the average return on its common stock. For ten firms the cover letter introduced a study of why organizations fail; for another ten it said the study addressed organizational success. Two of the fail questionnaires were returned compared to six of the success questionnaires, despite the fact only public information was requested. In another study (Salancik, 1979) contractors were asked to provide information about the extent of their hiring of women into management. The more affirmative were more responsive. And Speak (1964) has shown that the probability of a response to a job satisfaction questionnaire was related inversely to the vulnerability of an employee's position in the organization. The less-skilled workers from glutted labor markets were the most reticent. It does seem, then, that if researchers approach organizations only by interviewing them through their front doors, they will get to know them much as an occasional guest knows his host — politely, not too intimately, and with the distant affectation of parlor charm.

Although we strongly object to blanket reliance on survey methods we do not advocate their ban. Questionnaire inquiries can be revealing and might better be thought of as a special form of field stimulations. Certainly they prompt occasions for responding. From this perspective, the content is less intriguing than the voluntary reactions. Does a manager leave blank the items on job design and expound feverishly on government regulation? Do the returns come with cover letters apologizing for delays? Do returns come at all?

One early field stimulation study based its analysis on responses to questions, though primarily to discredit them. LaPiere (1934) questioned "establishment" hotels in a letter about their policies toward accommodating a member of a minority race. Most hotels replied apologetically that they would refuse service. But when LaPiere presented a person from a minority race to register, he was accommodated. Although LaPiere did not explore the organizational features which could account for these data, it would seem that the letters were answered by the hotel managers while the rooms were being let by the desk clerks. The clerks would have been acting within their roles and registering guests when rooms were available. The managers, with their broader concerns for the whole enterprise, however, may have been reacting to the prospect of undesirables upsetting the hotel's more regular clientele.

RESPONSE RATES AS INFORMATION

Many organizational researchers use questionnaires but fail to exploit the information stimulated by the request. The review of *ASQ* indicated response rates go as low as 25 percent, and some researchers actually cite authorities (Kerlinger, 1964) to validate the achievement of 56 percent as normal. Of 31 articles we noted, nine fail to report response rates, 14 fail to discuss the fractional samples obtained, and only three reveal the subgroup differences in responding.

Such lack of attention is unfortunate for response rates do reveal theoretically relevant information. The nonresponse is as much a behavior which needs explaining as a response. Much nonresponding is predictably random. Respondent loss, for instance, usually follows an exponential function with time. Thus Roos (1978), who traced the occupational influences of Turkish students across 18 years, reports respondent losses at a rate of $.948^{YR}$, where YR is the number of years since the sample was drawn. Similarly, for the five waves of data collected by Van Maanen (1975), participation decreased at a rate of $.901^{A(i)}$, where A(i) is the first through the fifth administration. Such exponential reductions mean that the study populations have some constant probability of not responding, implying randomly distributed inhibitions.

Other responses to inquiries, while not exactly random, take on the character of being mindless results of programed requirements from cultural or organizational roles. Thus when Phillip R. Kunz from Utah mailed 600 Christmas cards to midwestern addresses taken from a telephone book, it speaks volumes on the nature of this seasonal ritual when 117 families replied with cards of their own, with pictures of families, glad tidings, and imagined reminiscences of shared friends (San Francisco Examiner & Chronicle, 1975). Many households apparently organize this holiday chore into a routinized task system which accepts return addresses as input and produces stamped and labeled envelopes as output. The clerks' handling room requests from minority guests mirrors a similar organizational routine. Langer, Blank, and Chanowitz (1978) explored such routinized responding more systematically. They determined from discarded office memos that there was a typical manner of writing memos to secretaries, which they called "impersonal requests." Persons directing the work of a secretary write in a "Please do this" mode and with no signature. Believing that individuals respond to cues which invoke a certain "action script," Langer and her associates suggested that secretaries would respond to a field stimulation which cue this "impersonal request" script. They sent this unsigned note: "I would appreciate it if you would return this paper immediately to Room 238 through interoffice mail." Ninety percent of the secretaries did, fifty percent more than those who received notes which did not tap into the impersonal request script.

Many an investigator's hypothesis can be tested from just the response to his questionnaire. To illustrate this, we reanalyzed several *ASQ* reports. Ondrack (1975), for example, was interested in socialization in nursing schools and sent questionnaires to teachers, graduating students, and entering students of three nursing schools. The socialization effects are evident in the participation rates to his survey. If socialization were operating, the decisions of nursing students to participate would be predictable from the decisions of the teaching staff. The underlying notion of socialization is that the teachers pass on their expectations or models of conduct to the students. Since this transmission takes time, it is correct to deduce that the participation of the graduating students would be predicted by the participation of the teachers but that the participation of the entering students would not. The graduating students' response rates were significantly related to the teachers' according to $RR_{gs} = .986 \, RR_t .438$. In contrast, the response rates of the new students were independent of the teachers' $(r = -.16)$.

Ouchi and Johnson (1978) reveal similar theoretically relevant response differences from their study of Type A and Type Z companies. Type A managers are said to be independent and manage as they please as long as they are successful. Type Z managers, however, are expected to behave cooperatively and humanistically. If true, such distinctions should have affected participation in Ouchi and Johnson's study. Such appears to be the case. Ouchi and Johnson reported that Type A managers were more erratic in making appointments and kept them waiting longer for the interview to start. Moreover, cooperation from the managers' spouses in the survey was greater for Company Z than for Company A (chi-squared, corrected for continuity = 3.96; p = .047).

Another case is the response to Van Maanen's (1975) police socialization study. He administered questionnaires to four different groups of police recruits, which had been on the force either 0, 1, 3 or 4 months when he began to survey them for five months more. Thus Van Maanen has participation rates for police on the job for 0 through 9 months. His interest focuses on the commitment of the police recruit to his job over these nine months of experience, and he suggests that enthusiasm at first increases and then drastically drops with experience. As Van Maanen notes, an attitude develops over time which advises, "Lay low, hang loose, and don't expect too much" (p. 225). If this attitude develops as indicated, then the participation rates should reflect it by fitting to a quadratic function of the number of months in the organization, such as $a_0 + a_1 MO + a_2 MO^2$, where MO is the number of months. Just such a function fit the data reasonably well (R^2 = .62), with the peak at four or five months.

Field Stimulation Experiments

The major value of field stimulation as a strategy for research lies not merely in analyzing the basis for responses but in the freedom which the method allows in manipulating the conditions of a response, and hence the conditions for organizational behavior.

Field stimulation methods invite a much needed playfulness into research. Too many social scientists fantasize about "what would happen if . . ." and then pour devoutly over survey returns as if life were trapped beneath the pencil marks. It might be far better to tamper with organizations just to find out what makes them tick. Instead of wondering what will happen if a firm had to face a crisis, one might consider going out and organizing a crisis for it.

A playful approach has uncovered some interesting social phenomena for the field of social psychology. For instance, Bryan and Test (1966) learned a lot about why people stop to help a motorist in distress by parking a car on the free-way and letting the air out of a tire. And Romer (1977) learned that suburbanites will call an automobile repair ser-vice for a distressed motorist if he first informs them that it is a Lincoln that suffers rather than a Chevrolet; but, in the slums, the mention of a Chevrolet will get more help. Mann and his students (1977) have learned that Israelis will not queue up for a bus unless six confederates first started a neat and proper English line. And Pennebaker and Sanders (1976) learned that an effective way to get university men to write graffiti was to put a sign in the toilet stall which said "DO NOT WRITE ON THE WALLS," and attribute it to a high authority. But Moriarty (1975) discovered that beach-bathers will more likely chase a thief who stole another's radio if the victim first delegates responsibility for his things to the bathers — a good lesson for managing subordinates. Uranowitz (1975) learned that a person's enthusiasm for helping others is dampened when he first helps someone else. And Garfinkel (1967) has shown his students that if they call a supermarket manager over to the canned peas and say, "Tell ya what: I'll give ya 25 cents for these instead of 35 cents," they are quite likely to get a reduction.

These above studies focus on individual behavior and de-spite their light nature, are based in theoretical rigor. Fewer field stimulation studies have dealt with organizational be-havior. But such methods can reveal something about an organization, its structures, its routines, what it attends to and what it ignores, and about its relations with other or-ganizations. The telephone company, for instance, seems best able to deal with unusual circumstances when those circumstances can be transformed to fit their routine of balancing computer billing cards against computer payment received cards. And Langer and her associates (1978) illus-trated how organizational scripts enable a person to cope with receiving a letter that said nothing more than to mail it back.

The extent to which organizations are capable of transform-ing external stimuli into events for which they are designed to respond is almost too great to comprehend. We first ob-served this in a series of studies on book companies. We wrote publishers about the status of a book order, and indi-cated degrees of urgency by noting the class would meet in two weeks (summer) or in two months (fall). The replies were invariant to urgency, averaging two weeks. In another experiment we intimated that we were canceling orders that existed if we couldn't be assured of the material within certain time periods. We received the same invariant two-week reply. Even a message that says, "Contact me immediately about my order!" provokes little. One infers from these replies that the firms are responding to their own rhythms. A grand display of this came when we wrote a magazine to cancel the remainder of a nonexistent subscription. Two messages were received in return. The first thanked us for our recent order and informed us that delivery might require several weeks to begin; the second regretted our recent cancellation but assured us the unused portion of our subscription would be returned. With such impeccable logic working for us, we couldn't resist penning another note on the cancellation card: "Please cancel my cancellation. I have decided not to move after all." Magazines flowed thereafter.

The invariances in organizational responses are informative because they suggest what an organization takes to be its routine environment. But it is often more interesting to find similar organizations which respond differently, for they inform us about how the organization conceives of its environment. Thus, for instance, book publishers respond faster and through a different system when letters of concern are sent indicating a carbon is being sent to a bookstore that handles a lot of their business. Many of the organizational differences can be quite visible. Goodsell (1976) observed postal clerks in Costa Rica and the United States conducting business for confederates posed as high or low status customers. He found that U.S. clerks greeted clients neutrally without regard to their status but that the Costa Rican clerks greeted the high status confederate positively and low status confederate neutrally or negatively. Moreover, when the customer protested the cost of a stamp and claimed the price quoted was inaccurate, the Americans defended themselves with manuals against the high status clients while the Costa Ricans maintained a polite deference.

Goodsell's study tells us about cultural roles, but similar methods can be used to study organizational roles. In another study, we sent a note to the presidents of ten firms which read in part, "A colleague of yours told me that you might be the most appropriate person to ask . . . . What was the exact date of the founding of your firm?" Eight presidents responded within three weeks. However, when we inserted "An employee" in place of "A colleague" and sent the letter to another ten firms, only two presidents and three secretaries wrote back.

Another use of the field stimulation method is to select different types of organizations to stimulate. A recent study of the affirmative action programs by U.S. industrial firms used this variation (Salancik, 1979). Department of Defense contractors were sent an inquiry about management opportunities for women MBAs. The speed and quality of their replies were used to assess how affirmative were their attempts to attract women job candidates. The analysis concerned the effects of the firm's dependencies on the U.S. government for contract sales. The more affirmative firms were those which were more dependent on the government, consistent with typical theories of interorganizational power.

Another study reveals how different firms partition their environment. Marketing firms were asked to send information about their services. The requests were made either by a potential job candidate, a potential client, or university researcher. The point of analysis was to examine if the agencies differentiated these three publics in their replies. About half did; more importantly, firms with longer histories were more likely to differentiate the audiences. The longevity of a firm was estimated from the presence of its name for over fifteen years in the telephone book.

The studies described thus far might give the impression that field stimulations are useful only for examining the external relations of organizations. This unfortunate conclusion, however, would be a slap in the face of our intentions to encourage imagination. The numerous studies on client relations reflect our interest. Studies of internal organizational processes can be done with field stimulations but require a little more doing. The analysis of participation rates illustrates analysis of internal processes. Additionally, Schwartz and Skolnick (1962) gave application folders of bogus job seekers to 100 employers, and varied the presence of information about criminal records. They asked the employers if the applicant could be used in their firms. The number answering yes diminished when a criminal record was indicated, even when the record indicated acquittal. Similarly, we found that women were less likely to be found suitable for management positions than men using bogus profiles (Salancik, 1979).

It is also possible to study employees' attitudes through field stimulation methods. In a study conducted by Sue Trieber and myself, employees of an organization were telephoned several times during the year. The conversations induced them to attribute their absenteeism from the job to either intrinsic personal causes or extrinsic environmental causes. The intrinsically induced persons were more likely to still be in their jobs one and a half years later, a result contrary to the theory that underlies the study. In another study of employee attitudes, I am organizing an attempt to develop positive feelings toward jobs in fast food restaurants. The design calls for a confederate to order a drink from the cashier/ordertakers of MacDonald's and Hardee's and in the course of the transaction to interject, "You seem to like your job. Don't you?" This leading question invites the workers to search for confirming evidence from their knowledge of the situation. The effects will be observed over time on service and turnover. Of course, it is not necessary to use such elaborate methods in order to induce positive moods in people. Isen et al. (1978) did so merely by handing free gifts to patrons of a shopping mall.

A CONCLUDING NOTE ON ETHICS AND EFFICACY

This outline of possibilities for field studies may raise questions about the ethics and scientific status of stimulating behaviors for study. While we cannot answer them for everyone, we offer some thoughts about them in conclusion.

On the surface, it seems remote that survey participation rates reflect socialization practices. Similarly, the possibility that a firm's letter about management opportunities for women reflects its compliance with public laws seems tenuous and removed. Indeed, most of the data from field studies seem distant from the concepts they purport to reflect — because they are. In fact, it is true about any data (Brunswik, 1934). The relationship between an observation and the interpretation of that observation exists always as a tenuous proposition. It might seem therefore that field stimulations should be avoided because they cannot be interpreted clearly. The questionnaire method thus may seem a favored alternative. However, one does not escape such hard realities by the fact that one collects data by asking people questions. There too data link tenuously to theory. Consider asking "Do you like me?" and finding someone answer "yes." Does the response therefore answer the question? It sounds as if it does. It follows the question and relates back to the question. All seems quite orderly, and it would be easy to conclude that the causal basis for the answer is exactly what the question implies. And yet, there are alternative causal bases for this as for any response. The answer could be demanded by cultural propriety, or reflect a personal desire not to disappoint a fellow human being. Or it could reflect a misattributed momentary arousal. It could also be quite irrelevant because the concept of "like" intended by the interviewer is not shared by the respondent.

In short, there is no difference in the problem of linking data to theory for different methodologies. All that really differs might be the ease with which investigators accept particular causal assumptions. Questionnaire responses can seem far more real to us because they are more familiar and we have stopped questioning their bases. For this reason alone we would recommend researchers consider stimulating other responses from organizations and individuals. It will place upon them a burden of thought to attend to the details of the subject, its actions, and the context of those actions.

Field stimulation studies also raise serious ethical matters. But here too issues are murky and directions uncertain. For one, experiments represent the continual flow of human action, practiced by all individuals and organizations. OPEC's increase in the price of crude oil, for instance, is an experiment of sorts in that it introduces a new event into people's lives. It is done for the theoretical effects it will have on those same people's lives. Similarly, when a firm's management moves an organization from a five-day to a four-day work week an experimental intervention is being made. Indeed, even the U.S. government's guidelines for research on human subjects is an experiment affecting researchers and the results they obtain from their experiments (Gardner, 1978).

Since we cannot escape these interruptions, additions, and deletions from our lives, it becomes more sensible to ask under what conditions such manipulations are to be considered ethical or not ethical. One common guideline is that research subjects have informed consent, that participation be voluntary. This guideline, however, would disallow the administrative experiments to which we are subjected without consultation. Last winter, administrators we know closed their organization's furnaces periodically to see how it could save on fuel. Not only were employees not consulted but protests from them brought polite advice to wear sweaters. Is this ethical? Some might suggest that turning down a thermostat to evaluate cost savings is proper execution of managerial prerogatives and not in the realm of experiments, or ethics. If so, then anything within the domains of a "true" experimenter's prerogative must by logical extension also be excluded as subject to guidelines of informed consent. But this would exclude most anything a researcher might consider doing.

The above point and counterpoint could be extended indefinitely, but it would be more useful to recognize instead that the ethics of an action do not vary by the fact that they are part of a research project or not. Some acts are simply unethical or illegal. And others are merely indecent. Middlemist, Knowles, and Matter (1976), for instance, studied the effects of the presence of another on the micturations of men. They noted, as several theories would predict, that the speed and duration is reduced, and observed this when a confederate was present or not through an effectively concealed periscope. While this study was quite within an experimenter's rights and purview, it is, in our opinion, also distasteful. But so too, in our opinion, is handing out gifts in shopping malls.

REFERENCES

Brunswik, Egon
1934 Perception and Representative Design of Psychological Research, 2d ed (1956). Berkeley: University of California Press.

Bryan, J. H., and Mary Ann Test
1966 "A lady in distress: The flat tire experiment." Unpublished manuscript, Department of Psychology, Northwestern University.

Campbell, Donald T.
1965 "Pattern matching as an essential to distal knowing." In K. R. Hammond (ed.), The Psychology of Egon Brunswik. New York: Holt, Rinehart and Winston.

Gardner, G. T.
1978 "Effects of federal human subjects regulations on data obtained in environmental stressor research." Journal of Personality and Social Psychology, 36: 628–634.

Garfinkel, H.
1967 Studies in Ethnomethodology. Englewood Cliffs, NJ: Prentice-Hall.

Goodsell, Charles T.
1976 "Cross-cultural comparison of behavior of postal clerks towards clients." Administrative Science Quarterly, 21: 140–150.

Isen, A. M., T. E. Shalker, M. Clark, and L. Karp
1978 "Affect, accessibility of material in memory, and behavior." Journal of Personality and Social Psychology, 36: 1–12.

Kerlinger, F. N.
1964 Foundations of Behavioral Research. New York: Holt, Rinehart, and Winston.

Langer, Ellen, A. Blank, and B. Chanowitz
1978 "The mindlessness of ostensibly thoughtful action: The role of 'placebic' information in interpersonal interaction." Journal of Personality and Social Psychology, 36: 635–642.

La Piere, Robert T.
1934 "Attitudes vs. actions." Social Forces, 13: 230–237.

Mann, Leon
1977 "The effect of stimulus queues on queue-joining behavior." Journal of Personality and Social Psychology, 35: 437–442.

Middlemist, R. D., E. S. Knowles, and C. F. Matter
1976 "Personal space invasions in the lavatory: Suggestive evidence for arousal." Journal of Personality and Social Psychology, 33: 541–546.

Moriarty, Thomas
1975 "Crime, commitment, and the responsive bystander: Two

field experiments." Journal of Personality and Social Psychology, 31: 370–376.

Ondrack, D. A.
1975 "Socialization in professional schools: A comparative study." Administrative Science Quarterly, 20: 97–103.

Ouchi, William G., and Jerry B. Johnson
1978 "Types of organizational control and their relationship to emotional well being." Administrative Science Quarterly, 23: 293–330.

Pennebaker, J. W., and D. Y. Sanders
1976 "American graffiti: Effects of authority and reactance arousal." Personality and Social Psychology Bulletin, 2: 264–267.

Romer, D., M. Bontemps, M. Flynn, T. McGuire, and C. Gruder
1977 "The effects of status similarity and expectation of reciprocity upon altruistic behavior." Personality and Social Psychology Bulletin, 3: 103–106.

Roos, Leslie L., Jr.
1978 "Institutional change, career mobility, and job satisfaction." Administrative Science Quarterly, 23: 318–330.

Salancik, G. R.
1966 Selective Responding in Survey Situations. Master's thesis, Medill School of Journalism, Northwestern University.
1979 "Interorganizational dependence and responsiveness to affirmative action: The case of women and defense contractors." Academy of Management Journal, 22: 375–394.

San Francisco Sunday Examiner and Chronicle
1975 "Cards for proper strangers." December 21: page 11.

Schwartz, R. D., and J. H. Skolnick
1962 "Two studies of legal stigma." Social Problems, 10: 133–142.

Speak, Mary
1964 "Some characteristics of respondents, partial-respondents, and non-respondents to questionnaires on job satisfaction." Occupational Psychology, 38: 173–182.

Uranowitz, S. W.
1975 "Helping and self attributions: A field experiment." Journal of Personality and Social Psychology, 31: 852–854.

Van Maanen, John
1975 "Police socialization: A longitudinal examination of job attitudes in an urban police department." Administrative Science Quarterly, 20: 207–228.

Webb, E. J., D. T. Campbell, R. D. Schwartz, and L. Sechrest
1966 Unobtrusive Measures. Chicago: Rand McNally.

Webb, E. J., and G. R. Salancik
1970 "Supplementing the self-report in attitude measurement." In G. F. Summers (ed.), Attitude Measurement: 317–330. Chicago: Rand McNally.

Unobtrusive Measures in Organizational Theory: A Reminder

Eugene Webb
Karl E. Weick

The purpose of this article is to review and tighten the relationship between unobtrusive measures (Webb et al., 1966) and organizational inquiry and, in the process, to remind investigators that these measures continue to be workable, credible components of multimethod inquiry.

The object of interest is found in this illustration:

You know, I am really stupid. For years I have looked for the perfect pencil. I have found very good ones, but never the perfect one. And all the time it was not the pencils but me. A pencil that is all right some days is no good another day. For example, yesterday I used a special pencil soft and fine and it floated over the paper just wonderfully. So this morning I tried the same kind. And they crack on me. Points break and all hell is let loose. This is the day when I am stabbing the paper. So today I need a harder pencil at least for a while. I am using some that are #2 & ⅜. I have my plastic tray you know and in it three kinds of pencils for hard writing days and soft writing days. Only sometimes it changes in the middle of the day, but at least I am equipped for it. I have also some super-soft pencils which I do not use very often because I must feel as delicate as a rose petal to use them. And I am not often that way. But when I do have such moments I am prepared. It is always well to be prepared. Pencils are a great expense to me and I hope you know it. I buy them four dozen at a time. When in my normal writing position the metal of the pencil eraser touches my hand, I retire that pencil (Steinbeck, 1969: 35–36).

The recent enthusiasm for variations on Murphy's Law has produced marvelous exhibits of unobtrusive measures (Faber, 1979):

1. The more sophisticated the equipment, the bigger the adjustment department needed (p. 34);
2. The quality of food and service is inversely proportional to the captivity of the clientele (p. 37);
3. The quality of food in a restaurant is in inverse proportion to the number of semi-colons and exclamation marks on the menu (p. 38);
4. You can tell how bad the musical is by how many times the chorus yells hooray (p. 46);
5. The number of agency people required to shoot a commercial on location is in direct proportion to the mean temperature of the location (p. 50);
6. The length of a country's national anthem is inversely proportional to the importance of the country (p. 71);
7. In war, victory goes to those armies whose leaders' uniforms are least impressive (p. 112).

If we think of organizational inquiry as involving three steps — design, data collection, and analysis — an assessment of the field will show that there has been a substantial increase in the complexity and requisite variety of design (e.g., Cook and Campbell, 1979) and analysis (Tukey, 1977). But there has not been a corresponding increase in the complexity of data-collection techniques. Data collection in organizational inquiry is characterized by satisficing, and people who value unobtrusive measures are restless in the face of that conclusion.

The term unobtrusive measures has become something of a ceremonial citation that signifies sympathy toward multi-method inquiry, triangulation, playfulness in data collection, outcroppings as measures, and alternatives to self-report. The search for alternatives to self-report directly joins unobtrusive measures to current issues in organizational inquiry.

While investigators regularly detail the limits of self-report they also regularly say that despite these limits, the methods are good enough. They acknowledge that self-report involves small ideas generated by overly surveyed people that are overinterpreted, yet they continue to collect such data. This contradiction originates in several places.

Self-report also remains the dominant style of measurement because investigators have dealt continually with articulate populations. Less articulate populations, because they had neither time nor interest nor talent to work with self-report measures, are underrepresented in organizational research. Self-report measures seem to be used with higher levels of organizations, unobtrusive measures such as turnover with lower level portions of organizations such as the assembly line. In the latter case, the usage of unobtrusive measures seems to allow investigators to avoid talking to people and finding out what really goes on and what work is really like. If self-reports were extended downward, and unobtrusive measures upward, inquiry should become more valid as well as more interesting.

Finally, self-reports persist partly because the field relies heavily on cognitive concepts, concepts that are more readily operationalized by talk than by other traces.

Unobtrusive measures seem to be associated with and induce a different set toward data collection than is true for self-report measures. Some characteristics of this set are implicit in earlier discussions by Palmer and McGuire (1973), Bouchard (1976), Sechrest (1976), and Webb and Ellsworth (1976); this article makes six of these characteristics explicit.

1. Investigators construct and impose multiple indices that converge. The concern with multiples turns on the fact that it takes multiples of some form to capture and preserve multiples in the phenomenon of interest (i.e., organizations). These sensing multiples can be multiple hypotheses (people who use unobtrusive measures are convinced it is as important to develop banks of hypotheses as banks of data), multiple theoretical degrees of freedom (Campbell, 1975), multiple indicators, and multiple methods. The person concerned with multiples faces the question that if organizations are complex, does that mean that many different complex methods should be directed simultaneously at the phenomenon of interest or that many different indices within a single method (e.g., a battery of unobtrusive measures) should be used? In either case the intention is to match the variety of the source with variety in the sensing device that is applied to it (e.g., Weick, 1979: 188–193).

The tight coupling between multiples and unobtrusive measures, however, sometimes works against adoption of this procedure. Some people avoid using unobtrusive measures because they assume you can use them *only if* you also use a multimethod battery. And since a multimethod battery is complex and time consuming, to avoid it is to avoid unobtrusive measures. People may also avoid unobtrusive measures because they feel they add little information to that gained from other methods in a multimethod inquiry. Or unobtrusive measures are avoided because, when used in combination with other measures, the fact of multiplicity increases the likelihood that the resulting data will be inconsistent. To avoid the difficult task of interpreting contradictions, people avoid multiple measures.

2. Investigators assume that noise is rare. People who use unobtrusive measures think in terms of a signal-to-noise ratio, but tend to be generous in their definition of signal. The person using unobtrusive measures presumes that most of the world contains informative indicators and that it is silly to ignore outcroppings because they seem nonserious, untraditional, or puzzling. The image of a signal-to-noise ratio reminds people that they reject much information that is available, that the definition of what is signal and what is noise is variable, and that there will be dross in any observational setting.

An example of an unobtrusive measure is the number of bar transactions in Chicago's O'Hare airport before and after an air tragedy. It exemplifies the signal-to-noise ratio in the sense that those bar transactions do not involve just purchases of hard liquor. Nonalcoholic beverages, snacks, cigarettes, sweets, aspirin, and remedies for upset stomachs are also requested on those checks. To some investigators those "extras" are a nuisance whereas those who are sympathetic toward unobtrusive measures see no reason to assume a priori that such extras are meaningless as indicators of shifts in anxiety. Unobtrusive measures buy a lot of dirty details. To some that is their strength, to others it is their greatest liability.

3. Investigators believe in amortization. Unobtrusive measures are sometimes viewed as flawed because they are generated outside of the investigator's direct control. If an investigator manufactures data by the means of an experiment or an interview then those data are thought to be more scientific than if the data were manufactured by someone else and were picked up opportunistically by the investigator. The way to preserve this point is to argue that "hard scientists don't believe in amortization." Hard science seems to be based on the premise that there can be only a single purpose for data and that the investigator should be the one who designs and defines that purpose and creates the universe so that it is ideal for scientific purposes. Data created for other purposes are seen as neither scientific nor hard. People who favor unobtrusive measures find that stance counterproductive and naive.

4. Investigators find foolishness functional. Unobtrusive measures have come to be associated with a light-hearted, playful stance toward the world in data collection. This stance furthers science in several ways. If the same event, for example, is regarded as both absurd and serious then more of it is likely to be seen because, in fact, it contains both qualities. Foolish interludes generate novel inputs and permit people to recognize and break the singular focus toward a problem in which they had persisted. Foolish interludes disconfirm assumptions thereby creating interest (Davis, 1971), put distance between the observer and the phenomenon, sustain morale, recruit interest in the topic, aid retention, facilitate the content and process of free association, expose assumptions, forestall criticism that degenerates into cynicism, offset the preoccupation with rational models that is characteristic of organizational inquiry, and insert topics into inquiry (e.g., managing as Chinese baseball in Siu, 1978) that wouldn't be acknowledged or accepted if introduced in a more straightforward manner.

Enthusiasts for unobtrusive measures can be openly playful, which means that they can be playful with vigor, which means they can extract all of the benefits that flow from humor when it is done well. Playfulness becomes more exhibitionistic, less constructive, and more artful the more it is done hesitantly, self-consciously, and apologetically. Playfulness is risky among colleagues hardened to cute experiments, clever concepts, and artful prose. But to compromise playfulness with seriousness is to engage in neither and to offend enthusiasts of both.

5. Investigators ponder the variance rather than the mean. People who use unobtrusive measures presume that the variance is at least as interesting as the mean and typically more so. For people interested in organizations, the key question is, how do you get low variation? If individual differences are so abundant, then how can it be that for some populations in some settings, there is so little difference visible? This is the kind of question that lends itself to unobtrusive measures and it is the kind of question that interests people who use unobtrusive measures to understand organizations. For example, many theories of power are conspiratorial (e.g., Pfeffer, 1977) and one of the best indicators of conspiratorial power is a lack of variance. Governance of Washington, often said to be insensitive yet consistent, can be indexed by the fact that much of the district's governance is done by people who have zip codes clustered in areas *outside* the district (Washburn, 1967). The unobtrusive measure of similarity of zip code (low variance) when the expectation is a higher variance suggests the presence of organizing and pattern where none was suspected.

6. Investigators use expectancy as a control. Expectancies are the controls of both common sense and science; surprise is an indicator of the abuse of expectancies. What people don't do, who isn't in a network, practices that weren't made, are data and they become data because of the a priori expectations that existed. Thus, sophisticated and successful use of unobtrusive measures requires that investigators lay out in advance what they expect to find so that the surprise when they don't find it is visible and documented. Everyone, for example, appoints a chairman for meetings, especially when those meetings are consequential. However, given this expectancy as a control, the fact that Kennedy didn't appoint a chairman of the deliberations on the Cuban Missile Crisis becomes an indicator of added interest. To identify an omission and to judge its significance is to have an elaborated set of expectancies readily at hand. Enthusiasts for unobtrusive measures tend to be eclectics, and one reason for this is the presence among eclectics of wide-ranging sets of expectancies, some of which become disconfirmed and attract attention no matter what the organizational event.

DEADLINES: UNOBTRUSIVE MEASURES AT WORK

As an example of a phenomenon articulated and studied by a family of investigations — some direct, some unobtrusive, — we can consider work on the effect of deadlines. The history of the word deadline shows it to be grounded in an engagingly attractive organization control mechanism. Its nineteenth-century beginning was as a line drawn in the soil around a group of prisoners. Anyone stepping outside that line significantly shortened his life span. Currently, deadlines are less noxious. They serve as general control devices for both individuals and organizations, signaling the seasons of some organizations and setting a rhythm for the activities of the organization's members.

The characteristics of that rhythm setting were the concern of a group of students at the Stanford Business School in the early 1970s. The group converged around Hull's marvelously simple idea: the goal gradient hypothesis. Hull (1934) had proposed that the approach velocity of a hungry rat increases exponentially as it nears a food source.

To explore that idea in naturalistic settings, both observational and archival approaches were used. The first check on Hull's hypothesis was a failure. The Minneapolis airport, and its long escalator, provided the setting for the informal test: do people accelerate speed (i.e, begin walking on the escalator) as the end of the ride nears? Does the density distribution look related to the goal gradient? A wasted 45 minutes showed no cross-species support for Hull's finding with rats. People started walking at all points on the ride, even after one partialled out the "how-many-in-front" effect.

But in the spirit of multiple measures (and don't give up the hypothesis) thinking, the goal gradient generality was tested by two organizational deadline investigations. The first (Jerrell, 1973) looked at the rate of applications to the Stanford Graduate School of Business. The second (Glenn, 1974) examined the "makeup" rate of incompletes in the School of Education at Stanford. Both archival checks showed support for the proposition that organizational deadlines do indeed appear to pull behavior from relevant populations.

In the business school study, Jerrell noted that two deadlines existed for applications; the first, if one applied for financial aid, and the second, for admission independent of financial questions. Plotting the rate of applications against these two deadline dates, Jerrell found a nicely scalloped curve. The applications slant up exponentially as the first deadline is approached, drop off and then start the exponential rise to the second and last deadline.

Glenn showed similar curves when students make up incomplete grades. The institution establishes a quarterly deadline to file the incompleted work and the behavioral activity curve races up in frequency as each deadline nears and then falls away as it passes. The patterns detected by Jerrell and Glenn were replicated over several years.

Lest one feel this to be an unduly limited probing — one limited to the unreal world of the academy and its occupants — the field of inquiry was extended to two very real-world settings: the New York Stock Exchange and the National Football League. Using available records, Grauer (1973) traced the intraday trading volume of the Big Board. Was the approaching final bell for trading associated with trading volume? Grauer found the expected pattern. Trading was heavy in the early hours (as overnight orders were executed), dipped in midday, and then escalated as the closing bell neared — simple support for the deadline effect.

This support was strengthened by asking what happened in the pattern of trading when the New York Stock Exchange extended its closing time from 3:00 to 3:30. The answer is that nothing happened. When the closing time was 3:00, the last two hours showed escalating trading. When the closing time was 3:30, again the last two hours showed escalating trading; the activity curve simply shifted half a notch to the right. The closing bell was the marker, the magnetic draw, not the economic variables of the hour. Grauer also demonstrated that the gradient of the end-of-day trading slope was greater on Friday than on other days. With two days of no trading ahead, Friday's closing bell had a particularly potent pull. (It should be noted that this is a pattern analysis independent of the absolute number of shares traded.)

Grauer took advantage of another naturally-generated time variable. Because of the inability of brokerage houses to process orders, the New York Stock Exchange closed on Wednesdays for a while in 1969 — thus moving to a four-day trading week. He had observed the Friday difference: end-of-day trading was higher with the prospect of two days of non-trading. But what now happens to the *shape* of the trading curve on Tuesdays? With no trading on Wednesday, does the deadline effect become more pronounced? The simple answer is yes. A second-difference analysis shows the end-of-day trading slopes steeper for four-day work week Tuesdays than for five-day work week Tuesdays.

In this allegedly most rational of worlds, trading on the Big Board, the deadline gradient effect was observed for individual day trading and for end-of-sequence (work week) trading.

Yet another natural occurrence of deadline behavior is on the football field. In his pilot study for a provocative dissertation on play-calling behavior, Fischer (1973) used archival records to track the number of plays executed per quarter in professional football games. The deadline characteristic is slightly different than that found in the stock market investigation. The market closes at 3:30 EST, but a football game ends when 60 minutes of elaborately calculated playing time has expired. Now rank those quarters in order of the mean number of plays executed by both teams. A subtle student of football (and/or an advanced cost-benefit analyst) might have predicted Fischer's findings. In order of frequency of total plays executed: Quarter 2 > Quarter 4 > Quarter 3 = Quarter 1.

By the nature of the rules of American football, the second and fourth quarters are deadline quarters, while the first and third quarters are not. Possession of the ball is unaffected by the end of the first and third quarters. So the data support the general notion that a deadline promotes higher activity. That the mean number of plays is greater in the second quarter than in the fourth quarter, illustrates that a deadline can be both a friend and a foe. For the team leading in points during the fourth quarter, there is a strong disincentive to execute plays, the goal being one of letting time expire while one is still ahead. The losing team does all it can to accelerate the rate of play as it attempts to catch up. Toward the end of the second quarter, there is no such strategy divergence. Both teams would like to run plays and make points before the closing of the half. Thus, the greatest number of plays is in the second quarter.

In a less playful vein, there is Weiner's (1973) study of the effect of an imposed deadline on organizational decision making. Weiner examined the properties of the desegregation actions of the San Francisco Unified School District. Working within a garbage can model (Cohen, March, and Olsen, 1972) Weiner traced the appearance of the desegregation issue, the lack of decisive action, and the final organizational move triggered by a judge's mandate — a 50-day deadline by which a desegregation plan was to be submitted. Students of the theory of organized anarchies might attempt a prediction of organizational processes before consulting Weiner's study as a genuine tumbling garbage can at work.

We conclude this discussion of deadline research with two studies, neither of which is unobtrusive, but both of which are within the same research group. Dowling (1973) was interested in cultural differences in time perception and exploited the available subject pool of foreign students at Stanford as subjects. Using a questionnaire approach, he asked about time behavior in one's home country. How late can one be for work without being "too" late? How much time must pass beyond the scheduled start of a concert before it is "late starting"? What time would one appear at the restaurant for a 12:15 lunch date? Dowling showed a cultural difference, with Northern Europeans stating that they adhere more closely to time cues. One must keep all of this in perspective, however. Dowling plugged the notion of role into his questioning and asked what time one would show up for a 12:15 lunch if one person were a prospective employer and the other were a prospective employee. It will surprise few readers to learn that there was a difference in reported punctuality; the potential employee is reported to arrive earlier.

Arvedson (1974) has conducted the most thorough investigation of deadline effects. He studied the effect of setting various deadlines for the solution of an anagram and the influence of suggesting to subjects that the allocated time was short or long. This factorial study is studded with interesting findings about deadlines, but two are of particular note here. One relates to the property of deadlines that keeps people working, the other to the success rate when subjects think they have a short or long deadline.

Arvedson ran 51 subjects in a control condition in which no time deadline was mentioned. Six of these 51 nondeadline subjects gave up and said they could not solve the anagram; only one of the 157 subjects who had a deadline gave up. They may not have solved the problem but they were still working. Whatever else it may do, the deadline has an energizing function.

A second finding is that performance rate is greater when people are led to believe that they have a "long" versus a "short" time to do the job. When a constant eight minutes was available to work the anagram problem, 42 percent of those who were told their time was "short" completed the task. For those told they had a "long" time to do the task, 55 percent completed the job. A deadline, as in eight minutes to do a job, is not a deadline; it depends on the social reference. It should surprise no student of organizations that a labeling exercise, even if false, of what is an appropriate criterion of time in which to do a job has an effect.

CONTROL: UNOBTRUSIVE MEASURES AT WORK

Unobtrusive measures can both reshuffle thinking about traditional organizational topics and introduce nontraditional topics such as deadlines to the field. To illustrate how traditional themes are reopened when measured unobtrusively, consider the issue of control. Organizations are effective to the extent that they control variation in the actions of their employees by constraints and comparisons. This key principle of organizational theory has been explored primarily by asking who has muscle and how is that muscle exhibited? Efforts at control leave other traces, however, and our purpose here is to list some of these.

Control is indexed most literally by how easy it is to get into and out of the physical plant of the organization. Organizations concerned with trade secrets (e.g., toy manufacturers) have fewer entrances to their premises than do less concerned organizations. More constraint is visible when calls go through a central switchboard rather than directly to the people being contacted, when home phone numbers are not given out by office switchboard operators, when background checks become more extensive, when the number of master keys in circulation decreases and the number of gradations in the master key system increase, and when "security risks" are defined more broadly. Written documents index control in such ways as explicit discussions of control in annual reports, coercive elements in employee handbooks, and in the thickness of procedure manuals distributed by headquarters to branch organizations as well as the degree to which those manuals have been thumbed and marked. If, for example, Lufthansa employees in North America receive manuals that are four inches thick while the desks of Air France employees contain manuals only one-half inch thick, we can infer the presence of differences in constraint. Discretionary behaviors provide unobtrusive measures of control. The amount of money people allocate before they are subject to review is sensitive to differences in constraint. As a variant, one could ask, "How much money does it take to get the attention of the provost at Cornell, the Secretary of the Army, the president of Bechtel?" While these sums are diagnostic in their own right, all such figures will have exceptions (e.g., the Secretary wants to know about *all* allocations involving programs for women) and these exceptions are clues to the political realities faced by such people.

Structural traces reveal control emphases. Organizational charts identify nominal controls and who figures in whose plans to bypass an immediate superior and get a wider hearing. The labels on organizational charts represent efforts to control expectations, requests, and accountability. The presence of oversight committees represents an effort to reduce the power of outsiders and to increase the diversity of views considered. Formal arrangements to bypass portions of an organizational chart, as when managers are required to go to their subordinate's subordinates to get input for any major decision, represent an effort to reduce the effects of filtering and to discover bad news before it becomes a disaster.

As noted earlier, low variance signifies the potential presence of control and this low variance can meaningfully range across items as diverse as dress, wall trappings, names, departments through which interdepartmental mail envelopes have previously circulated, zip codes of residence, time of arrival or departure, sports preferences, seating at meetings, format of daily calendar, jewelry, formality of telephone greeting, etc. These measures, all of which are obvious, tend to be overlooked in favor of what people say about the control they exert and receive. Since that talk may itself be controlled in such a way that crucial phenomena are selectively inattended and/or represented in innocuous images, cross-checking by other less influenceable measures is especially crucial (Edwards, 1979).

CONCLUSION

Our reconsideration of unobtrusive measures suggests that, for organizational questions, ceremonial citation should be turned into substance. Heavy prior reliance on self-report has excluded crucial populations from organizational inquiry, postponed cross-checking of propositions, inflated the apparent consequentiality of minor irritations in the workplace, and imposed a homogeneity of method which raises the prospect that the findings of the field are method-specific. Further development and application of unobtrusive measures should offset the tendency to satisfice in data collection and should add variety to inquiry that registers a greater proportion of the variety in ongoing organizations (Daft and Wiginton, 1979). The provocativeness of that registry is evident in a final illustration which comes from a description by Lazard (1946:168) of the psychological consequences of living for two years under an assumed name in occupied France to avoid being arrested by the Germans.

I have already said that I was friendly with the priest in the neighboring village whom I had taken into my confidence. I asked him one day what he thought of an existence which placed one constantly under a deliberate lie. He knew what I meant and replied that as far as he was concerned it was of no importance theologically, that the only truth was that due to God. I stayed more than an hour with him, speaking of a thousand things. When I was leaving, the woman (who had some suspicions about my identity) entered by the garden. He said to me, "Wait five minutes in that little room on the side there before coming out. It will be better if you are not seen now. After such a conversation as we have had there sometimes remain on the face things which one would prefer to hide."

REFERENCES

Arvedson, L. A.
1974 Deadlines and Organizational Behavior: A Laboratory Investigation of the Effect of Deadlines on Individual Task Performance. Doctoral dissertation proposal, Graduate School of Business, Stanford University.

Bouchard, T. J.
1976 "Unobtrusive measures: An inventory of uses." Sociological Methods and Research, 4: 267–300.

Campbell, D. T.
1975 "Degrees of freedom and the case study." Comparative Political Studies, 8: 178–193.

Cohen, Michael D., James G. March, and Johan P. Olsen
1972 "A garbage can model of organizational choice." Administrative Science Quarterly, 17: 1–25.

Cook, T. D., and D. T. Campbell
1979 Quasi-Experimentation: Design and Analysis Issues for Field Settings. Chicago: Rand McNally.

Daft, R. L., and J. C. Wiginton
1979 "Language and organization." Academy of Management Review, 4: 179–192.

David, M. S.
1971 "That's interesting: Towards a phenomenology of sociology and a sociology of phenomenology." Philosophy of Social Science, 1: 309–344.

Dowling, J. B.
1973 "The social context of time behavior." Unpublished manuscript, Graduate School of Business, Stanford University.

Edwards, R.
1979 Contested Terrain. New York: Basic.

Faber, H.
1979 The Book of Laws. New York: Times.

Fischer, P. C.
1973 "A report on the influence of deadlines on the behavior of the professional football team." Unpublished manuscript, Graduate School of Business, Stanford University.

Glenn, J. R.
1974 Presidential Time Allocation in American Colleges and Universities. Doctoral dissertation proposal, Graduate School of Business, Stanford University.

Grauer, F. L.
1973 "On deadline effects: Intraday trading volume on the New York Stock Exchange." In E. J. Webb (ed.), Papers for the March 1973 Deadline Conference. Unpublished manuscript, Graduate School of Business, Stanford University.

Hull, C. L.
1934 "The rat's speed-of-locomotion gradient in the approach to food." Journal of Comparative Psychology, 7: 393–422.

Jerrell, S. L.
1973 "Goal gradient illustration: MBA admission applications." In E.J. Webb (ed.), Papers for the March 1973 Deadline Conference. Unpublished manuscript. Graduate School of Business, Stanford University.

Lazard, D.
1946 "Two years under a false name." Journal of Abnormal and Social Psychology, 41: 161–168.

Palmer, J., and F. L. McGuire
1973 "The use of unobtrusive measures in mental health research." Journal of Consulting and Clinical Psychology, 40: 431–436.

Parmenter, R.
1968 The Awakened Eye. Middletown, CT.: Wesleyan.

Pfeffer, Jeffrey
1977 "Power and resource allocation in organizations." In Barry M. Staw and Gerald R. Salancik (eds.), New Directions in Organizational Behavior: 235–265. Chicago: St. Clair.

Sechrest, L.
1976 "Another look at unobtrusive measures." In H. W. Sinaiko and L. A. Broedling (eds.), Perspectives on Attitude Assessment: Surveys and Their Alternatives: 94–107. Champaign, IL.: Pendleton.

Siu, R.G.H.
1978 "Management and the art of Chinese baseball." Sloan Management Review, Spring: 83–89.

Steinbeck, John
1969 Journal of a Novel. New York: Viking.

Tukey, J. W.
1977 Exploratory Data Analysis. Reading, MA.: Addison-Wesley.

Washburn, W. E.
1967 "Power in Washington: A zip-coded directory." Washington Post, Potomac Magazine, 132: 48–54.

Webb, E. J., D. T. Campbell, R. D. Schwartz, and L. Sechrest
1966 Unobtrusive measures. Chicago: Rand McNally.

Webb, E. J., and P. C. Ellsworth
1976 "On nature and knowing." In
H. W. Sinaiko and L. A. Broedling (eds.), Perspectives on Attitude Assessment: Surveys
and their Alternatives: 223–
238. Champaign, IL.: Pendleton.

Weick, Karl E.
1979 The Social Psychology of Organizing, 2d ed. Reading,
MA.: Addison-Wesley.

Weiner, S. S.
1973 "Deadlines and school desegregation in San Francisco."
In E. J. Webb (ed.), Papers for
the March 1973 Deadline
Conference: unpublished
manuscript, Graduate School
of Business, Stanford University.

Metaphors of the Field: Varieties of Organizational Discourse

Peter K. Manning

LANGUAGE AND SOCIAL ANALYSIS

There is a tradition in the analysis of social life that treats the social world as an independently perceivable phenomenon, something that observers delineate, describe, and make coherent. Observation and the observer stand removed. Recent trends in social philosophy challenge this subject-object distinction, viewing as isomorphic the seer and the seen, the knower and the known (Ryan, 1970). The correspondence theory of truth is rejected, for within a phenomenological perspective, there is no single "correct" reading of the "external world," no proper way in which facts must be selected and presented, and no arrangement, emplotment or presentation, or encodation that is uncontrovertibly correct or valid. The implications of this position for fieldwork should be recognized. The utility of this position has not been fully appreciated for although most sociologists would accept this "perspectival" view of social analysis, they are unaware of the range of interpretive options. They remain wedded to the correspondence version of truth.[1]

The problem of qualitative analysis based on fieldwork is that of avoiding solipsism on the one hand and avoiding positivism on the other. One approach to this problem is to make language the locus of analysis and not to confuse the language systems used to "explain" or formulate the world with the objects of study. The error here would be to mistake modes of analytic or scientific discourse for relationships among objects inhabiting a posited semantic domain such as the input-output world of Leontief, the operational-experimental world of the behaviorist, or the world of state in Hobbes. The thrust of phenomenological analysis is to make the language system into which experience, behaviors, symbols, and facts are cast a subject of concern.

In organizational analysis, the issue of perspective is raised once one contrasts the imagery used to "see" or represent organizations. The basic idea of perspective, or a way of viewing the social world, is infrequently discussed in organizational analysis. When distinctions are drawn between schools, frames of reference, or approaches (cf. Perrow, 1972; Haas and Drabek, 1973; Etzioni, 1975; Zey-Farrell, 1979), they are described as if the language systems by which they are characterized were ways of reflecting facts in the social world rather than as metaphors for constituting the facts. Important criticisms of the assumed world captured by these writers are found in the works of several scholars (Benson, 1975, 1977a, 1977b; Brown, 1976; Manning, 1977, 1980a; Pondy, 1977), especially the recent, provocative writings of Weick (1976, 1977).

THE MASTER TROPES

There are several implications of the criticisms of Weick and others of organizational analysis and of the place of language in social research. The most profound issue raised is what is an organization. If "organization" is a label with a set of domain assumptions about the semantic space in which it operates, and a set of implicit meanings that are tacitly assigned to behaviors, then it cannot be a concrete, unequivocal, phenomenologically invariant thing. The environment cannot be usefully seen as a single object, nor can the organization. The various ways in which language mediates between the world and perceptions of the world are a primary locus of analysis. Methodological analysis must discover discourse. Styles of discourse must be examined as they play roles in the gathering and analysis of field data. These styles or *tropes* are central to literary or textual analysis. Social analysis involves both creating and criticizing texts. White (1978) has suggested, in a brilliant collection of essays, that tropes (following Burke, 1962) are stylistic means by which discourse constitutes the objects which it "pretends" only to describe "realistically" and analyze "objectively." Master modes or tropes are metaphor, metonymy, synecdoche, and irony, and as such they represent the means of encodation and emplotment of the narrative and the way in which facts are made arguable. Each of these tropes will be examined here as the basis for analyzing and gathering field data.

From metaphor, or ways of seeing things *as if* they were something else, flow the related tropes. Metaphor asserts a "similarity in difference and, at least implicitly, a difference in similarity" (White, 1978: 72). Metaphor is the broader principle under which metonymy and synecdoche "operate." By asserting a similarity through the use of metaphor, the author sets something apart from other things; establishes its differences from them; but also, by seeing the object in terms of the metaphor, the object is seen as partaking of the qualities or properties of that by which it is labeled. Implicit meanings are transformed across linguistic boundaries. Metaphoric thinking maintains "double vision" (Brown, 1976: 175). By holding an object simultaneously in two or more points of view, it is enriched. We can vacillate between two levels of understanding while being aware that each has an "as if" quality. Metaphoric work should involve transfer of meanings from one domain to another, should prick our awareness, should be consciously "as if" and still be understood (Brown, 1976). Within the metaphoric context, metonymy and synecdoche are secondary forms which further specify the differences between elements said to compose the whole (metonymy) or to expand the similarities within the context (synecdoche). In the latter case, the part, by extension, becomes increasingly encompassing, integrative, and consuming.

Synecdoche, or seeing the part for the whole, in a sense, involves expanding a partial indication of the whole into the whole — "red sails in the sunset" for a boat. One may thus take a single example and use it as a microcosm of a larger process. It works through the principle of the expansion of meaning from part to a larger whole about which the reader is meant to be concerned.

Metonymy, on the other hand, takes a whole and reduces it to constitutive parts. It works through the mechanism of reduction, with the adduced parts being linked in some fashion with some explicated force which causes their identified patterning. Both metaphoric variations, synedoche and metonymy, proceed on the assumption of an established context of a known whole or distinction.

Irony, the fourth of the master tropes, is an explanation in terms of difference rather than the posited similarity of metaphor (Burke, 1962: 503–517). Irony is a "linguistic strategy" in which what appears to be the case is contraposed to some "more real" explanation or dynamic. Irony sanctions opposition to literalism, the acceptance of appearance, or makes a distinction within it, qualifies, converts, or transforms the apparent (White, 1978: 73).

Metonymy is the most common trope employed by social scientists when approaching organizational analysis. Metonymy takes the whole (an organization) to be indicated by its parts (e.g., the number of levels in an organization, the size of the body of rules governing procedures, the rates of mobility between and within organizational slots). The whole is thus represented by the parts; the essential features of a whole are reduced to indices. This whole is not itself sketched, but this "incorporeal" or intangible idea is converted into a visible, corporeal, or tangible "thing" (Burke, 1962: 506). Relationships between the indices or variables form the infrastructure of the thing, or the processes and functions. Complex cognitive, behavioral, and emotive matters are reduced to measurable spatial and temporal relationships. Metonymy dominates in an analysis when organizations are seen as composed of a series of relations represented by path coefficients that are argued to be the cause of organizational behavior (actions in uncertain markets, attempts to control resources, or other bridging metaphors of explanation for the statistical series). Numerical analysis is always indexical or standing for something in series.

The organic concept of organizations is a synecdoche. The idea is that the organization is an organic part transacting across boundaries with a larger environment to which it is closely linked with evolution. The organic metaphor, developed by Terreberry (1968), links the differentiation and growth of organizational structure to responses and adaptation of the organization to the environment. The organization is taken as a synecdoche for all living and adapting units. The apparent distinctiveness of organization behavior is resolved by seeing it/them as mere cases of general principles of evolution, adaptation, and/or natural laws.

Irony is to some extent used by all social sciences, since all trade on debunking, conversion, transformation, and making the apparent no longer apparent. The rational system view of organizations (Gouldner, 1959) trades on irony in that it sees the organization as maintaining a degree of rational control over its environment by the specification of determinant rules, procedures, and goals. Organization stands in contrast to its environment: it represents a rational island in the midst of irrational counterforces.

Each of the four master tropes organized my fieldwork (and my analyses), although my understanding at the time of the precise mechanisms they involved was limited.

FIELDWORK[2] AND THE TROPES

The modes of discourse discussed selectively conceal and reveal aspects of the social world. Alterations in style, by framing the world, also may throw putative features of it into contrast or even contradiction. Variations in tropes produce alterations in readings and show the relativism of each. When inspecting field research and the analysis of field data, one should bear in mind the analogs between literary and social criticism; both assume and play upon the root metaphor that language, or the structure of language, provides the structure of the social world. Language is the model for all human communication.[3]

In the organizational analyses undertaken by myself and colleagues, different modes of discourse were employed singularly or in combination during the course of the field research and in different sections of subsequent publications. It should be noted that the use of these tropes was not sequential in the sense that one followed the other, or that any is the preferred or correct one. Furthermore, I do not believe that any one of them is "higher," more abstract, or illuminating than the others. It is clear in retrospect that they did not emerge one after the other; but rather they achieved degrees of salience from time to time over the course of the research. Unlike White (1978), I do not argue that there is a hierarchy of tropes — from the most naive approach in metaphor in general, through metonymy, synecdoche, and, finally, irony — with each revealing more than the other.

On the other hand, ironic analysis is inevitable whenever one approaches any subject, sees it within another perspectice, turns it over, "takes it apart," compares, and contrasts it. Irony is the substantial metaphor of social research (Burke, 1962, 1965; Bruyn, 1966; Gusfield, 1976).

Metaphor: The Master Detective

The general metaphor "master detective," as applied to drug policing, was derived from the study of policing and, more specifically, detective work. In detective work, the conventional metaphor is one of the "super investigator" who encounters a crime, seeks clues, persons (witnesses, suspects, informants), motives, opportunities, weapons and other physical evidence, assembles the facts, correctly adduces a conclusion, and names a villain.[4] This master detective metaphor provides a lens through which drug policing can be viewed. Using this metaphor, a comparative table was developed to guide analysis of two organizations. With it, I intended to display a comparison of the sources, types, and numbers of cases investigated and cleared, and to identify the means by which they were closed. It was assumed, following the master detective metaphor, that the concept of and definition of a "case" were nonproblematic, that the sources of cases were limited and well controlled by administrative personnel, and that the procedures, means of investigation, forms of resolution, and clearance were standardized. Successful comparative analysis was predicated on these assumptions. What was envisioned was an organizationally-controlled investigative process. In time, however, a drug investigator-centered model was found to more accurately describe the process of enforcement (Manning, 1980a).

In one sense, of course, the organization creates the drug investigator-centered model of drug policing shown in Table 1 as much as it creates the organizational-centered model. In both, the case stands for the organization. The way in which the case is defined is the basis of the distinction within the metaphor. The concept of case took on different meanings in different contexts.

Synecdoche: The Case

Fieldwork in the first of the two sites revealed that this metaphor was only a partial truth for drug policing. The establishment of the existence or potential existence of a crime was the job of the drug investigator. In some sense, officers had to "make crime happen." They did not respond to or react to previously defined and investigated events as did detectives. Cases were not funneled or channeled to drug investigators in routinized fashion, unlike detective work where cases are assigned to investigators by their supervisors. Case materials were not kept in formal, shared, rationalized formats and stored in a central location. Instead, they were kept by individual officers in their desks or "heads," until and unless they personally decided to close them. In that instance, a case would be simultaneously opened or closed. Since emphasis was placed more on arrests than on solving cases, the "master detective" was much less the dominant role model than was the officer who was shrewd, fast-operating, and clever at constructing the scenes in which crimes might be seen, verified, or created. The synecdoche "case" for investigation was not an adequate expansion of the metaphor.

Conversely, the "case" or "detective" metaphor was a penetrating tool insofar as it dramatized the importance of informants as a means of gathering clues, of careful interviewing and of suspicious trust. The partial truth of the metaphor was revealed through interviewing key informants, the flavor of which can be suggested by a paraphrase from an early interview. When I asked an officer how he attained his cases he cautioned me that I should not make his comments "too public." He explained that cases came mainly from informants who had been charged with crimes and were willing to "work" or to "make cases." Making cases meant making buys from dealers to enable the police to

Table 1   Features of Narcotics Enforcement and Modes of Organizational Control

Features of Narcotics Enforcement and Modes of Organizational Control

Narcotics Crimes in General

1. Crimes are private transactions, usually with no complaints.
2. Agents are often distant from crime; must "make crime happen."
3. Agents do not rely wholly on voluntary information, but must obtain it through informants. Conditions for "working off" cases are not put in writing a priori nor is approval required before a "deal" is made between an investigator and an informant.
4. Selection of targets is discretionary and cases are infinitely expandable.
5. Calls to narcotics units are not tape recorded (i.e., can not be independently monitored).
6. Sergeants are usually not aware of the precise number of informants or cases of an individual officer.
7. Relationships between time, effort, money, and arrests are unknown; activity sheets are only a partial record of time and effort.

Investigator-Centered*	Organization-Centered
1. No initial information can be verified independently. Nothing in writing is required upon receipt of information.	1. Some clues are recorded on special investigative forms.

2. Those few cases that are assigned are considered special assignments.
3. No cases are officially "opened" or "closed."
4. Number, type, promise, and estimated "pay-off" of cases are known almost exclusively by an officer or investigating officers.
5. Arrests, charges, seizures, served search warrants, and buys indicate officers' activities only *after the fact.*
6. No clearance rate can be calculated since: Crimes are not independently investigated after an allegation. Cases are in effect self-initiated, self-defined, and self-closed.
7. Informants are known only by investigators, not evaluated by supervisors, and may not be placed in official files nor given an official number.

2. Cases are routinely assigned.
3. Assigned cases must be closed within a specified time.
4. Frequent checks are made on the number, type, and promise of cases (e.g., squad or section meetings).
5. Supervisors must give prior approval of buys and raids.
6. Partial clearance rate can be calculated for assigned cases.
7. Use of informants requires sergeant's approval, and a sergeant must meet informants. Performance of informants is evaluated and a central file is kept with records of payments and performance.

*Some squads may vary from this model, e.g., diversion, schools or squads on special "big case" assignments.

make a sales case, identifying dealers from whom officers might make buys (with an introduction made by the informant), or giving information which might lead to an arrest. These informants generally were paid, or they worked off their "beefs" (arrests) under the control of an officer. Other sources of cases were from paid informants, anonymous citizens who call, other agencies, and patrol officers. Many of these leads were not reviewed or controlled by supervisors. Officers made virtually all the significant decisions about their cases. In effect, the diversity of the leads, the control of the officer over the information received, the weak controls of supervisors over informants, and the paying of informants meant that, in most instances, the officer along with the informants, developed, worked, and closed cases independently.

"Working" informants is exciting and central to the everyday work of the units. It is a "key event"; in Burke's terms, it is one of a class of events that provided synecdocheal data or served as a source of "representative anecdotes." These were events on which the success or failure of the unit was believed to rest: search warrant raids; surveillance, especially moving surveillance of drug dealers; interrogation and debriefing of informants and recently arrested persons; and supervised controlled buys made by informants from dealers (the hope was to make the buys the basis for obtaining and serving a search warrant or making an arrest for drug sales). These were, in short, the synecdocheal events by which the entire organization was characterized by participants. Two lines of analysis were derived from these synecdocheal relations. The first involved locating the central features of the interactions between "narcs" and "informants" and to see those, in turn, as characteristic or central features of narcotics police work (as opposed to police work in general and to other sorts of specialized policing). Knowledge of this segment of police work became a basis for a second analysis, an investigation of the bases of the systematic differentiation of narcotic policing from other forms of policing.

Metonymy: Arrest Data

From this material, it was clear that there might be a number of ways of "getting cases," and that these, in turn, might be a function of the agent's perspective. Administrative personnel, when interviewed concerning the overall aim of drug enforcement would use a form of metonymy by referring, for example, to objectives, goals, and indicators of success. The perspective differed in an important way. The metonymic arrest data that was provided did not capture the officers' perspective since the nature of the object being called a case could not be reduced. Cases were constituted from different facts and the causal logic linking cases to outcomes was not that of the intelligent officer solving obscure cases in the Holmesian fashion.

The statements of goals provided by administrators are reductions or indices of the process of drug control. Enforcing drug laws, at least theoretically, is based on knowledge of the number of users, the size of their habits, the types of drugs they use, the distribution of the users and use levels across the ecological complex of the jurisdiction, the price, the market structure for each of the drugs at hand, the licit versus illicit sources of the drug, trends and levels of use, variations in the above "variables," and the overall causal structure that links them. Administrators did not possess such theoretic knowledge. When such processes and complexes can be transformed into metonymic indices, a model of these metonymic relations could be constructed (e.g., Preble and Casey, 1969; Wilson and Wheat, 1975; DuPont, 1978). Correlations between these figures have been found, and detailed and precise models had been developed by Silverman, Spruill, and Levine (1974), Levin, Roberts, and Hirsch (1975), and Moore (1977). In these models, indicators of larger processes were shrunken into microformats and modeled using crime statistics, seizure data, number of warrants served and the like. The construction of the drug problem in this fashion is an *equation* of two phenomena. "Drug use" is collapsed into "crime," "crime" is collapsed into the statistics and rates for drug arrests, and changes in drug arrest rates are taken to be indicators of variation in the magnitude of the drug problem. The "drug problem" is itself a synecdoche for all crime, while also standing in metonymic relationship to "drug use." When one works back and forth across the equation, parallels and differences can be made salient. Is drug use (e.g., marijuana, cough syrup, valium) a crime representative of all crimes? Of what part of what whole is it a reduction?

Irony: The Rational Organizational Model

Research was governed overall by the strategy called by Burke (1962: 69–163) "perspective by incongruity," or sensitivity to indications of basic irony. Two sorts of irony are built into this perspective on drug enforcement. The first irony is derived from systematically contrasting what is viewed as the morally proper and necessary enterprise of policing, to the structurally similar enterprise, the "drug business," which is viewed as immoral, improper, and certainly illegal. We found this a useful irony. The drug world and the police world were treated analogously. They were displayed as mirror-images of each other (see Table 2). The irony results from identifying parallel structures in two social worlds, one moral, the other immoral. Ironically, undercover narcs do not look like police officers: they keep strange hours, hang out with "bad guys," can drink, frequent bars, dress like criminals while on duty; are paid on a different basis; and attempt to become like the persons from whom they were meant to be different. By creating this set of comparable dimensions, the relativity of the norms, values, roles, motivations, and rules is dramatized. What ultimately distinguishes one from the other, once they are seen as similar on one level, different on another?

The second sort of irony is produced by a close examination of the rational model of organizational control. This model is one of the most common constitutions of organization found in the literature. From this model were derived notions about how the organization shaped cases, how they were obtained, how they were "worked," what was done to resolve them, how they were supervised and monitored from time to time, what the appropriate costs, techniques, and informants used were, and what the necessary training was. The source of my original view (or metaphor) is noted on the organizational-centered side (left) of Table 1 while the dominant pattern in the second organization (and in others later studied) is shown in the right column. The organizational-centered model was used to contrast with the officer-centered model.

Since these models were analytic ideal-types and did not shape all the cases worked in either of the two organizations compared (see Manning, 1980a), it was possible to extend the irony further. This was accomplished by contrasting a set of ways in which cases might be obtained with the organizational model by showing how, even when the aim was close organizational control, the impact of the organization of case selection, investigation and closure was minimal; that of the individual agent supreme. In addition to the irony that in neither type is the organization the controlling force guiding agents' actions and their choice of cases, one must consider the metairony that the police in general, and certainly the drug police, have little effect upon crime. Although the degree and type of effect of policing on crime varies, it is of marginal significance. From this master irony, the secondary irony of ineffectual drug control is a logical derivative (Manning, 1977, 1980b).

CONCLUSION

It has been argued that most social science does not take into account the way in which the master tropes shape the writing as well as the gathering of qualitative data. If, for example, the analysis of drug policing had proceeded as if the master detective metaphor were adequate, then, those cases which fit the tropes would have been sought out, followed, detailed, and written up as representative of drug work. This is in fact what the agencies themselves do in selectively publicizing their successful "busts," large raids, enormous seizures, and ingenious infiltration of sinister drug-dealing cabals. Perhaps placing together the two tropes is revealing in a dialectical fashion. It produces irony, which, in turn, touches off new possibilities in troping and new perspectives by incongruity (Burke, 1962). What metaphor is chosen will be modified in the course of field research and

Table 2   Analogs Between the Dealing-Using System and the Enforcement System

Narcotics-Dealing Organizations	Narcotics-Enforcement Organizations
1. Pressures for sales and production.	1. Pressures for sales, production of cases, search warrants, and arrests.
2. Concern for security and secrecy.	2. Concern for security and secrecy.
3. Dealings based on personal relationships; trust central to the work.	3. Dealings based on personal relationships; trust central to the work.
4. Entrepreneurial model of success.	4. Entrepreneurial model of success.
5. Feudal loyalty characteristic of organizational relationships; punitive mode of coercion prevails.	5. Feudal loyalty characteristic of organizational relationships; punitive mode of coercion prevails.
6. Pyramidal-like structure of operation: low, flat hierarchy with largest number of actors on the bottom of the organization being exposed to the greatest risks.	6. Pyramidal-like structure (varies by unit): low, flat hierarchy with the largest number of actors on the bottom being exposed to the greatest risks.
7. Distrust, lying, misrepresentation, and duplicity are dominant modes of interpersonal relations.	7. Trust/distrust, lying, misrepresentation, and duplicity are dominant personal modes. Formalization of relations across organizational segments.
8. Prices based on relationship to buyer; negotiated and not fixed.	8. Payment based on relationship to informant and case; prices somewhat negotiated, not fixed, but constrained by both the market and organizational policy as interpreted by the sergeants.

9. Violence, inter and intraorganizational envy, ambivalence, and revenge are dominant themes.
10. Street "rip-offs" of money happen frequently; law is a powerful force protecting narcs and sanctioning their revenge-retaliatory actions.
11. Work demands are sporadic and episodic; often nocturnal. Work is overdemanding and the clientele must be controlled by manipulation.
12. Clientele can be "turned" to be used by the "enemy." Can not be trusted (yet must be trusted); is viewed as tricky and deceitful, as are agents of control.
13. Prestige comes from targets, quality of one's past arrests and seizures, and knowledge of the drug scene.
14. Routines and the rationalization of practices are a basis for success.
15. Both caution and risk taking are essential to success.
16. Generally a young man's work, dominated by a young man's style of life and interests, on and off duty.

9. Violence, envy, ambivalence, and revenge are dominant emotional themes.
10. Street "rip-offs" of money and dope are common; law does not provide protection for such losses by dealers.
11. Work demands are sporadic and episodic; often nocturnal. Work is overdemanding and the clientele must be controlled by manipulation.
12. Clientele can be "turned" to be used by the "enemy." Can not be trusted (yet must be trusted); is viewed as tricky and deceitful, as are agents of control.
13. Prestige comes from associates, quality of one's clientele, dope, amounts dealt, style of life, and knowledge of drug scene.
14. Routines and the rationalization of practices are a basis for success.
15. Both caution and risk taking are essential to success.
16. Generally a young man's work, dominated by a young man's style of life and interests, on and off the job.

a note of irony rings through most such analyses. They contain self-confessional notes, new revelations, misunderstandings, reinterpretations and new sense(s) of the social settings being investigated (see Johnson, 1975; Manning, 1984). Much of the work of this paper was done by examples from field research and the modifications of tropes and relevant data. Converting this material into a written text creates a new set of problems and ambiguities, the discussion of which concludes the paper.

The presentation of an argument in this text is multi-reflective: The text communicates about observations made and interpreted, but it also reflects on itself as a written document which the reader must make sensible.[5] Variations in text or context produce variations in awareness, much as attention shifts in everyday experience. Each sign (something which indicates something else to some observer) — signifier (that which is indicated) combination (e.g., a rose (sign) indicates passion (signifier)), is linked in a context of conventional understanding of the signified relationship. Roses as a signifier are, as Barthes (1972) writes, "empty," but as the product of the signifier-signified relationship, they become a meaningful and powerful sign. The styles of discourse utilized here, the tropes, are symbolic contexts (ironically indicated). The reader is meant to take the discussion framed by the introduction of the term "synecdoche" as an illustration of the working of that trope (at least). However, since it is a context, it can be removed from that context or shifted from one set of rules for context framing to another.[6] The possibility that an instance or example might be seen other than as it is presented generates ambiguity. It can be seen as a metaphor on more than one level.

Patterned ambiguity of context, mode, or text, introduces surprise or awareness even of this possible variation in expository writing. Analogously, metaphoric or similar concepts presented as semantically frozen, that is, locked into a conventionalized semantic space of denotative meaning, can be jarred loose. Some of these concepts, "organization," "organizational," "environment" and the like, as indicated by Bittner in a brilliant and innovative paper (1965), are only frozen contextually. Lemert (1979), in an equally seminal paper, has outlined a promising semiotics of organizations and of organizational analysis. These highly original exercises in textual criticism are portentous. They suggest that concepts become frozen as a result of location. Do concepts in organizational discourse in a sense speak unequivocally because they reside in texts that are conventionally defined as "speaking science"?

It is also worth noting that while much is done in scientific writing to deny the individuality of the writer, to constrain the varieties of worlds possible which might be represented, and in fact to posit the reader as a mere recipient, any text can be viewed as producing the opposite effects. In "readerly" texts of science or of the classics in literature, as Barthes (1974) writes, the nature of social reality is static, given to be taken and reflects a single, hegemonic set of values and interpretations. Such texts heretofore have been the basis of social science. On the other hand, this conception of the text can be contrasted with "writerly" texts where the reader participates and takes an active part in the interpretation of the text. They actively create a sense of the signified through sharing the signifiers, or the text (see, for a useful summary of this argument, Barthes, 1976 and Hawkins, 1977: 106–122). Perhaps because this paper is a *text* in which the *linear* mode of communication is singularly employed, and where iconic variations are minimized, the transformation between codes does not occupy us much. The process may well be a worthy preoccupation. Writing contains two kinds of signs, Hawkins (1977: 136) reminds us, and

language, which is normally *auditory* in mode, is made *visual* when it is written down or given printed form. To the auditory sign's commitment to *time* as a structuring agent is therefore added (in one sense, the process is also one of reduction) to the visual sign's commitment to *space*. Thus writing imposes on language a linearity and a sequentiality and a physical existence in space which speech does not have.

The text is made an object of consideration, both as a production and representation, and as a physical entity with spatial reality.

NOTES

1

Field researchers in the tradition of symbolic interactionism such as Becker (1970), McCall and Simmons (1969), and Denzin (1979) view the world as an "out there" to be measured, that measurements possess various degrees of validity and reliability, and that measurement problems are ultimately to be resolved by data. Critics such as Cicourel (1964, 1968, 1973), Johnson (1975), and Douglas (1976) argue, in a position consistent with the argument presented here, that observers create a domain of interest through concepts and perspectives, affirm it by selective and selected measures and, in a sense, construct the social world through these actions. The critics raise the spector of solipsism by considering all analyses of the social world to be problematic accounts rather than objective descriptions subject to confirmation or disconfirmation through scientific investigation.

2

The material cited here comes from two studies. The first was undertaken by Manning as a visiting fellow at NILECJ/LEAA during 1974–1975 in two municipal police drug law enforcement units in the southeastern United States; one in a large metropolitan police department of over 4,000 officers, and one in a suburban (county) unit of over 500 officers. The units were composed, respectively, of more than 50 and under 20 officers (the number fluctuated). The second, a study of six municipal units, was carried out by Jay R. Williams, principal investigator, Lawrence John Redlinger, and Manning with a grant from NILECJ to the Research Triangle Institute during 1976–1977. In each site, we gathered field observations, interviews, records, forms, and participated in the round of work. Our focus in the field work was upon *key events* such as raids, surveillances, interrogations, group meetings, and arrest-and-charge situations. We also studied police-prosecutor relations through interviews with prosecutors. Details of the first study are found in Manning (1980a) and of the second in Williams, Redlinger, and Manning (1979).

3

This is a basic tenet of structuralism in its several forms. See the useful summaries of Jameson, 1972; Scholes, 1974; Culler, 1975; Leach, 1976; Hawkins, 1977; Pettit, 1977.

4

This Holmesian model has since been shown to be a very partial description of actual detective work by Greenwood, Chaiken, and Petersilia (1977).

5

Weick (1977, 1979) utilizes iconic variations to jog thought. Poems and drawings are set next to linear text. Visual-spatial signs "emit iconic messages about their nature through the visual means of typography over and above (or under and beneath) the symbolic messages of their content" (Hawkins, 1977: 136). To write, "this is 'ironic'" is an iconic sign signifying the concept irony (unexpected appearance of a message about the text itself in the text). It also signifies irony in the juxtaposition of facts it refers to in the text. The same iconic work is done by inserting figures to illustrate textual arguments: they provide a counter-point.

6

This process is elaborated in complex and elegant detail by Goffman in *Frame Analysis*, 1974; see also Derrida, 1976.

REFERENCES

Barthes, Roland
1972   Mythologies. New York: Hill and Wang.
1974   S/Z. R. Miller, trans. New York: Hill and Wang.
1976   Pleasures of the Text. New York: Hill and Wang.

Becker, Howard S.
1970   Sociological Work. Chicago: Aldine Press.

Benson, J. Kenneth
1975   "The inter-organizational network as a political economy." Administrative Science Quarterly, 20: 229–249.
1977a   "Innovation and crisis in organizational analysis." Sociological Quarterly, 18: 3–16.
1977b   "Organizations: A dialectical view." Administrative Science Quarterly, 22: 1–21.

Bittner, Egon
1965   "The concept of organization." Social Research, 32: 230–255.

Brown, Richard Harvey
1976   "Social theory as metaphor." Theory and Society, 3: 169–197.

Bruyn, Severyn
1966   The Human Perspective in Sociology. Englewood Cliffs, NJ: Prentice-Hall.

Burke, Kenneth
1962   A Grammar of Motives and a Rhetoric of Motives. Cleveland, OH: Meridian.
1965   Permanence and Change, 2d ed., rev. Indianapolis: Bobbs-Merrill.

Cicourel, Aaron V.
1964   Method and Measurement in Sociology. New York: Free Press.
1968   The Social Organization of Juvenile Justice. New York: Wiley.
1973   Cognitive Sociology. Harmondsworth, England: Penguin.

Culler, Jonathan
1975   Structuralist Poetics. Ithaca, NY: Cornell University Press.

Denzin, Norman
1979   The Research Act, 2d ed. New York: McGraw-Hill.

Derrida, Jacques
1976   Of Grammatology. Baltimore: Johns Hopkins University Press.

Douglas, Jack D.
1976   Investigative Social Research. Beverly Hills, CA: Sage.

DuPont, Robert L.
1978   "The drug abuse decade." Journal of Drug Issues, 8: 173–187.

Etzioni, Amitai
1975   A Comparative Analysis of Complex Organizations, 2d ed. New York: Free Press.

Goffman, Erving
1974   Frame Analysis. New York: Harper & Row.

Gouldner, Alvin W.
1959   "Organizational analysis." In R.K. Merton, L. Broom, and L.S. Cottrell, Jr. (eds.), Sociology Today: 400–428. New York: Basic Books.

Greenwood, Peter, Jan Chaiken, and Joan Petersilia
1977   The Criminal Investigation Process. Lexington, MA: Heath.

Gusfield, Joseph
1976   "The literary rhetoric of science." American Sociological Review, 41: 16–34.

Haas, J. Eugene, and Thomas Drabek
1973   Complex Organizations. New York: MacMillan.

Hawkins, Terence
1977   Structuralism and Semiotics. Berkeley, CA: University of California Press.

Jameson, Frederic
1972   The Prison-House of Language. Princeton: University Press.

Johnson, John
1975   Doing Fieldwork. New York: Free Press.

Leach, Edmund R.
1976   Culture and Communication. Cambridge, England: Cambridge University Press.

Lemert, Charles
1979   "Language, structure and measurement: Structuralist semiotics and sociology." American Journal of Sociology, 84: 929–957.

Levin, Gilbert, Edward Roberts, and Gary B. Hirsch
1975   The Persistent Poppy: A Computer-Aided Search for Heroin Policy. Cambridge, MA: Ballinger.

Manning, Peter K.
1977   Police Work: The Social Organization of Policing. Cambridge, MA: MIT Press.

1980a   The Narcs' Game: Informational and Organizational Constraints on Drug Law Enforcement. Cambridge, MA: MIT Press.

1980b   "Crime and technology: The role of scientific research and technology in crime control." In National Science Foundation, The Five-Year Outlook for Science and Technology, vol. III. Washington: U.S. Government Printing Office.

1984   "Making sense of field data." In Thomas J. Cottle and Robert Weiss (eds.), The Narrative Voice. New York: Basic Books (forthcoming).

McCall, George, and Jerry L. Simmons, ed.
1969   Issues in Participant Observation. Reading, MA: Addison-Wesley.

Moore, Mark
1977   Buy and Bust. Lexington, MA: Lexington.

Perrow, Charles
1972   Complex Organizations: A Critical Essay. Glenview, IL: Scott, Foresman.

Pettit, Phillipe
1977   The Concept of Structuralism. Berkeley, CA: University of California Press.

Pondy, Louis R.
1977   "Effectiveness: A thick description." In Paul S. Goodman, Johannes M. Pennings et al., New Perspectives on

Organizational Effectiveness: 226–234. San Francisco, CA: Jossey-Bass.

Preble, Edward, and John Casey
1969   "Taking care of business: The heroin user's life on the streets." International Journal of the Addictions, 4: 1–24.

Ryan, Alan, ed.
1970   The Philosophy of the Social Sciences. New York: MacMillan.

Scholes, Robert
1974   Structuralism in Literature. New Haven: Yale University Press.

Silverman, Leon, Norman Spruill, and D. Levine
1974   "Drugs and crime in Detroit." Unpublished paper, Drug Abuse Council.

Terreberry, Shirley R.
1968   "The evolution of organizational environments." Administrative Science Quarterly, 12: 590–613.

Weick, Karl E.
1976   "Educational organizations as loosely coupled systems." Administrative Science Quarterly, 21: 1–19.

1977   "Repunctuating the problem." In Paul S. Goodman, Johannes M. Pennings et al., New Perspectives on Organizational Effectiveness: 193–225. San Francisco, CA: Jossey-Bass.

1979   The Social Psychology of Organizing, 2d ed., Reading, MA: Addison-Wesley.

White, Hayden
1973   Metahistory. Baltimore: Johns Hopkins University Press.

1978   Topics of Discourse. Baltimore: Johns Hopkins University Press.

Williams, Jay R., Lawrence John Redlinger, and Peter K. Manning
1979   Police Narcotics Control: Patterns and Strategies. Washington: U.S. Government Printing Office.

Wilson, James Q., and Thomas Wheat
1975   "Heroin." In James Q. Wilson, Thinking About Crime: 125–161. New York: Basic Books.

Zey-Ferrell, Mary
1979   Dimensions of Organizations. Santa Monica, CA: Goodyear.

Epilogue: Qualitative Methods Reclaimed

John Van Maanen, Editor

Remarks appearing in an epilogue are usually meant to tie together whatever loose ends still exist in a book by providing a general yet final perspective on all that has come before. Sometimes these remarks do so by detailing in a crisp, abbreviated way events taking place after a book proper has been closed, events of the sort that presumably shed light on narrative detail. Sometimes these remarks work by revealing hidden meanings in the text, meanings a writer wants to be sure do not remain hidden for long. Sometimes an epilogue is but an epitaph that serves to commemorate if not celebrate the preceding words and ideas. Sometimes an epilogue is merely a convenient excuse for an author to try again to bring home some central argument or point of view. This epilogue is written in the spirit of all of these honorable, perspective-seeking traditions.

Time, however, is the master perspective provider. Like goals, intentions, or purposes, perspectives are best determined retrospectively. This applies particularly well to the products of scholarship that are both long in coming and long in attracting whatever attention (if any) they receive. Certainly, in academic life, we write papers, deliver them more or less on time, seek out the immediate reactions and opinions of selected others (usually friendly ones), and then lay back to wait and see

Editor's Note: Partial support for the writing of this epilogue comes from Chief of Naval Research, Psychological Sciences Division (Code 452), Organizational Effectiveness Research Program, Office of Naval Research, Arlington, VA 22217, under contract N00014-80-0905; NR 170-911.

what will happen to our own sacred words. Four years is not a long time to wait, of course, but it is long enough to allow for another look at the papers presented here, so that we might see purposes to their writing, beyond those initially staked out by their authors (and editors).

A good place to begin is with the commonplace observation that the literature in organization studies is put together by those who do the research, those who are researched, and those who read the research. Despite the variety of these groups (or perhaps because of it), this homily suggests that whatever sense a researcher is able to make of the researched is ultimately mediated by the readers of the research. They are the ones who must eventually come to terms with whatever sense is claimed in a study, for they are the ones who must put this sense to work. My first concern, then, is to report on some of the things I've heard from readers of this special issue.[1]

THEMES UNCOVERED

Readers have not missed the rhetorical purposes attached to the papers in this volume. There is more than a little "pontification" involved whenever our own methods are discussed, since, by presenting our own ways of seeing the world as more or less definitive, irony is cast on other ways of seeing (A. Becker, 1982). To some degree, then, these papers are part of a larger movement involving those who are attempting to rearrange and revalue the various symbols of the organization research world such that qualitative work will achieve a more prominent place than some think it now holds.[2]

Given that the rhetorical functions of social science writing are unavoidable (Gusfield, 1981: 83-108), the way in which those writing here attempt to persuade their audience also provokes reader comment. For example, noticeably absent in this volume is the use of passive constructions as a way of giving a manuscript something of a magisterial and impersonal air. The active voice is very much present in these chapters, thus identifying the agent from which a given pronouncement comes. Polysyllabic and turgid prose is infrequent. While the stylistic delicacy of the crafty novelist is hardly achieved, there is the sense among readers that the authors of these essays care as much about the presentation of their research reports as they do about the accomplishment of the research itself.

Two observations are relevant in this regard. First, each of the chapters is short; thus the social scientist's habitual use of twenty words when two will do is structurally (editorially) constrained. Second, missing from these essays are many of those vague phrases that convey, among other things, a general reluctance on an author's part to take the rap for what is being said or to specify precisely who is saying what. Examples in the existing literature are everywhere. "All things being equal, A tends to be related to B." "It is becoming increasingly apparent. . . ." "Differences are found. . . ." These fuzzy phrases portray research results as emerging from an external world of data unsullied by the researcher's presence. They also serve as all-purpose loopholes, such that if and when an author's position is questioned the nonspecificity of the writing will allow an easy out (H. Becker, 1982). The authors of the chapters presented here seem willing, if not eager, to take the rap by offering up their generalizations (and pontifications) in ways readers find refreshingly direct.

Similarly, method is personalized in the chapters of this book, and readers express some enjoyment with the idiosyncrasies displayed, the behind-the-scene revelations, and the mannered but distinct voices exhibited by the writers. The vertical pronoun "I" shows up with remarkable frequency for an academic publication, thus documenting the fact that there really is a person behind the technique discussed. This is not to suggest that each writer should be awarded some sort of intimacy trophy for baring all the sterling and sordid, brave and cowardly detail of his or her respective research adventures, but it does suggest, by telling anecdote, the presence of a most human element in the research process.

Another thematic point remarked on by readers is an apparent self-consciousness on the part of the authors. Specifically, the essays in this volume drive home the fact that qualitative research is hardly a process marked by an untroubled accumulation of detached, neutral, or purely descriptive fact. Indeed, those writing in this volume would no doubt claim that any kind of research endeavor is a social and cultural process with deeply rooted moral, political, and personal overtones. Such a perspective points to a deepening sophistication within the organizational research community and helps make the researcher a visible and discussable object of scrutiny rather than a shadowy, impersonal, and hence, rather feckless guide to enlightenment.

The variety of research approaches presented here also stimulates reader comment. The standard research cliché that points to the interaction of method, theory, and data throws some light on this diversity. For instance, if the data are messy, disordered, or otherwise difficult to pin down, these features seem also to be reflected in the methods and theories to which such data become attached. Bonini's paradox (as formulated by Bill Starbuck and discussed by Weick, 1979) provides a good way of making this point. The paradox itself refers to an accuracy comprehensibility tradeoff that occurs when organizational simulation models are constructed and run. The more accurate, detailed, and precise a given model, the more complex, untidy, and chaotic the simulation results. In field studies, a similar result is likely. The more complicated the social system studied, the more any description of that system must, to be true to the "real stuff" caught in the field, itself be complicated. Presumably, the methods selected for such study must also reflect what is to be examined. A simple method in a complex scene may well be inadequate (and vice versa).

Consider also how method mirrors data, as well as the reverse. A near perfect example of just this is *Boys in White* (Becker et al., 1961), the deservedly famous study of medical school education, conducted by a team of researchers of differing ages and academic status. As detailed by Hughes (1974), the research team gradually and without much planning came virtually to replicate the social structure of the institution it studied. Everett Hughes, the oldest and most prestigious member of the team, worked with the school's top administrators and senior faculty members. Howard Becker and Blanche Geer, the youngest and greenest of the researchers, took on the medical students. Anselm Strauss spent most of his time in the field among the residents and interns who occupied, as he did, the middle ranks of their respective social systems.

It is true, of course, that such mirroring effects can be disastrous when they are of a cognitive rather than a structural sort. As some of the authors of this volume note, with more than a little trepidation, there is always the danger that researchers will lose their uniqueness and distinctive mission and become (if only temporarily) little doctors, cops, or bureaucrats instead of the sociologists, economists, or psychologists they set out to be in the setting studied. There may be some field worker's pride in such a transformation, but, rest assured, there will also be some academic shame.

The role of surprise in research activities is yet another feature of these essays that has caught the attention of at least some readers. Unlike the Prince of Serendip stories that litter the unserious asides in many research methods textbooks, the authors here search out and, to a degree, count on finding what Agar (1983) nicely tagged "reality disjunctures." This points to the essential, if not fundamental, role incongruity plays in research of the qualitative sort.[3] In fact, a sort of general research model is visible running through these chapters, wherein lines of study and theory building are occasioned by the breakdown or failure of the researcher's manifest and latent expectations. Sometimes the breakdowns are accidental ("serendipitous"), but more often they are mandated in the sense that the researcher directly seeks them out. Unexpected variance is the heart and soul of qualitative work, for it brings about a conscious search for resolution. When a researcher's surprise becomes understood, theories of the studied scene (and perhaps of method as well) are enriched. To seek the exceptional is to discover the routine.[4]

Disturbing to some readers is the often maddeningly emergent or unfolding character of the research discussed in this volume.Grant givers, among others are often furious at qualitative researchers for doing Study B when they were funded to do Study A. Yet qualitative work is, by design, open ended. It is also skeptical. Researchers in this domain are a fairly contentious lot, typically unwilling to grant much credence to another's observations or theories. Thus the perspectives and topics originally informing a proposed program of research are quite likely to shift as the research runs its course. Part of the issue is the just-mentioned central role played by incongruity and surprise in qualitative work, but another part of it concerns the largely unstandardized reporting formats that mark qualitative research. In the absence of conventionalized formats, the researcher must work through a lengthy chain of choices when preparing research reports for public consumption. Most of these choices are private ones that derive from the emergent nature of the project itself.

Impressions and potential themes of the research, for example, must continually be sorted out. Various interpretive schemes need to be tried for relative fit and their ability to condense and order data. Propositions and hypotheses are typically worked up and examined while the data are still being collected. At the same time, the researcher is also absorbing and culling new ideas that may be included in the writing that punctuates any investigation. The interpretations and ideas that will eventually be included in the research report come slowly into view as the writer sits down and decides what impressions are to be given voice, what analytic constructs are to be taken up, what words are to be used to illuminate them, and so on. Writing up the results of qualitative work is as much a discovery process as it is a summary of what has already been discovered (Mills,

1959). A Weickian maxim is appropriate in this regard: "Qualitative researchers often do not know exactly what they have studied until they have written it up and passed it around."[5]

Finally, readers of these reports frequently remark on what they think is the misleading label applied to the examined research methods. They point out (and I would agree with them) that to use the label "qualitative methods" as a descriptive device presumes the presence of an opposite and contrary set of methods with, perhaps, an equally misleading label, "quantitative methods." Whatever one is, the other is not. Yet as many readers suggest, any given researcher typically works in a number of ways. Moreover, whatever distinctive unity either camp possesses, it is a unity seen primarily by members of the other camp. As I noted in the Preface to this volume, qualitative strategies are essentially those emphasizing an interpretive approach in which data are worked with (and on) both to pose and resolve research questions. From this standpoint, there is nothing hard or soft, objective or subjective, about a qualitative orientation; within its reach are found a broad range of craft-like approaches to particular research problems.

ON PRINCIPLE AND CRAFT

As qualitative research unfolds, it sidesteps the hypothetico-deductive model in favor of an interpretive eclecticism designed to resolve whatever incongruities a researcher has managed to uncover in a given domain. This is high-sounding sentiment. Counterclaims exist, and certainly a portion of what passes under the qualitative banner leaves much to be desired. To the degree that qualitative researchers are a source of embarrassment to some, it is often because, in the strictest sense, their methods are untried and, therefore, lack reputability. Professional standards, it seems, are best safeguarded (and probably enhanced) by the thoughtful articulation, encouragement, and enforcement of what is already known and practiced.

The researchers represented in this volume cannot, however, easily be dismissed for not understanding or not being familiar with conventionalized research presctiptions. In fact, almost all the writers of this book have a past history (no matter how secret or shady) of using a variety of research designs and tools. Moreover, if qualitative work is increasingly attractive to the recruits in the field, it cannot be argued that it is because they do not have the training to do anything else. Even the most lax Ph.D. programs devoted to the training of organizational researchers typically require a semester or two of statistics, a course on research design, some exposure to philosophy of science (usually positivist), and, of course, a daily diet of the "classics" in the field.

If, as I suspect, qualitative work represents an explicit rejection of certain research models, what is being accepted by students as good practice? This is not as yet altogether clear. To move toward a definition for qualitative work is obviously difficult. Consider some of the specific research techniques that are linked by organizational researchers to the qualitative label: participant observation, content analysis, formal and informal interviewing, clinical case studies, life-history construction, videotaping behavioral displays, archival data surveys, historical analysis, the invention and use of varied unobtrusive measures, and various formal schools of thought and procedure in social science such as dramaturgic analysis, semiotics, frame analysis, ethnomethodology, and conversational analysis. Even these fairly precise technical tags are not always as telling as one might think. Participant observation, for example, really says more about the situation of the researcher than it does about what is done in a particular setting (Emerson, 1981). All forms of interviewing beg descriptions of just how the interview responses are heard, coded, and linked to theoretical interests or constructs (Cicourel, 1964). Even historical analysis often employs quite refined numerical procedures, although these activities rarely become the centerpiece of a research report (Bailyn, 1982).

If anything, qualitative research is marked more by a reliance on multiple sources of data than by its commitment to any one source alone. Technique-dependent definitions, then, are faulty, since they cannot absorb the diversity of uses to which the qualitative label applies. It is my view that we are best off thinking of qualitative research in terms of some of the organizing principles surrounding the activities (and topics) of those who do the work. Gleaning from the chapters of this volume, I have seven principles in mind (although a reader can certainly add to this list).[6]

1. Analytic induction. Qualitative work begins with the close-up, firsthand inspection of ongoing social life. Specific and local features of the studied scene are sought as a data base from which patterns may or may not be imposed. Generalizations are to be built from the ground up and offered tentatively on the basis of their ability to contain fully the data in hand. In the ideal, no variance remains unexplained.

2. Proximity. Researchers place importance on concrete occurrences and episodes, not on reports of such. Investigators should witness firsthand much of what is studied and, presumably, understood.[7] To the extent possible, people should be observed engaged in activities that matter to them, the performance of which is, to them, of more importance than the fact that they are performing in front of the researcher.

3. Ordinary behavior. Topics for qualitative study are located within the natural world of those studied. Qualitative research is interested in everyday activity as defined, enacted, smoothed, and made problematic by persons going about their normal routines. Whatever interrupts or otherwise disturbs or distorts ordinary lines of action is to be minimized.

4. Temporal sensitivity. Patterns of collective behavior must be seen from both a topographical (relational) and historical perspective. Any given social action is unique and unlikely to be repeated in precisely the same way. It may be that the more critical the event, the more rare its occurrence. Thus qualitative researchers must pay attention to historical antecedents as a way of understanding just what a given event or pattern represents, in contrast to what came before and what may come after. Such sensitivity takes many forms, from the living in a social system over a nontrivial amount of time, to the careful survey of system-specific historical materials, to the close inspection of broader historical records (and commentary).

5. Structure as ritual constraint. Qualitative work takes it as axiomatic that given patterns of social activity are essentially arbitrary, a result of custom, present circumstance, situated motives, and ongoing interaction. From this perspective, there is no primal social order or set of fundamental survival functions that exist for a collective against which some "natural deviation" might be defined. Human actions and the organization that surrounds them) are intentional, mediated by what people think they are accomplishing. To ignore these meanings and the context within which they are contextually relevant is to impose structure rather than to discover it.

6. Descriptive emphasis. Qualitative work involves ontological inquiry. This is merely a fancy way of saying that, at root, qualitative research seeks descriptions for what is occurring in any given place and time. "What is going on here" is the most elementary qualitative research question, yet the most difficult to answer adequately because, typically, there are many voices and perspectives to be heard. Qualitative work, as is true for social science in general, is then essentially ironic, since it aims to disclose and reveal, not merely to order and predict.

7. Shrinking variance. Qualitative research is geared toward the discovery and explanation of similarity and coherence. Reasons behind the absence of variance are often both the subject and goal of qualitative study. Instead of asking questions about those who, in Lévi-Strauss's wonderful phrase, "do things to whiten mother's hair," qualitative researchers ask first why it is there seem to be so few people who do whiten mother's hair. In this sense, qualitative work is concerned more with commonality and things shared in the social world than it is with differentiation and things not so shared.

These principles are, of course, quite rudimentary. They may even obscure, as much as they sharpen, the image of qualitative work, since to state a principle is not to say how it is used. The aim to produce a coherent description of a claimed reality (and the truths it contains) may be shared by qualitative researchers, but there are, indeed, many ways such a mandate can be addressed. Fiction may be as useful as fact.[8] In his essay "False Documents," E. L. Doctorow (1977: 219) suggested that novelists "compose false documents more valid, more real, more truthful than the 'true' documents of the politicians or the journalists or the psychologists. Novelists know more explicitly that the world in which we live is still to be formed and that reality is amenable to any construction that is placed upon it."

Qualitative researchers would surely agree with these remarks, pointing out that Doctorow is simply saying that all descriptions purporting to be true carry with them their own interpretive standards. Here, of course, is where qualitative research becomes a craft very much dependent on the public and private standards (aesthetic, moral, and professional) held by the researchers. Any given piece of work might violate a few or many of the principles I just enumerated, yet still be prized and valued within the qualitative research community. It seems that the most memorable and influential works in organization studies are just those that do violate standards and principles of both the qualitative and quantative sort. Some examples are Gouldner's *Patterns of Industrial Bureaucracy* (1954), Dalton's *Men Who Manage* (1959), and Goffman's *Asylums* (1961). More recent examples are Kanter's *Men and Women of the Corporation* (1977) Willis's *Learning to Labor* (1977), and Starr's *The Social Transformation of American Medicine* (1982). These works defy easy classification. They wander from the numerical to the interpretive, from the production of facts to the essay, from the synthetic and theoretically derivative to the strikingly original, and so on.

The craft of these works seems to reside in the avoidance of a compulsive orthodoxy or rigid methodology. There is an apparent passion and concern for the topics of study standing behind the writing. There is an unbending commitment to authenticity and close detail, but without ducking the writer's responsibility (and authority) for establishing the meaning of such detail. Yet theory never runs away with the story in these works. Theory is, in fact, used rather sparely as a secondary theme, not as a primary one. Moreover, the theory drawn on represents something of a *bricolage* coming from psychology, political science, sociology, economics, and so forth. To call any of these works functionalist, Marxist, interaction-ist, or structuralist would be to do a disservice to the many analytic traditions the authors draw on in the telling of their respective tales.

What does come through in these works is a commitment to go beyond method, to venture out beyond principles of conventional procedure or topical constraint. There is, I think, a general truth here, because it seems the heros in any field of endeavor are those who break with the principles, disobey the advice of their standard-bearing elders in the field, and question what is currently regarded as proper, smart, or useful. Most of us fail in unspectacular ways, of course, when we leave the comfortable confines of advisable practice. But not everyone fails, and those who do not become the guides for proceeding in new and exciting ways. A field grows and advances its craft to the degree that there are those on the margins looking outward, not inward, for clues as to how to move ahead.[9]

At a somewhat more pedestrian level, one function of qualitative work is to enlighten a reader without disfiguring the social life that is described in a research report. Part of the craft of qualitative work lies, then, with the ways in which the data are handled after they have been more or less gathered. Harvesting the data of qualitative work means essentially two things: writing and rewriting. These efforts also require the soliciting of critical commentary so revisions will become more coherent and logically persuasive. This is hard work. One must also be something of a statistical atheist to work well in this domain, since it requires the continual forming and reforming of possible hypotheses (a practice that is anathema to the dedicated statistician). Each iteration of a research report is designed to better resolve analytic and empirical inconsistencies. This commitment to full or at least hardy explanation lies behind Howard Becker's (1966) oft-quoted quip about methodology being too important to be left to the methodologists. Yet even when it is not left to the methodologists, the craft of qualitative work necessarily remains partially veiled. Presumably, if we knew exactly what to do, we would go do it and stop offering advice.

For those with high status in a field, to prescribe a method is essentially to recommend powerfully what is already more or less a matter of actual experience. Such advice is most often little more than saying, "It worked for me, it'll work for you." Even the relatively loose prescriptions of the sort reprinted in this volume fail to account for the biographical particulars of potential researchers, the changing scenes in which the research takes place, the ever-shifting principles of practice that, when put to work, define the craft. This prescriptive dilemma reflects more than just my own timidity or private doubts about what it is we do. It reflects, I think, the changing basis of social science research, a change that is moving us from a rather fossilized paradigm of method to the acceptance of many methods, each of which allows paradigmatic but unique descriptions and explanations to emerge from empirical sources.

PARADIGM LOST

It is again worth reminding ourselves about the fundamental character of the sorts of things we study in organizational analysis. The kind of science possible surely depends on the kinds of things with which it must deal. In this light, consider the study of, say, plant life as it takes place in the natural sciences. Plants have a physical presence. They are there. You can turn your head away from them, look back, and they are still there. They can be measured for their stable and not-so-stable characteristics. Moreover, you can put one plant alongside another and clearly have two plants.

Now, things examined in organization studies, like industrial plants, just do not predictably live and die within some known and normal range of environmental variation. They come and go of course, but not in any fixed or unalterable sequence. Suppose a sociologist watches these plants for a while and watches, in particular, plant closures. Two closures are seen. Has the plant sociologist seen the same thing twice? Has anything been seen? What if this plant sociologist sees that it takes four administrators six weeks to close one plant. Will it take two administrators twelve weeks to close another plant of similar dimensions? The absurdity of these questions is the very point of this discussion. Like winks, blinks, and nods, the "thingness" of industrial plants is distinctly problematic.

In a marvelous but discomforting essay on the same theme, political scientist Lloyd Etheredge (1976) pointed to the pluralistic and competing knowledge base that underlies our studies. He posed a not-so-hypothetical problem: "The Case of the Unreturned Cafeteria Trays," wherein the manager of a college cafeteria seeks advice from behavioral scientists as to what is going on in his plant, why it is happening, and what he might do to stop it. Thirty or so different explanations are provided, along with somewhere around twenty different policies designed to get cafeteria trays back to where the manager thinks they belong. This is the structure of our knowledge.

As uncomfortable as Etheredge's little parable is, I suspect most organizational theorists have no trouble grasping the argument. There are many fragmentary theories in our field and any imaginative (and ambitious) proponents eager to put a given theory to work. To take another somewhat more familiar example, consider the kinds of explanations that might be proposed to the question, "Why does Sam Stone work hard?"

He works hard becase he is given appropriate training, leadership, and direction.

He works hard because he gets lots of sleep, eats well, and keeps regular hours.

He works hard because his friends work hard.

He works hard because he fears being fired if he doesn't.

He works hard because his parents encouraged him to do so as a child.

He works hard because he likes what he does.

He works hard because he is well paid.

He works hard because he doesn't know any better.

Almost instantly a number of quite different answers can be generated to this rather straightforward inquiry. All are valid responses, since they address the "why" questions with the proper and respected "because" answer. More to the point, we can easily imagine situations that would make any particular "because" a cogent and compelling response. This is a simple way of noting that ours is not only a field in which multiple theories can coexist with a degree of impunity but it is also a highly context-sensitive field.

The "paradigm lost" to which this section title refers is essentially the experimental, positivist, and empirical correspondence paradigm of the natural and physical sciences. It is the prescription to generate propositional statements first and then test them by reference to observable fact. The inextricable dilemmas surrounding this approach are fairly well documented, but two problems are worth quick restatement.[10]

The first problem of the paradigm is that the required independence of theory, fact, and method simply will not hold for the social sciences (if it will hold anywhere). Like

Sam Stone's hard work, social actions can be read in multiple ways. The responses of a worker to a questionnaire on job performance for instance, can be viewed by the plant sociologist as an informant report on specified features of a given organization. The same responses can also be viewed by the ethnomethodologist as evidence about the routine properties of form completion, an everyday task more or less routinized and, therefore, itself a subject of analysis. The data are given meaning by a researcher, then, only by reference to the theory to which they are made relevant.

The second problem of the paradigm is that suggested by Popper (1963), who wondered mightily about where given theories originate. If the simple-minded illustrations used here can generate a lengthy set of plausible propositions, how does one go about selecting from among them those most worthy of empirical test? Science won't help us here. Consider Pirsig's (1974) delightful little novel, *Zen and the Art of Motorcycle Maintenance,* in which the protagonist abandons science when he realizes that science always leads to the development of far more theoretical questions than can possibly be tested or solved. this is not to suggest that we abandon our pursuits, as some readers felt the frontispiece ("The Seminar") of this volume recommends. It is to suggest, however, that we undertake our studies with a degree of appropriate modesty and restraint.

Perhaps some of this modesty and restraint can be had by viewing our theories as mere similes, able to catch a part of the object of study, but only a part. Take my favorite simile of "impression management" or "life as theater," as analyzed by Messenger, Sampson, and Towne (1959). Such a simile treats naturally occurring episodes of social interaction "as if" such episodes were occurring on stage. Dramaturgic analysis then becomes useful. Thus props, plots and plops are sought out, rehearsals and opening nights discovered, backstage and frontstage regions plotted out, faulty as well as splendid performance critiqued, instances of stage fright and overacting catalogued, and so forth. While this is a particularly potent simile, it captures and analyzes only a few of the purposes to which a given interaction might be put. People may, indeed, wish to manage their impressions in order to make good ones, but they may also wish from their interactions to make money, make time, make cars, make haste, make change, make out, make children, make clear, or make fun.

If treating theory as simile helps inform qualitative work, we still are faced with Popper's problem: where do we go for good ones? Here is where I think we must go directly to the social world itself and attempt to uncover what people are up to at any given time in differing contexts. Moreover, we must be careful in so doing not to bring too many purposes beyond the descriptive with us, or some of the distinct advantages of qualitative work will be lost. If for example, a man rests his head on a chopping block expecting to get a haircut, the fact that his head drops off is not of great interest to the qualitative researcher. Losing one's head under such circumstances is mere behavior, not social conduct (White, 1976). This is to say that questions surrounding the consequences of behavior may be very different from the questions surrounding the nature of human conduct. It seems to me the study of conduct or social action will remain the special province of qualitative research, since it necessitates an interpretive approach. The study of behavioral consequence is also important, whether or not we aim to design efficient barber shops or guillotines. But to emphasize consequence is to bypass, by omission or intention, the ontological question of "what is going on."

In looking for interesting theory, it is obvious that we do not have any shortage in organizational studies. There are certainly more than enough around to keep us busy testing and elaborating, well into the next century. This is not the only path to be followed. If my sense of paradigm lost is accurate, we must not expect great theories again to rise and fall in the social sciences. We are now far too segmented, specialized, suspicious, and savage to allow any one theory group to dominate the field. Theory building will continue of course, but given what I suspect is a general disenchantment with social theory of all sorts, those theories that are constructed will most likely be used selectively as similes to order data in a particular and fairly narrow domain. To hold out for the grand paradigm in the human sciences is akin to being a member of some cargo cult.

THE FINAL WORD(S)

To conclude, a cautionary note. Time seems always to erode purpose and highlight form. Method discussions, such as this one, also erode purpose. the danger of pushing method is that it may become an end in itself. This is as true for those in the self-proclaimed empathetic and humanistic enclaves of qualitative research as it is for those merry pranksters of the social psychology laboratory, those diabolic taxonomists of the population ecology schools, or even those practical and zealous theorists on missions to save organizations. One doesn't have to be the crudely (perhaps cruelly) stereotyped number-crunching, model-building theory tester to allow form to overcome function. If Woody Allen is right in his claim that 90 percent of success lies in getting it done and turned in on time, we must not make an obsession of our methods. To get on with our various research programs is the thing of foremost concern. If we can do so with a bit more appreciation for the diversity of these programs, then perhaps the detour through this land of many methods will have been worthwhile.

NOTES

1

As always. the methods used to build a particular description deserve scrutiny. In this case, they don't deserve much. What I have done in the following section is merely to organize thematically some of the comments I have heard about this special issue over the past few years. There is nothing systematic about my hearing except those sociological biases that are mobilized around my specific place in space and time, and those not-so-very-peculiar psychological biases that probably make me a better hearer of the celebratory and laudatory comments coming from readers than those of a defiling and critical kind. At some time or other, I have used all of the writings in this volume as fodder for graduate students in research seminars and, as a result, have been perhaps overimpressed by what recruits to the field, rather than their sage elders, have to say.

2

Since this special issue was published in December of 1979, the attention provided qualitative methods seems not to have waned. If anything, there is greater interest today than there was then. Emerson (1983) has a new fieldwork reader on the market. Spradley (1979, 1980) has two method texts available (regrettably, posthumous). Agar (1980) has another. Webb et al. (1981) have released a second version of their unobtrusive measures book, this time called "nonreactive" measures. Of more direct relevance, two of the six monographs published in the Sage series Studying Organizations: Innovations in Methodology deal with qualitative methods (McGrath, Martin, and Kulka, 1982; Van Maanen, Dabbs, and Faulkner, 1982).

3

The principle of incongruity as fundamental to the awareness process was perhaps best addressed by Burke (1965). There are, of course, important philosophical distinctions to be made concerning such a process (e.g., Schutz, 1970; Gadamer, 1975). If, however, readers feel philosophy is important enough to be left to the philosophers, Glaser and Strauss (1967) put forth a discovery technique of general value. Of more recent vintage, I find the theories of descriptio provided by Agar (1982, 1983) most useful.

4

I have developed this point somewhat more systematically elsewhere (Van Mannen, 1979). The theory on which it rests and the methodological implications that follow are best described in Becker (1970).

5

Such retrospection may be partially responsible for the repeated insertion of substantive findings in the essays of this volume. Method and result are closely intertwined in qualitative work, and it is difficult to discuss one without considering the other. Readers seem to appreciate this linking of substance and method because it represents something of a break from any of the prescriptive writings that ritualize data collection, institutionalize analytic tech-

nique by isolating it from fresh data, and sterilize research reporting by linking it to a fixed format. If nothing else, the writers here push for a more playful, experimental approach to the doing and reporting of organizational research. The best treatment on cognitive aspects of all phases of social research and on the merging or analysis and findings in the reporting of empirical work is Bailyn (1977).

6

Some of these "principles" are put forth in Van Maanen, Dabbs, and Faulkner (1982: 16-17). That I am easily able to add to the list (or take away from it) suggests, as I do later in the text, that there is nothing holy being discussed here.

7

It is worth noting that this principle urges the principal investigator to go into the field and collect data. There is no substitute for firsthand inspection in qualitative work. The real thing is not to be found in other people's data, even if these other people are hired hands (and maybe especially then). This runs counter to custom in the organizational research tribe. Schwartz and Jacobs (1979: 310) suggested an inverse relationship between the collecting of data and the fame and reputation of the researcher. In many quantitative studies, for example, anonymous graduate student "workers" catch and run the data while the name-brand "professional theorists" analyze it. This is thought to be good training for the recruits and efficient use of time for the veterans who, after all, "already know what is happening out there." Most disturbing in light of the proximity principle is, however, the fact that it is quite possible to get a Ph.D. in any of the fields concerned with organizational study without ever observing organizational life in any detail, up close, for any length of time.

8

Krieger (1983: 173-199) had some wonderful things to say about the role of fiction in social science. Among the intriguing points raised in her brief essay is the view that current social science does not allow many dimensions of the outside world to enter into its discourse. While our methods are supposed to prevent this, Krieger suggests that our insulation stems from allowing our evidence to follow our arguments, rather than the reverse.

9

This matter of craft bears further attention, for it cuts to the core of the purpose of this volume: to promote worthy qualitative studies of organizations. As Hughes (1958) suggested, in virtually every sphere of vocational competence, people are judged by peers using standards that go well beyond whatever minimal levels of skill are required to meet basic tasks. That these standards cannot be fully formulated in advance of performance does not seem to bother, for example, most medical doctors, garage mechanics, teachers, clerics, policemen, fishermen, or social workers. Such standards, in general seem to form around the ability of practitioners to meet and master the unexpected. In short, craft calls for the exercise of judgment and

skill when one is faced with puzzling and pressing matters. To say we cannot prepare organizational researchers for tasks that have no names is altogether specious, since other occupations do so by deliberately preparing would-be members to seek out and come to terms with the unexpected, the dramatic, the anomalous. Parachuting graduate students into organizational fields from which they are expected to bring back qualitative field reports might be one way to begin such preparation.

10

See for example, Burrell and Morgan (1979) on the meaning of multiple paradigms in organizational analysis. One possible line of resolution consistent with the empirical and more or less positivist traditions of our field is the Lakatosian approach to theory validation, which, in light of current practices, makes relatively little use of the rack of nature. Theories win out in only context-specific ways. Facts are suspect in such a research approach, because validation rests on theory-to-theory comparisons rather than theory-to-fact comparison per se (Lakatos, 1970).

REFERENCES

Agar, Michael H.
1980 The Professional Stranger. New York: Academic Press.
1982 "Toward an ethnographic language." American Anthropologist, 84: 779-795.
1983 "Ethnographic evidence." Urban Life, 12: 32-48.

Bailyn, Lotte
1977 "Research as a cognitive process." Quality and Quantity, 11: 97-117.

Bailyn, Bernard
1982 "The challenge of modern historiography." American Historical Review, 87: 1-24.

Becker, Allen L.
1982 "On Emerson on language." In David Tanner (ed.), Analyzing Discourse: 39-62. Washington, DC: Georgetown Univeristy Press.

Becker, Howard S.
1966 "Whose side are we on?" Social Problems, 14: 239-247.
1970 Sociological Work. Chicago: Aldine.
1982 "Freshmen English for graduate students." Unpublished paper, Department of Sociology, Northwestern University.

Becker, Howard S., Blanche Geer, Everett Hughes, and Anselm Strauss
1961 Boys in White. Chicago: University of Chicago Press.

Burke, Kenneth
1965 Permanence and change, 2d ed. Indianapolis, IN: Bobbs-Merrill.

Burrell, Gibson, and Gareth Morgan
1979 Sociological Paradigms and Organizational Analysis. London: Heinemann.

Cicourel, Aaron V.
1964 Method and Measurement in Sociology. New York: Free Press.

Dalton, Melville
1959 Men Who Manage. New York: John Wiley.

Doctorow, E. L.
1977 "False documents." American Review, 5: 215-232.

Emerson, Robert M.
1981 "Observational field work." Annual Review of Sociology, 7: 351-378.

Emerson, Robert M. (ed.)
1983 Contemporary Field Research. Boston: Little, Brown.

Etheredge, Lloyd S.
1976 The Case of the Unreturned Cafeteria Trays. Washington, DC: American Political Science Association.

Gadamer, Hans G.
1975 Truth and Method. New York: Continuum.

Glaser, Barney G., and Anselm Strauss
1967 The Discovery of Grounded Theory. Chicago: Aldine.

Goffman, Erving
1961 Asylums. New York: Anchor Books.

Gouldner, Alvin W.
1954 Patterns of Industrial Bureaucracy. New York: Free Press.

Gusfield, Joseph R.
1981 The Culture of Public Problems. Chicago: University of Chicago Press.

Hughes, Everett C.
1958 Men and their Work. Glencoe, Il: Free Press.
1974 "Who studies whom." Human Organization, 33: 327-334.

Kanter, Rosabeth Moss
1977 Men and Women of the Corporation. New York: Basic Books.

Krieger, Susan
1983 The Mirror Dance. Appendix: "Fiction and social science." Philadelphia: Temple University Press.

Lakatos, Imre
1970 "Falsification and the methodology of scientific research programs." In Imre Lakatos and A. Musgrave (eds.), Criticism and the Growth of Knowledge. New York: Cambridge University Press.

Messenger, Sheldon E., Harold Sampson, and Rober D. Towne
1962 "Life as theatre: Some notes on the dramaturgic approach to social reality." Sociometry, 25: 98-110.

McGrath, Joseph E., Joanne Martin, and Richard A. Kulka
1982 Judgment Calls in Research. Beverly Hills, CA: Sage.

Mills, C. Wright
1959 The Sociological Imagination. Appendix: "On intellectual craftsmanship." New York: Grove Press.

Prisig, Robert 1974 Zen and the Art of

Prisig, Robert
1974 Zen and the Art of Motorcycle Maintenance. New York: Morrow.

Popper, Karl
1963 Conjectures and Refutations. London: Routledge & Kegan Paul.

Schutz, Alfred
1970 On Phenomenology and Social Relations. Chicago: University of Chicago Press.

Schwartz, Howard, and Jerry Jacobs
1979 Qualitative Sociology. New York: Free Press.

Spradley, James P.
1979 The Ethnographic Interview. New York: Holt, Rinehart & Winston.
1980 Participant Observation. New York: Holt, Rinehart & Winston.

Starr, Paul
1983 The Social Transformation of American Medicine. New York: Basic Books.

Van Maanen, John
1979 "The self, the situation, and the rules of interpersonal relations." In Warren Bennis, John Van Maanen, Edgar H. Schein, and Fred Steele (eds.), Essays in Interpersonal Dynamics: 43-101. Homewood, IL: Dorsey.

Van Maanen, John, James M. Dabbs, and Robert R. Faulkner
1982 Varieties of Qualitative Research. Beverly Hills, CA: Sage.

Webb, Eugene J., Donald T. Campbell, Richard D. Schwartz, Lee Sechrest, and John Grove
1981 Nonreactive Measures in the Social Sciences. Boston: Houghton Mifflin.

Weick, Karl E.
1979 "Summary comments on observational methodology and NIE funding." Washington, DC: National Institute of Education.

White, Sheldon H.
1976 "The active organism in theoretical behaviorism." Human Development, 19: 99-107.

Willis, Paul
1977 Learning to Labor. London: Saxon House.

About the Authors

Diane Brannon is Assistant Professor at the University of Washington School of Social Work, Seattle, WA 98195. Her current research interests focus on the organizational analysis of public welfare systems. She received her M.S.S. from Bryn Mawr and her Ph.D. from Cornell University.

H. Kirk Downey is Professor of Management and Chairman of the Management Department at Texas Christian University, Fort Worth TX 76129. His current research interests include the role of cognition in the structuring of organizations and task design in high-technology organizations. Professor Downey received his Ph.D. from The Pennsylvania State University.

R. Duane Ireland is the W. A. Mays Professor in the Hankamer School of Business at Baylor University. His current research focuses on strategic issues in both large and small organizations. In particular, he is interested in examining relationships among strategy, several contextual variables, and performance. Professor Ireland received his D.B.A. from Texas Tech University.

Todd D. Jick is Associate Professor of Organizational Behavior and Industrial Relations in the Faculty of Administrative Studies, York University, Downsview, Ontario, Canada M3J 2R6. His research interests include the management of decline and change, stress, and the various effects of cutbacks on publicly funded organizations. He received his M.S. and Ph.D. from Cornell University.

Donald Light, Jr., is Associative Professor in the Sophie Davis School of Biomedical Education at The City University of New York, New York, NY 10031. His research interests concern the interplay between organizational structure and professional relations. He is the author of *Becoming Psychiatrists: The Professional Transformation of Self*

(Norton, 1982). Professor Light received his Ph.D. from the University of Chicago.

Peter K. Manning is Professor of Sociology and Psychiatry at Michigan State University, East Lansing, MI 48824, former Fellow of Balliol College, Oxford, and Research Associate at the Centre for Socio-Legal Studies, Oxford. His areas of interest include social organization and comparative studies of health and illness. He is the author of *Police Work*, (M.I.T. Press, 1977) and *The Narc's Game* (M.I.T. Press, 1980), and is working on a new book, *Signifying Calls*. Professor Manning received his M.A. and Ph.D. from Duke University.

Steven Maynard-Moody is Assistant Professor of Political Science, and Research Associate and Coordinator of the Survey Research Program in the Center for Public Affairs at the University of Kansas, Lawrence, KS 66045. His current research involves the application of case study and survey methodologies to examine the role of street-level bureaucrats in shaping public policy and the organizational influences on the implementation of innovations. He received his Ph.D. from Cornell University.

Charles C. McClintock is Associate Professor in the Department of Human Service Studies, College of Human Ecology, Cornell University, Ithaca, NY 14853. His current research interests include the use of survey methods in program evaluation and the development of internal systems for program evaluation and operational audits in public and private organizations. He received his Ph.D. from the State University of New York at Buffalo.

Matthew B. Miles is Senior Research Associate at the Center for Policy Research, Inc., 475 Riverside Drive, New York, NY 10115. Recent books are *Innovation Up Close* (Plenum, 1984) and *Analyzing Qualitative Data* (Center for Policy Research, 1983). His present research interests focus on the implementation of "Effective Schools" improvement programs. He received his M.A. and Ed.D. from Teacher's College, Columbia University.

Henry Mintzberg is a Bronfman Professor of Management at McGill University, Montreal, Canada H3A 1G5. His current research is concerned with the strategy formation process in large organizations. He is completing a series of books on the theme of studies in the theory of management policy of which *Power in and around Organizations* (Prentice-Hall, 1983) is the most recent. Professor Mintzberg received his M.S. and Ph.D from the Massachusetts Institute of Technology.

Andrew M. Pettigrew is Professor of Organizational Behaviour in the School of Industrial and Business Studies, University of Warwick, Coventry CV4 7AL, England. He is the author of *The Politics of Organizational Decision Making* (rev. ed., Blackwell and Prentice-Hall, 1984) and (with Enid Mumford) *Implementing Strategic Decisions* (Longman, 1975). His latest book, *The Politics of Creating Organizational Change* will be published by Blackwell and Prentice-Hall in 1984. Professor Pettigrew received his Ph.D. from Manchester University.

Michael J. Piore is Professor of Economics at the Massachusetts Institute of Technology, Cambridge, MA 02139. His research interest centers on labor markets and industrial relations. His most recent books include *Birds of Passage: Migrant Labor and Industrial Societies* (Cambridge University Press, 1979) and *Inflation and Unemployment: Institutionalist and Structuralist Views* (Sharpe Press, 1979). He received his Ph.D. from Harvard University.

Gerald R. Salancik is the IBE Professor of Organizations at the University of Illinois, Champaign, IL 61820. His current research interests include organizational power and control, cognitive foundations for organization beliefs, and ideologies evolved to justify administrative control practices in organizations. Professor Salancik is the coauthor (with Jeffrey Pfeffer) of *The External Control of Organizations* (Goodyear Press, 1979). He received his Ph.D. from Yale University.

Peggy Reeves Sanday is Associate Professor in the Department of Anthropology at the University of Pennsylvania, Philadelphia, PA 19104. Her research interests include cognitive anthropology, the cross-cultural study of sex roles, and the use of anthropological techniques to study public education in the United States. Professor

Sanday is the editor of *Anthropology and the Public Interest: Fieldwork and Theory* (Academic Press, 1976) and author of *Female Power and Male Dominance* (Cambridge University Press, 1981). She is currently completing a book, *Cannibalism and the Problem of Evil.* She received her Ph.D. from the University of Pittsburgh.

John Van Maanen is Associate Professor of Organizational Psychology and Management at the Massachusetts Institute of Technology, Cambridge, MA 02139. His current research interests include socialization practices in work organizations, varieties of police work in urban areas, and the occupational culture of American fishermen. He is a coauthor (with Warren Bennis, Edgar H. Schein, and Fred I. Steele) of *Essays in Interpersonal Dynamics* (Dorsey Press, 1979) and is also a coauthor (with James G. Dabbs and Robert R. Faulkner) of *Varieties of Qualitative Research* (Sage, 1982). Professor Van Maanen received his M.S. and Ph.D. from the University of California, Irvine.

Eugene Webb is the Lane Family Professor of Organizational Behavior in the Graduate School of Business at Stanford University, Stanford, CA 94305. His current research interests include the vagaries of implementation programs and the bargaining features of jury trials in the California courts. Professor Webb is the senior author (with Donald T. Campbell, Richard D. Schwartz, and Lee Sechrest) of *Unobtrusive Measures: Nonreactive Research in the Social Sciences* (Houghton Mifflin, 1981). He received his Ph.D. from the University of Chicago.

Karl E. Weick is the Nicholas H. Noyes Professor of Organizational Behavior in the Graduate School of Business and Public Administration and a professor in the Department of Psychology, Cornell University, Ithaca, NY 14853. His research interests are directed toward cognitive processes and the problems of organizing human activities. He has recently published the second edition of *The Social Psychology of Organizing* (Addison-Wesley, 1979). Professor Weick received his Ph.D. from The Ohio State University.